SOFIA COPPOLA

First published in Great Britain in 2025 by Greenfinch
An imprint of Quercus
Part of John Murray Group

A CIP catalogue record for this book is available from the British Library

ISBN 978-1-52944-690-6
EBOOK ISBN 978-1-52944-691-3

10 9 8 7 6 5 4 3 2 1

Cover design by Luke Bird
Interior design by Ginny Zeal
Printed and bound in Dubai by Oriental Press

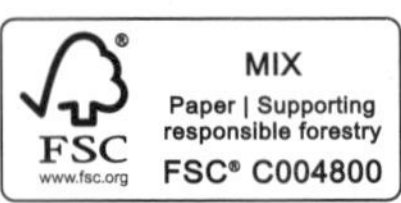

Papers used by Quercus are from well-managed forests and other responsible sources.

Quercus
Carmelite House
50 Victoria Embankment
London EC4Y 0DZ

John Murray Group
Part of Hodder & Stoughton Limited
An Hachette UK company

The authorised representative in the EEA is Hachette Ireland,
8 Castlecourt Centre, Dublin 15, D15 XTP3, Ireland (email: info@hbgi.ie)

ICONIC DIRECTORS SERIES

SOFIA COPPOLA

THE COMPLETE UNOFFICIAL GUIDE

CHRISTINA NEWLAND

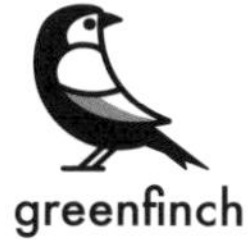

greenfinch

CONTENTS

'I think you can be substantial and still be
interested in frivolity.'
SOFIA COPPOLA

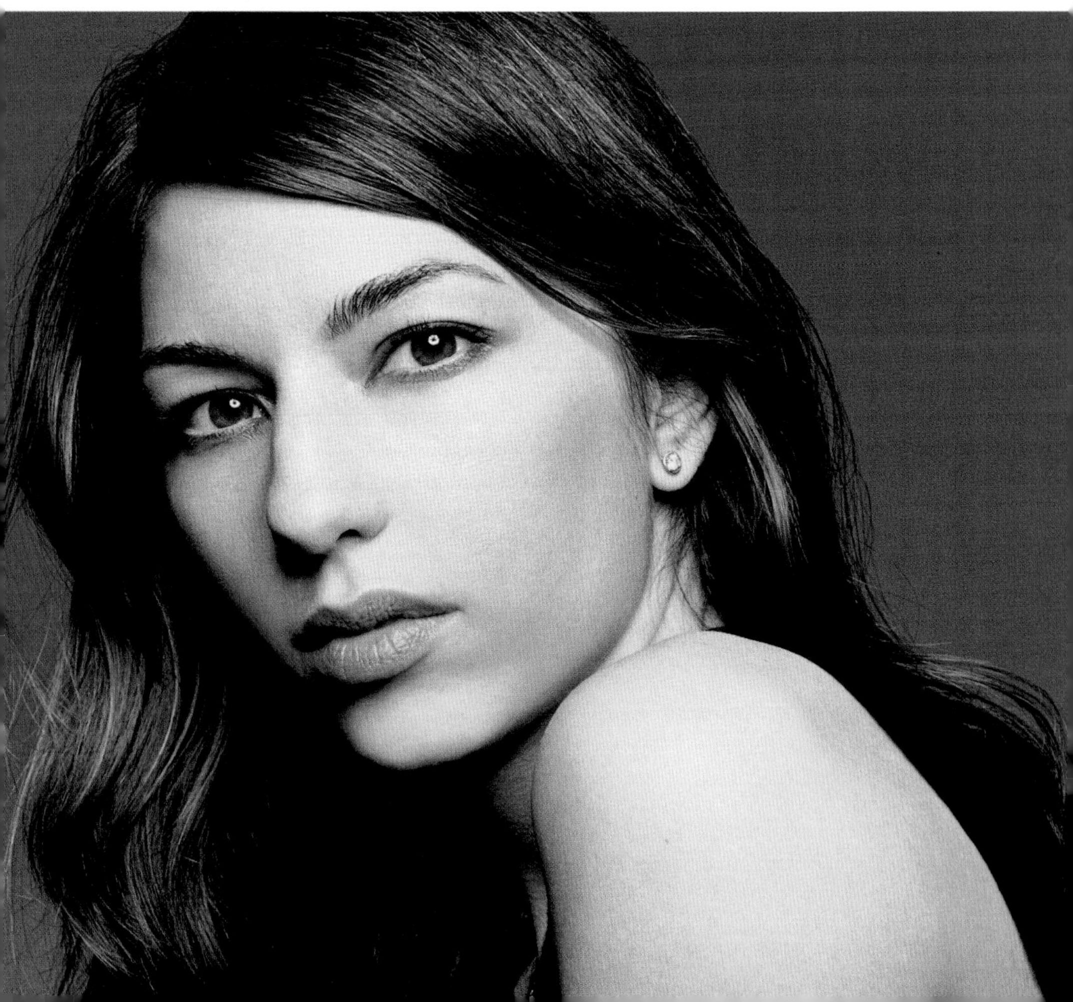

INTRODUCTION

When I think of Sofia Coppola's films, the well of imagery blossoms fresh and vivid: the giddy, somnambulant thrill of leaving a masked ball at dawn, with a rosy-cheeked Marie Antoinette smiling to herself at her evening's flirtations; *Somewhere*'s long, slow shot of a dad and daughter sunbathing by the Chateau Marmont pool; the moth-to-the-flame flutterings of women in white frills in the candlelit gothic *The Beguiled*; the cramped heat and itchy grass on bare legs of suburban summers in *The Virgin Suicides*.

In a career of eight feature films which has brought her from strength to strength, Sofia Coppola has demanded to be taken seriously as a woman and a filmmaker on her own terms. She has continued to make films with a uniquely feminine slant, about subject matter which varies in setting but remains consistent at heart. She's an auteur in a true sense, making films about what intrigues and excites her as an artist and growing alongside the work; as such, her films' trajectory has moved from girlhood to womanhood in many ways. For her second film, *Lost in Translation*, she won an Academy Award for Best Screenplay, becoming only the third woman to do so in Oscar history. And in 2017, for *The Beguiled*, she won Best Director at Cannes, again making history as only the second person of her gender to triumph as director there. But these feminist advancements, important as they are, only tell a fraction of the story.

As an artist, Coppola has proven to have as much aesthetic and visual integrity as she does devotion to her subject matter.

LEFT: Sofia Coppola, 2003.

Whether it's Lance Acord or Philippe Le Sourd, her regular collaborators on camerawork are painterly, precise and execute the utmost care. Even with tiny budgets, Coppola's careful moodboarding, visual finesse and focus on the importance of framing and composition are clear. It's important to her that her work is not only beautiful but is also capable of speaking without words; she is truly a visual thinker.

I might not have much in common with Sofia Coppola and her upbringing (not many of us do). Crucially, though, her work and its dreamy ambiguity can be latched onto by so many of us. As a teenage girl, I, like Coppola, was obsessed by fashion and music magazines and the faraway glamour of big-city bohemianism. Like her, I cut out images from those magazines, and then I plastered posters of The Strokes and ripped-out photoshoots of runway models and Andy Warhol screen prints all over my bedroom walls. They gave me something to dream about, to envision a future with Coppola's teen-dream image-making is so powerful for this very reason.

Many of Coppola's detractors, over the years, can be characterized as dismissive of what they may deem as superficial or inconsequential elements of her work. But it's this very dismissiveness that drove Coppola in the first place: a demand to take women and young girls' lives and interiority seriously. Like so many filmmakers known for a distinctive style, it's easy to reduce Coppola's body of work down to stereotypes: she's interested in teenage girls, she's preoccupied with the pretty and the frilly; that her films are 'cool' but not 'deep'. Too often, the tone of the criticism of Coppola's work has only proven how ahead of her time she has been. (And the huge popularity of her work and its aesthetic on Gen Z social media speaks volumes on this front.)

RIGHT: *Lost in Translation* US poster, 2003.

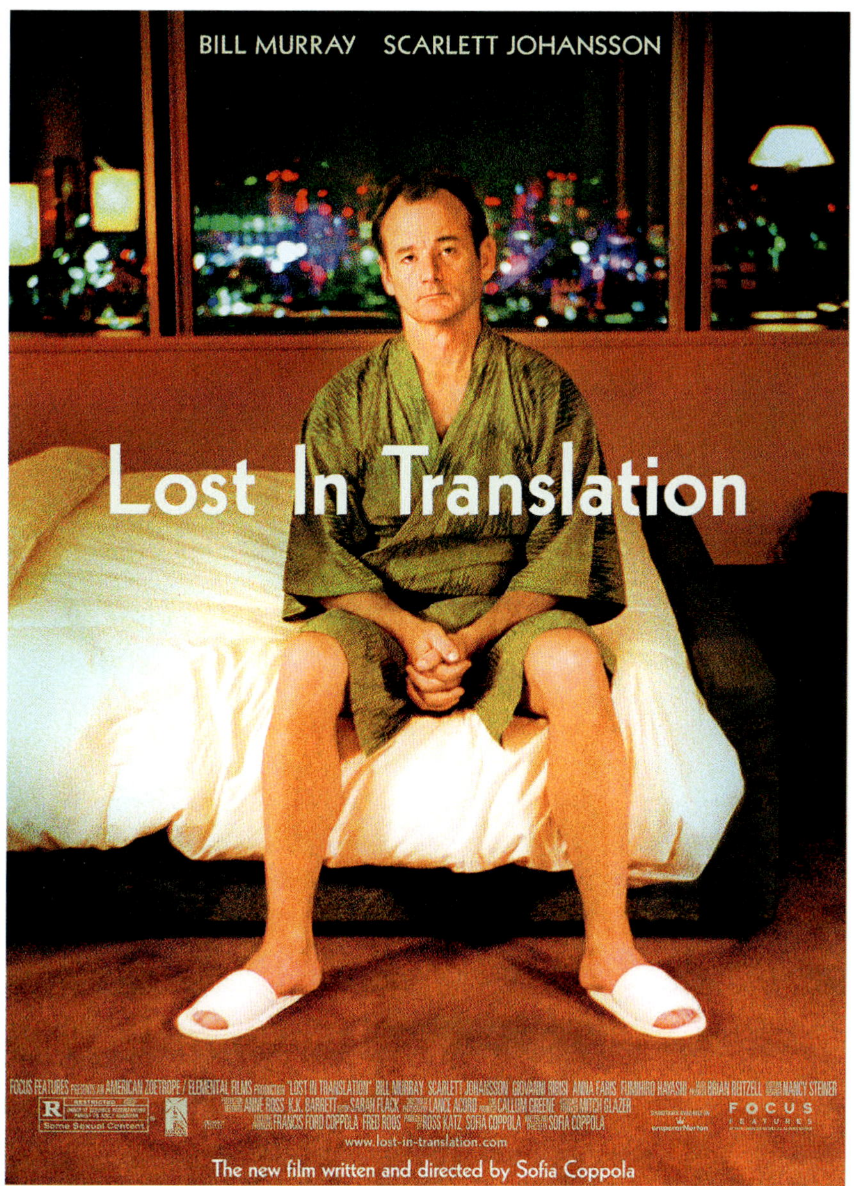
BILL MURRAY   SCARLETT JOHANSSON
Lost In Translation
The new film written and directed by Sofia Coppola
www.lost-in-translation.com

Throughout her career, Coppola has demonstrated a complex understanding of girls and young womanhood. That might be uncertainty and anguish; the way our parents shape us; the pubescent exhilaration of successful early flirtation; the throbbing faux-innocence of going 'boy crazy'. But more than any other contemporary filmmaker, she captures the fragility and the wisdom of teenage girls, their yearning and their process of becoming.

In *The Virgin Suicides*, Lux's mother burns her rock 'n' roll records as a punishment. Coppola films it for the tragedy it is and grasps the histrionic extremity of emotion that comes for a lonely teenage girl who has lost one of her avenues of escape. Coppola knows that if you'd have burned my vinyl as a teenager, it would have been the end of my world. She takes girls seriously, and most especially she takes them seriously at their most frivolous, materialistic, girly-girl inclinations. That, to me, is rare and wonderful.

In taking on this unofficial guide to her films and in returning to so much of her work, I have been moved again and again to see how the things in Coppola's films which spoke to me as a teenage girl take on new life as a grown woman. I see now how much empathy and love she shows all of our younger selves for making the choices we did then, and what informed them. How beauty culture, fashion, boys and music can both define and confine us. Whether you're an avid fan or a newcomer to her work keen to learn more, I hope that the chapters to follow will spark interest, rewatches and debate. I hope you will find the same frivolous pleasures and fascination with the dark hearts of girlhood as I found within Sofia Coppola's work. And that you find a whole mysterious feminine world to explore within.

RIGHT: Sofia Coppola in 2004, with her Academy Award for *Lost in Translation* Best Original Screenplay.

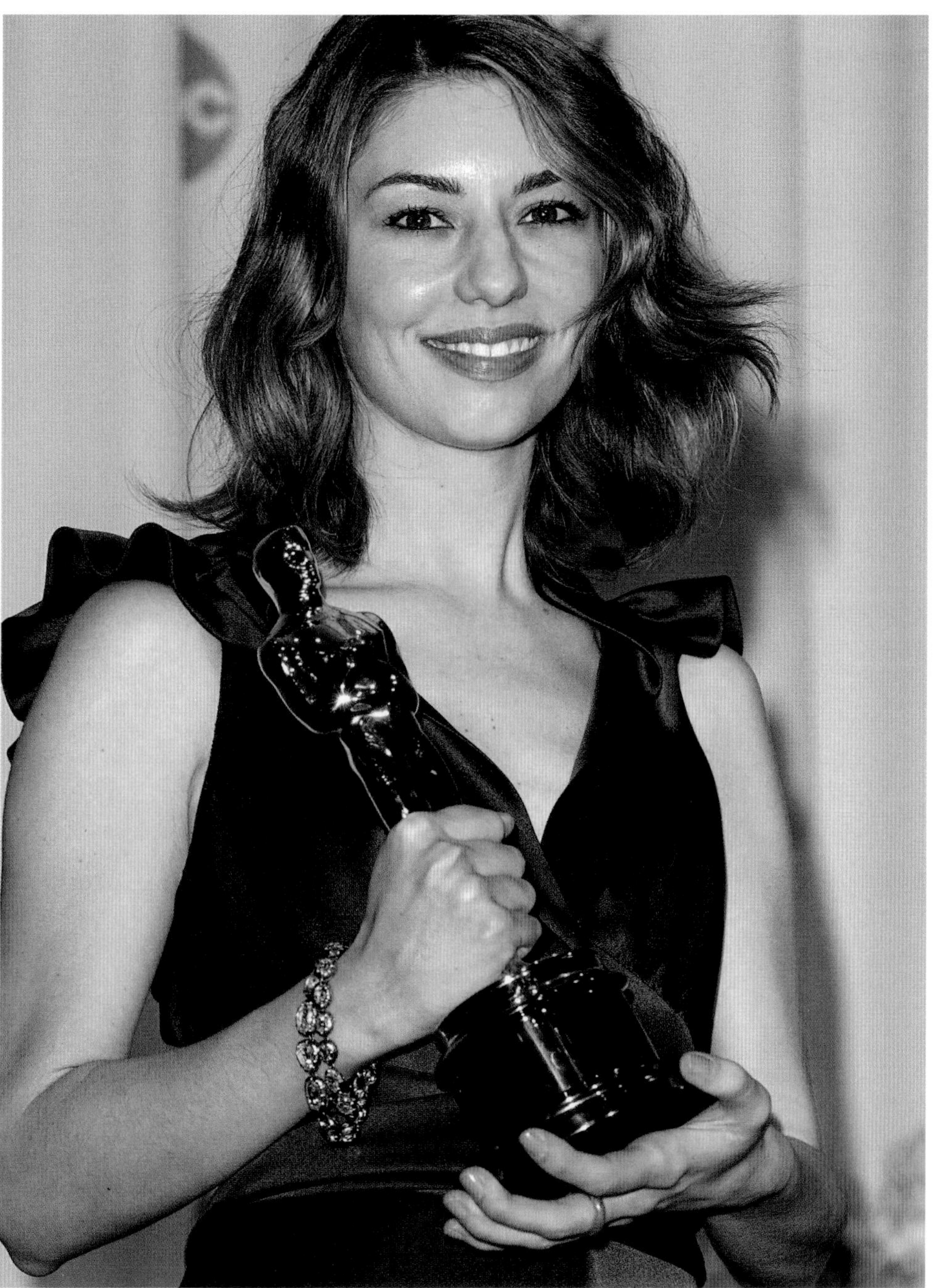

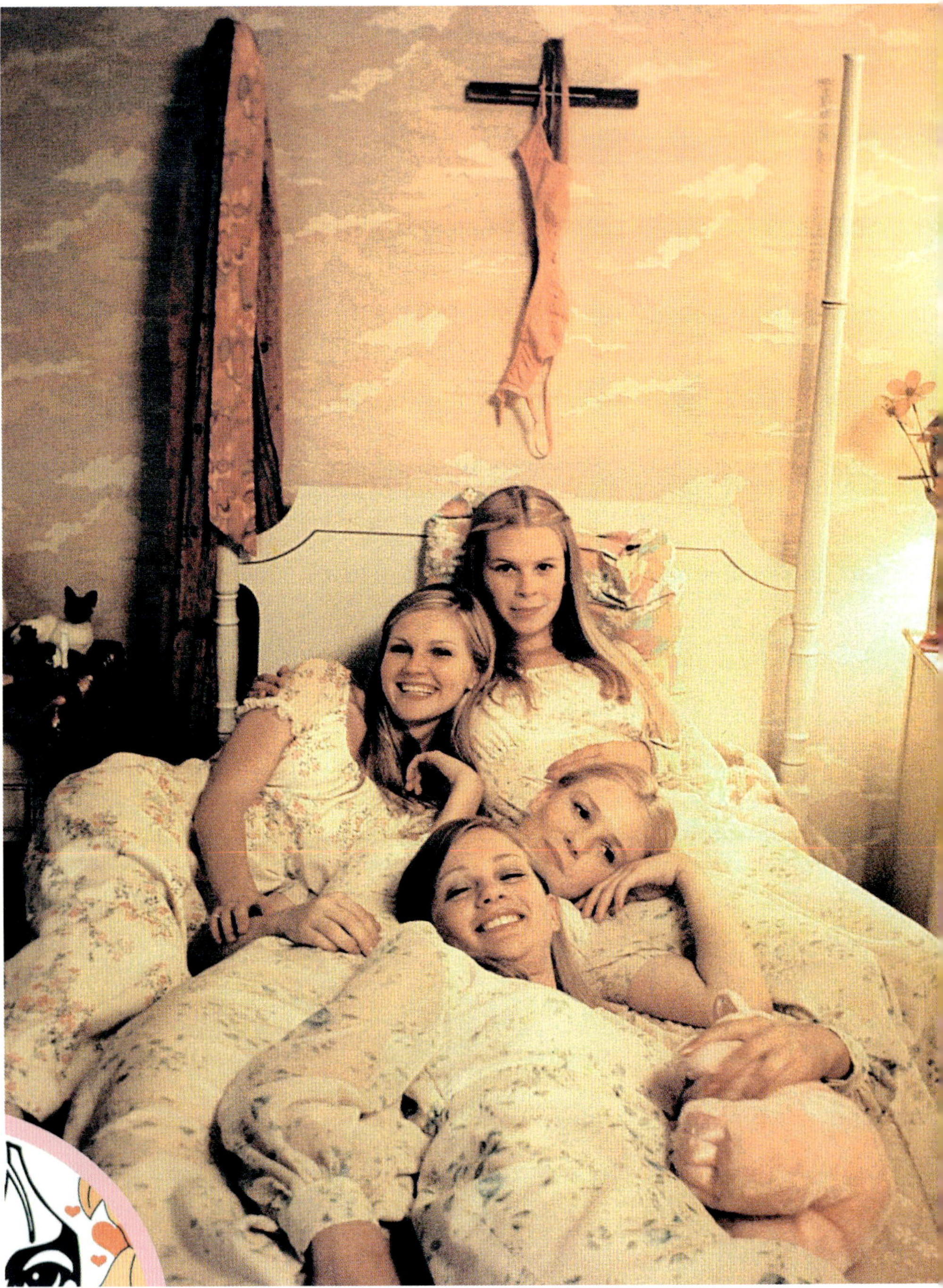

'Obviously, doctor, you've never been a thirteen-year old girl.'

THE VIRGIN SUICIDES
2000

It all began as an experiment. A woman of 28 – a CalArts college dropout with a keen interest in design, photography and music whose father had considerable experience in adapting novels for the screen – heard through the grapevine that one of her favourite books might get the Hollywood treatment. She found herself so fixated on whether they'd get it right, she thought she might take it upon herself to try. She began to highlight and outline the first few pages of an adapted screenplay, and found she couldn't stop.

That young woman was Sofia Coppola, daughter of Hollywood legend Francis Ford Coppola, and not yet the elegant and accomplished filmmaker we now know her to be. That book – and that experiment – was *The Virgin Suicides*. The novel, published in 1993 by first-time author Jeffrey Eugenides, was a troubling, lyrically written tale about an ordinary suburban family – the Lisbons – in 1970s Detroit. Told from the vantage point of 25 years later, from the perspective of a group of local then-teenage boys, it tells the story of the Lisbons' five beautiful daughters. They are a source of lusty fascination for the boys, particularly given their strict Catholic upbringing, which does not allow them to date. And then each of them, seemingly inexplicably, commits suicide.

The Lisbon sisters, introduced to us in the film in a dreamy haze, faces superimposed across images of blue summer sky, and through the besotted eyes of the boys who are watching them

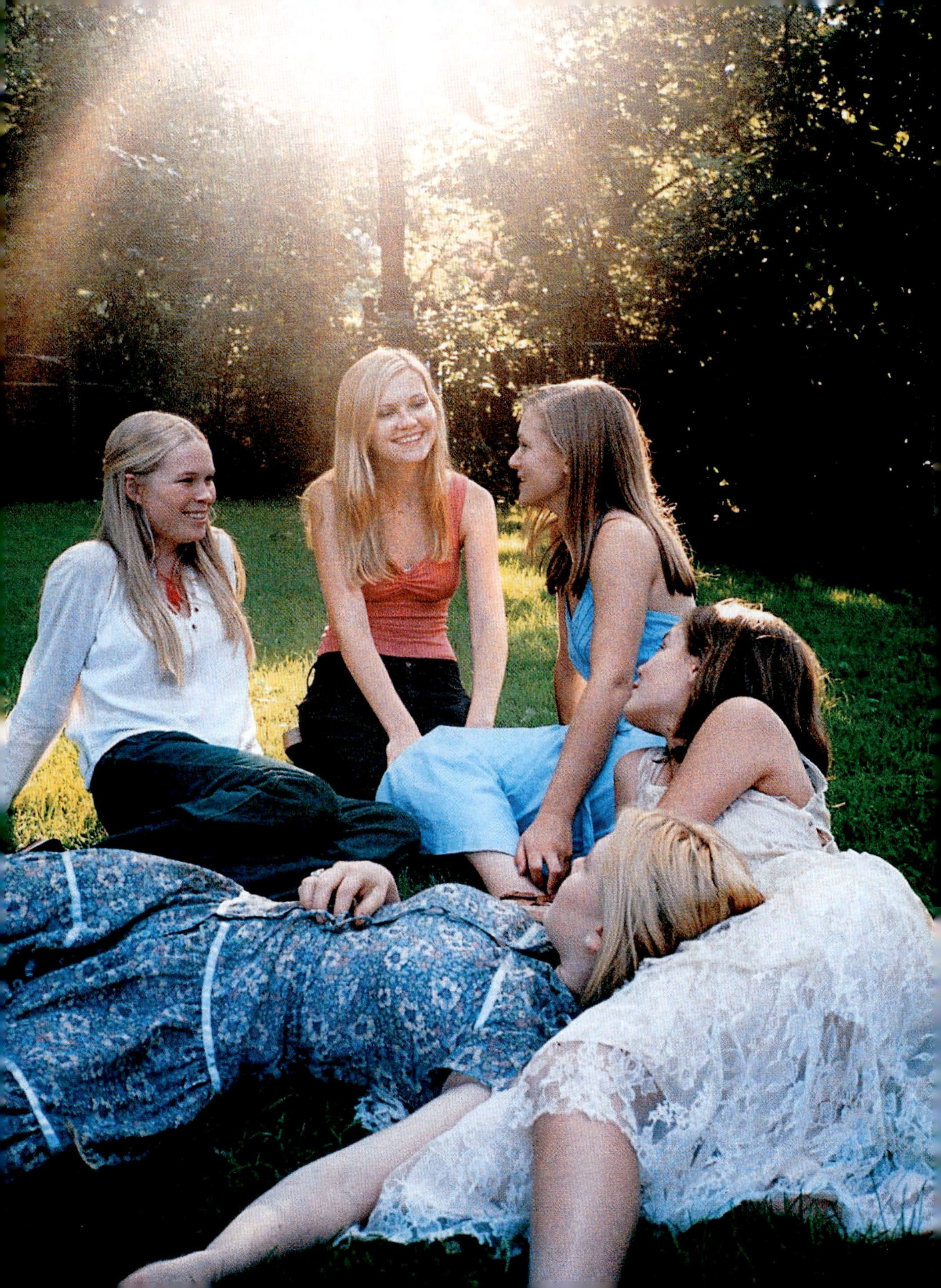

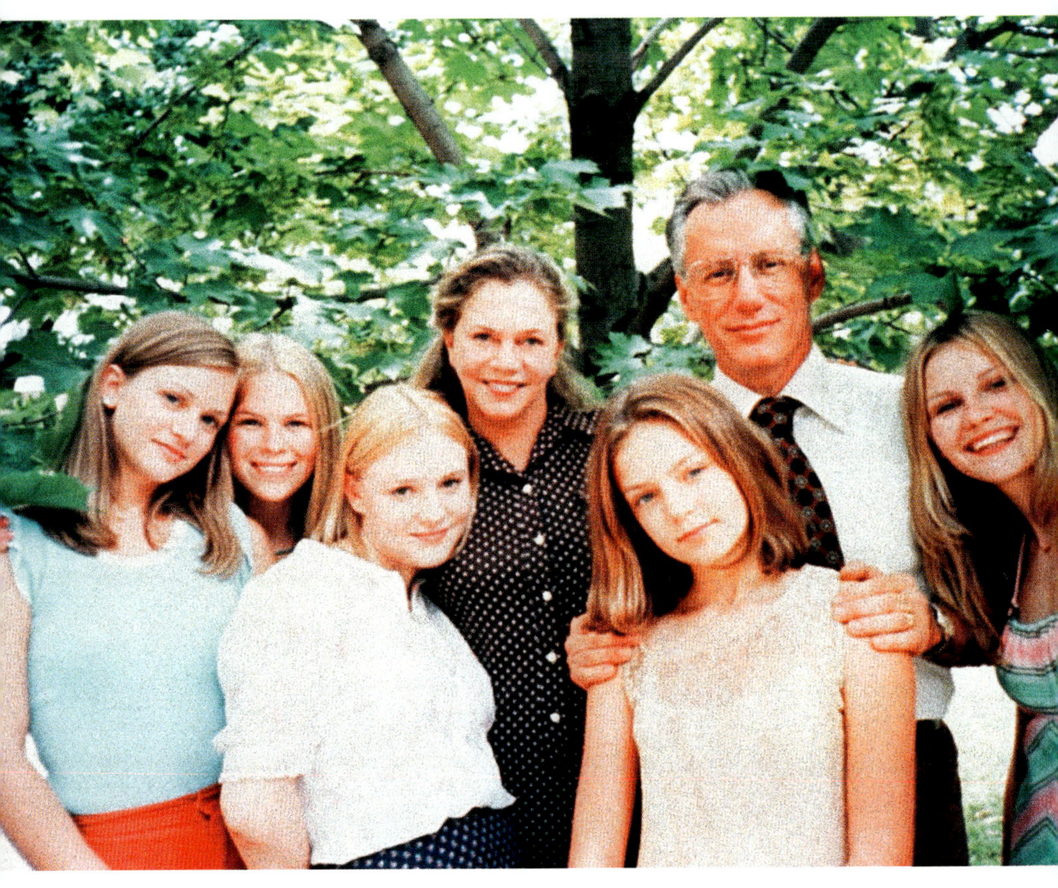

ABOVE: A Lisbon family photo, featuring James Woods and
Kathleen Turner as Mr and Mrs Lisbon.

from across the street. Coppola captures their swooning all-American beauty; sun-bleached dirty-blonde hair and lissome long limbs in the suburban breeze. There's 17-year-old Therese (Leslie Haymon), and then, in descending order of age, Mary (16, A J Cook), Bonnie (15, Chelse Swain), Lux (14, Kirsten Dunst) and youngest child Cecilia, 13 (a memorably sullen Hanna Hall). It's Cecilia who first attempts suicide, sending the entire middle-class community reeling in horror.

Coppola sought to remain faithful to the spirit and letter of the source material, inviting author Jeffrey Eugenides on set for several days as an adviser of sorts. The film unfolds with an ongoing, foreboding voiceover (voiced by actor Giovanni Ribisi), and it never hides the truth of the tragedy to come. The haunting question becomes the how and the why of it – inasmuch as there ever is a concrete how and why to a thing like taking one's life. And in using the storytelling framework of the boys' point of view, Coppola offers a perfect allegory to express how much boys, men and, ultimately, society, project onto young women; how much their behaviour and appearances are hyper-analysed in order to pathologize them. In terms of the film itself, the major 'events' or plot points are only the ones which would be memorable to teenagers, in the same dreamy haze as a high-school yearbook flashback: a shuffling, awkward house party that ends in sudden disaster; fumbling make-outs in cars; and a homecoming dance where Lux loses her virginity.

In terms of casting such a big – and young – ensemble, perhaps the most fortuitous of Coppola's choices was the 16-year-old Kirsten Dunst. Coppola first saw Dunst as a child actor in *Interview with a Vampire* (1994) and was struck by the contrast between Dunst's wholesome cheerleader-esque blondeness and a certain depth – even darkness – behind her eyes. Coppola was right: Dunst's depiction of Lux, the boldest and eventually most promiscuous of the girls, gives the film warmth and texture even as the storytelling often regards her as something of an enigma. Dunst later expressed her own anxiety around playing the role: she herself had not, she says, had much experience with boys or played such a grown-up part before. The apple of all the boys' eyes, Lux knows how to flirt better than the other girls; she plays footsie under the table and sunbathes in her bikini on the front lawn. Ultimately, though, it is her burgeoning womanhood and sexual curiosity that will lead to her parents' increasing, suffocating punishment.

Coppola's first feature is one of remarkably complete directorial vision. In 1999, a year when American teen high-school comedies and romances were at a frenzied peak – *American Pie, She's All That, 10 Things I Hate About You* and *Never Been Kissed* all appeared that year, to name a handful – she offers a darkly compelling image of teenage girlhood and defies any conventions of this high-school obsession. In a film culture where, generally speaking, sex, virginity and teen girls' bodies tended to be simple objects of male lust or crude punchlines, Coppola took teenage girls seriously. Nor, in her characterization of the Lisbon girls, does she lean into some of the more familiar tropes or trends of the 1990s teen film. These are not goths or witches or mean girls or quipping femmes; they are bored, nervous, hormonal adolescents with braces on their teeth and boys' names doodled on their notebooks (and, in Lux's case, her bra).

RIGHT: Kirsten Dunst, aged 16, on set.

OVERLEAF: Sofia Coppola and Kirsten Dunst, on a break between scenes.

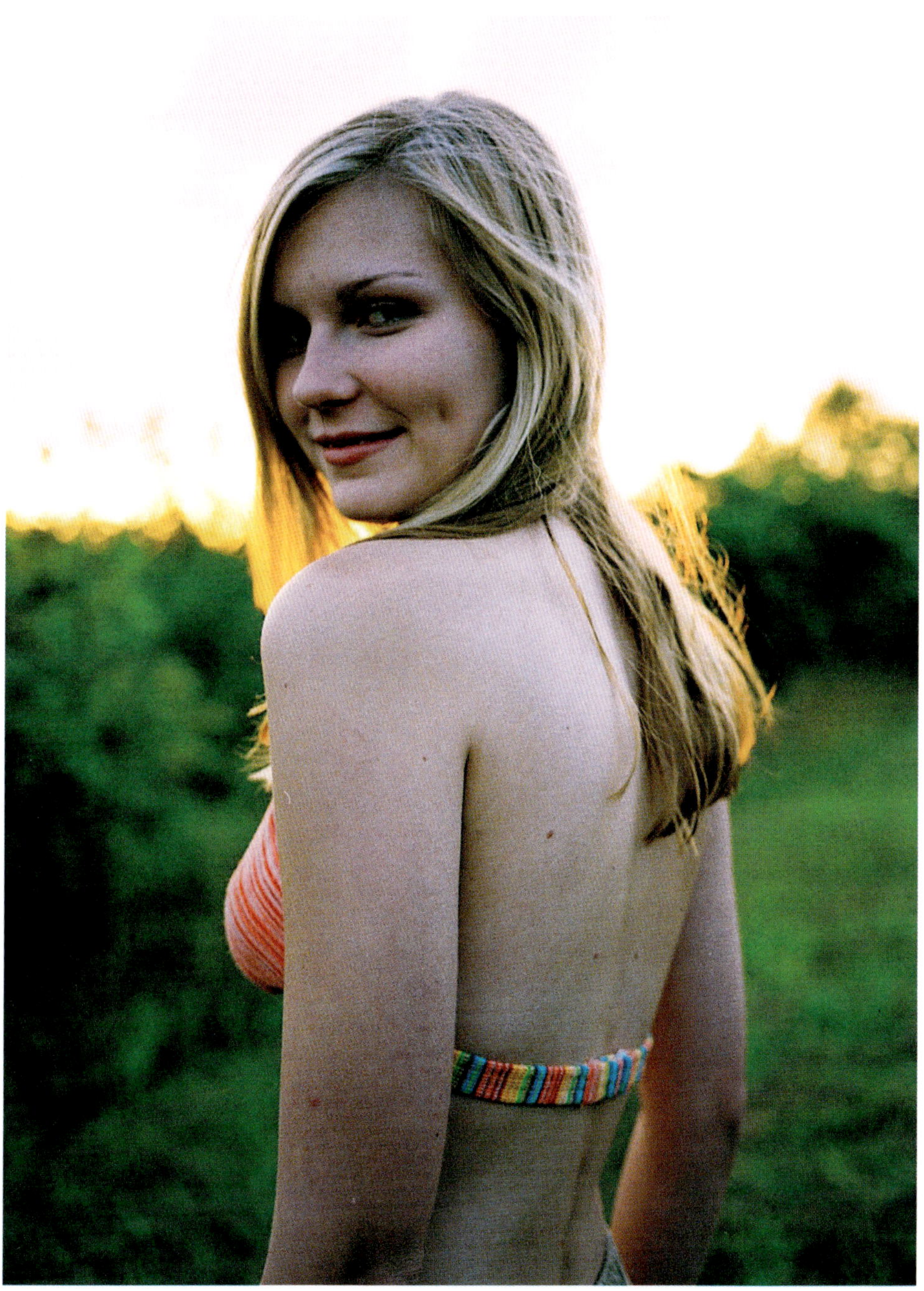

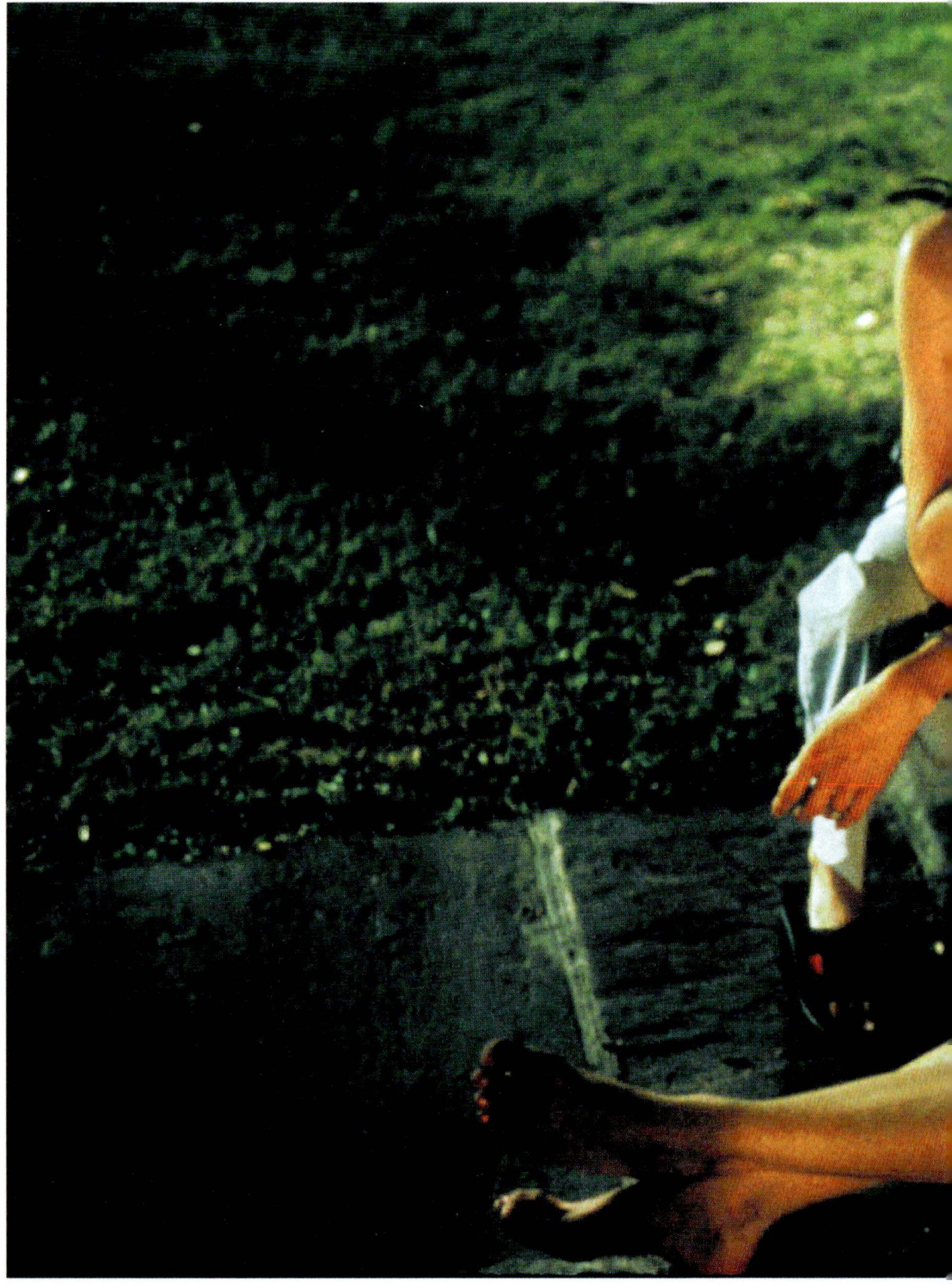

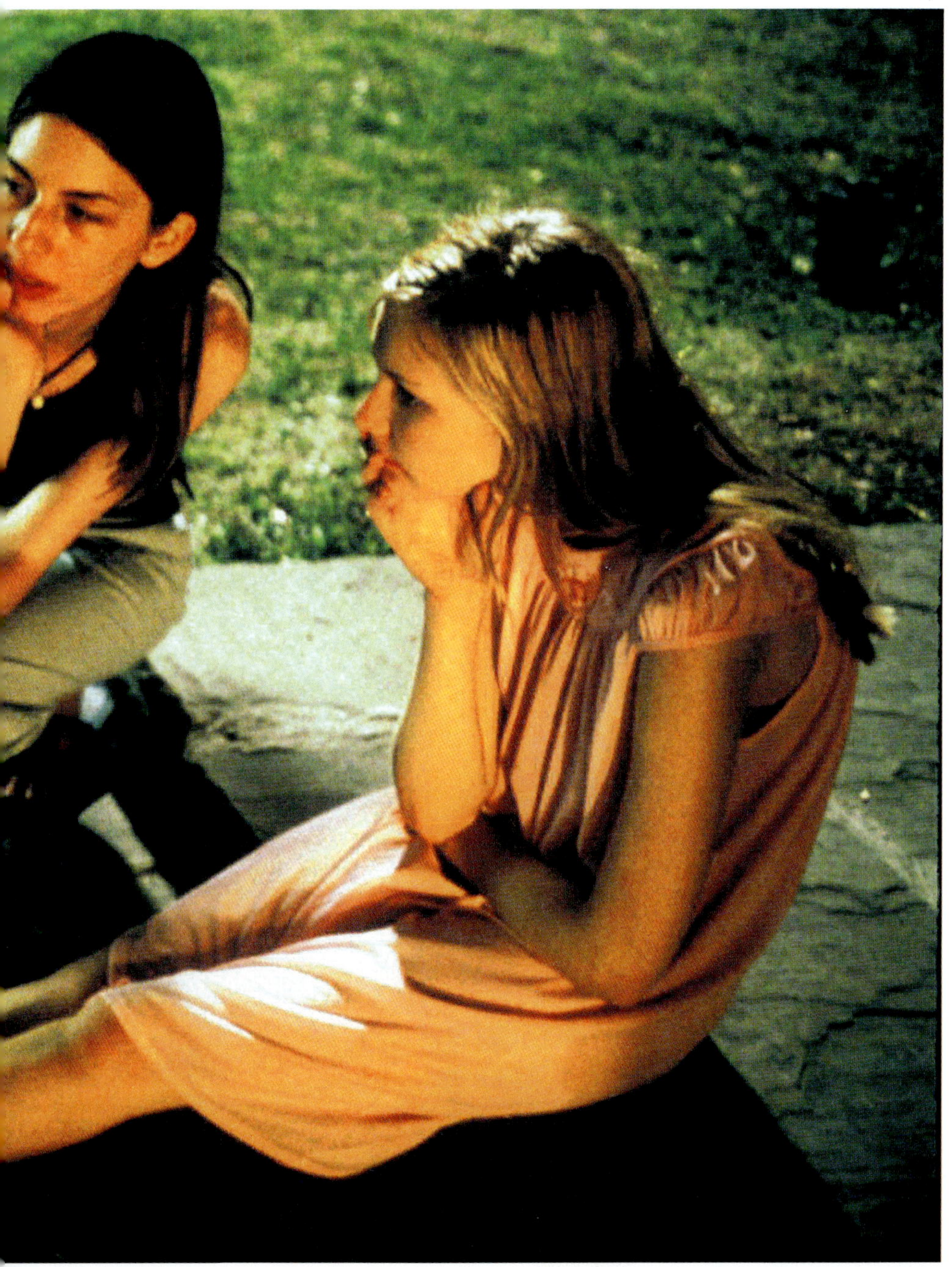

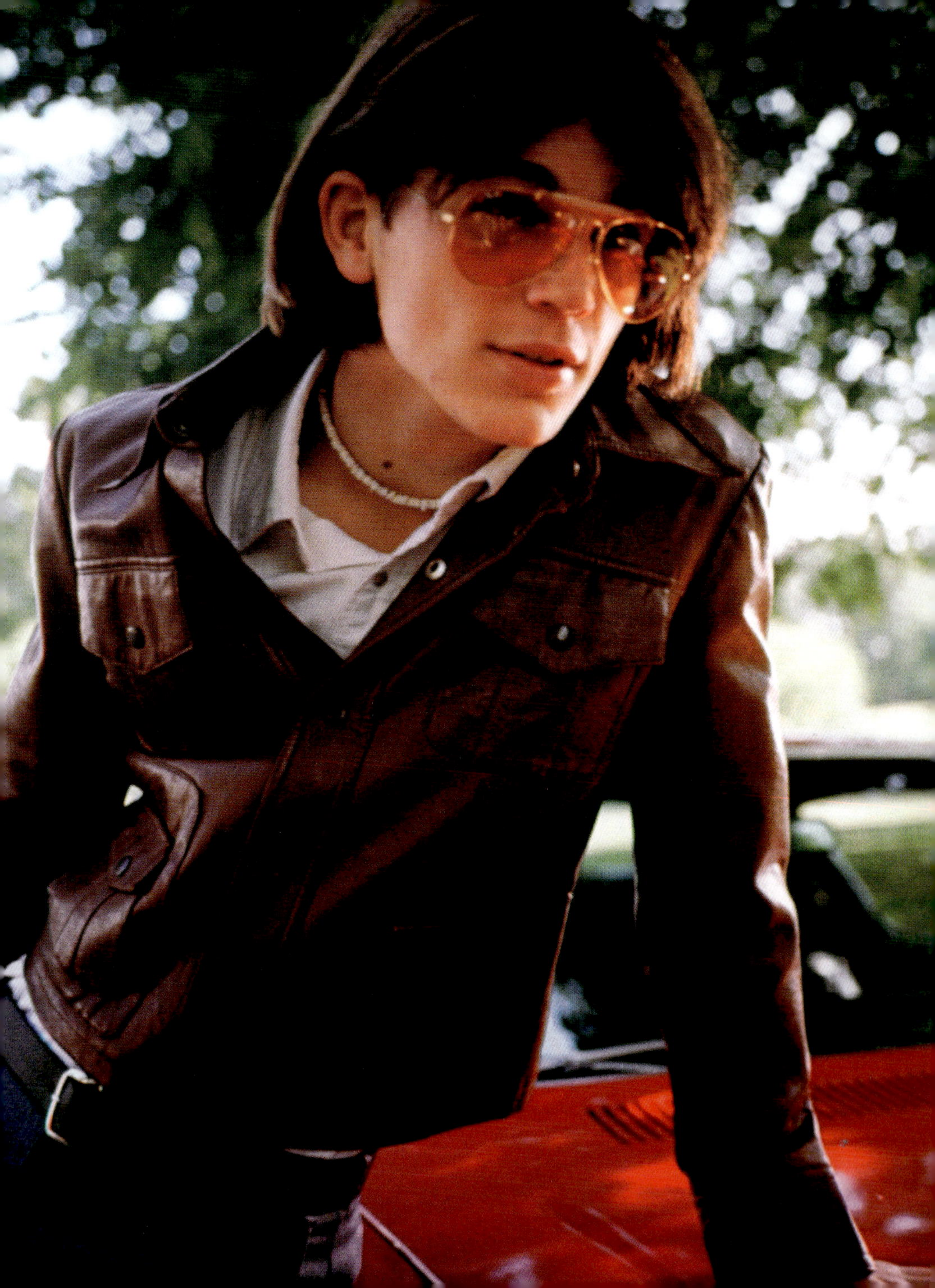

Beyond this, *The Virgin Suicides* was also a project which employed so many of the visual and thematic interests she would express further in her career: the so-called gilded cage of young women in varying degrees of wilting isolation and repression, even while often in materially comfortable surroundings. Sexual repression is another major theme (from *Marie Antoinette* to *Priscilla*, it's a distinct theme and one Coppola has acknowledged); the trappings of so-called frivolity and femininity that these characters reclaim as sustenance, looking for pleasure in pretty things where they can find it. Coppola has a distinctive eye for nail polish-and-makeup-covered dressers, the charming mystery of girly adolescent bedrooms, the idle magazine reading and lolling bare feet of the sisters in their isolation; we see this in *The Virgin Suicides* and repeatedly throughout her work, regardless of the setting.

For Coppola, surrounded as she was by the masculine Italian-American cabal of her father's world – cousins, friends and brothers alike – she couldn't help but be drawn to the girly confection of a subject like the one in the book. She revelled in Eugenides' novel and its fascination with the cosseted world of girlhood. As a revealing line from the book, repeated in voiceover in the film, goes: 'We began to understand the imprisonment of being a girl, how it made your mind active and dreamy, and how you understood what colours went together.'

Even if you've seen only a handful of Sofia Coppola's films, you know what a prophetically perfect summary it is of so much of

LEFT: Josh Hartnett as teen heartthrob Trip Fontaine.

OVERLEAF: Leslie Hayman, Kirsten Dunst, Hannah Hall and Chelsea Swain.

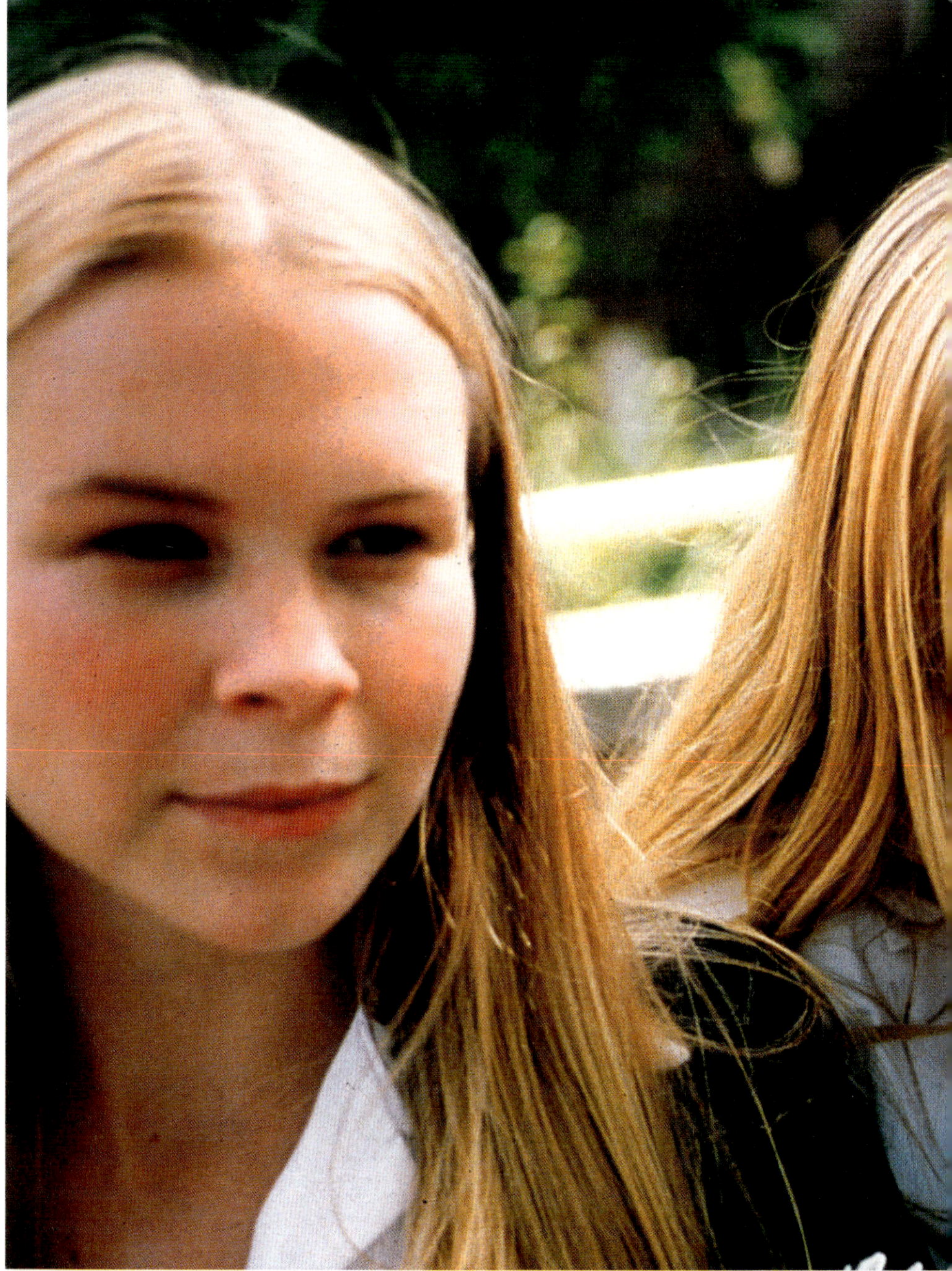

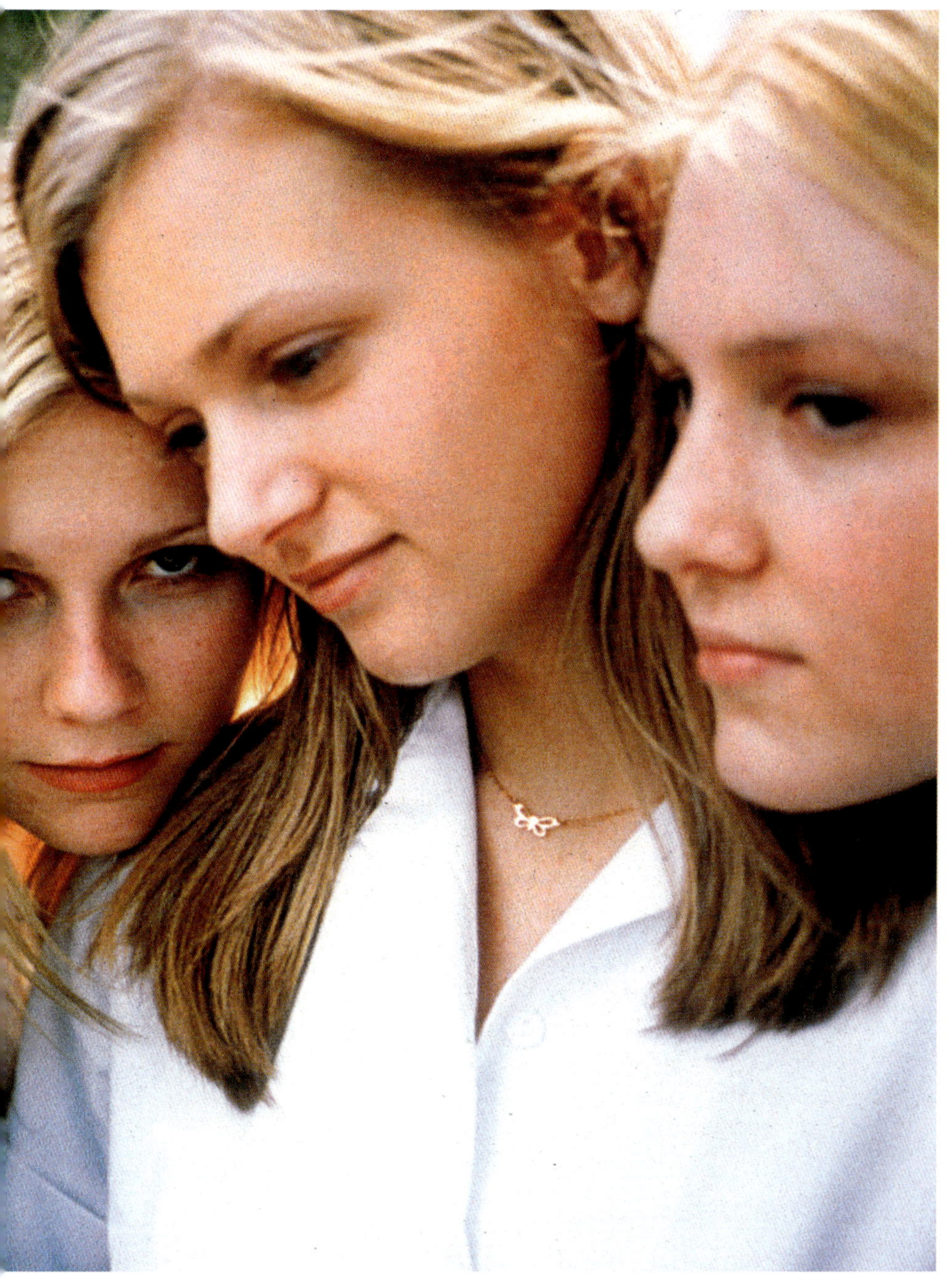

her work; how it describes both the constraints and the pleasant frivolity of girlhood, and how one might become a way to deal with the other. For his part, Jeffrey Eugenides felt Coppola captured his book wonderfully and added her own spin to it. In a 2018 interview, he expressed the idea that the point of his book in many ways is that these boys don't see or understand the girls very well at all, but that lack – that emptiness – is exactly what many young women readers seized onto. Perhaps that is exactly what Sofia herself saw as an opportunity within. Its impenetrability is precisely its point: when it comes to girlhood, there's a lot of conjecture and very little understanding. 'Maybe growing up with so many strong men around me meant I felt, I don't know, closely connected to being feminine,' Coppola said in a 2017 interview. 'In my first movie I felt like making something for teenage girls.' In her film, the gap between looking and actually *seeing* – between an external fascination with these young women and the actual truth of their lives – is made clear. She achieves this not only through the voiceover of these middle-aged men reminiscing over a female tragedy, but also through the exterior shots of the Lisbon house, its windows and its seemingly towering enigma.

Beyond its gendered element, there is also the story's obvious preoccupation with sudden and premature death. When Sofia, who is the youngest sibling in her family, was the tender age of 15, her oldest brother Giancarlo, who was 22, was killed in a boating accident. The shockwaves of that grief seem to have informed some of her attachment to the project; one presumes she knew, at a painfully young age, what it was like to experience the heaviness and darkness of this kind of loss. It gives a particular anguish and poignancy to Coppola's depiction of the sisters' reaction to the loss of their youngest, Cecilia. Framed carefully, mostly in nocturnal darkness, Mr Lisbon cradles the girl's crumpled body in the front yard as the others are held back by their mother,

Early work and *Lick the Star*

It took Sofia Coppola a little while of dabbling and moonlighting before she decided to turn her hand to filmmaking. Growing up fascinated by music, fashion, photography and the arts, she spent some time as a supporting actor in her father's films – and then starring memorably and controversially in *The Godfather Part III* (1990) – before turning to other pursuits. She went to college, dropped out, started a fashion label; she both appeared in and directed a handful of music videos. But it wasn't until 1998 that Coppola would make a film – a stylish 14-minute short called *Lick the Star* – that she realized she 'just knew' what it was she should be doing.

The short concerns a group of vicious, disaffected seventh-grade girls who take it upon themselves to poison the boys in their class, led by their imposing queen bee. Inspired by V C Andrews' *Flowers in the Attic* – a popular gothic novel of teen incest and arsenic poison – the girls go about their business to the needle drops of girl-punk and Riot Grrl bands like The Go-Go's, Free Kitten and The Amps, fronted by Kim Deal, formerly of the Pixies. Filmed in handheld, black and white 16mm, the grainy observational style might initially seem rough-around-the-edges for the usually pristine Sofia; but there are still revealing moments of the filmmaker's future within. A lackadaisical, poetic slow-motion sequence comes into play at one point; but perhaps more than anything else, *Lick the Star* is thematically of a piece with much of Coppola's later work. It's a real window into what would prove to be lasting auteurist preoccupations for her: death, teenage girlhood and the more unseemly and raucous behaviours and desires of young women. The fun had only just begun.

who has her arms thrown wide around them in a protective huddle. She is trying to shield them from the image of their dead sibling as they stand on the threshold of the family home, changed beyond measure. It's one of the most striking and memorable moments in the film.

As such, Coppola's approach is a curious mixture of melancholy memory and dark irony. In some elements, there's a real swoon of nostalgia, a rose-tinted affection for these doomed young women looking aloof in their 1970s summertime to the radio rock of Styx and Heart. But it also coolly uproots any of the usual cinematic affectations around nostalgia (compare and contrast to the tone of Richard Linklater's notably boyish 1970s teen flick, *Dazed & Confused*). This is a film where awkward high-school house parties turn into sites of horror and death; not quite gothic but verging on the territory, with its abrupt reveal of two stockinged feet hanging from the rafters or the waifish youngest sister tumbling from a window.

If all of that sounds serious, it's also worth noting that Coppola is never without a twinkle of sly humour. One of the boys (played by Robert Schwartzman) does the quasi-smooth flirtatious classic – a wall-lean – to talk to one of the sisters; the airless, mean-spirited gossip of suburban

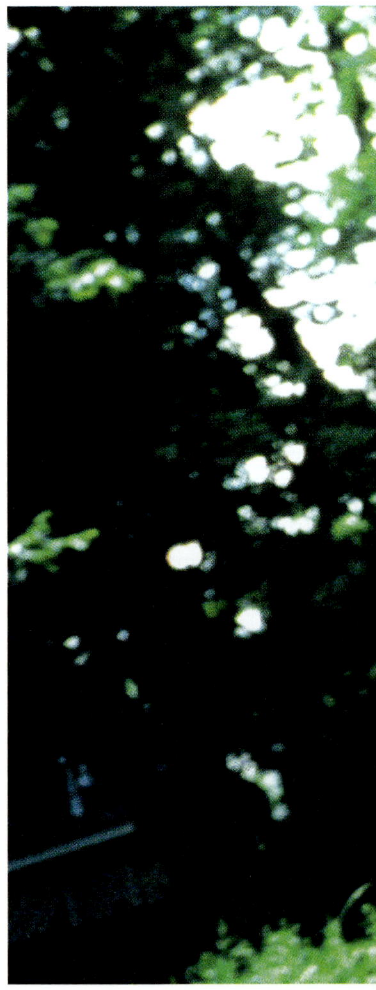

BELOW: A candid photo of Kirsten Dunst on set.

housewives and neighbours, with Coppola cutting between various domestic spaces to underscore the absurdity and cruelty of their prurient interests. And certainly the deadpan line from Cecilia, when she's being questioned about her motivation for attempting suicide, is a comic reading for the ages: 'Obviously, doctor, you've never been a 13-year-old girl.'

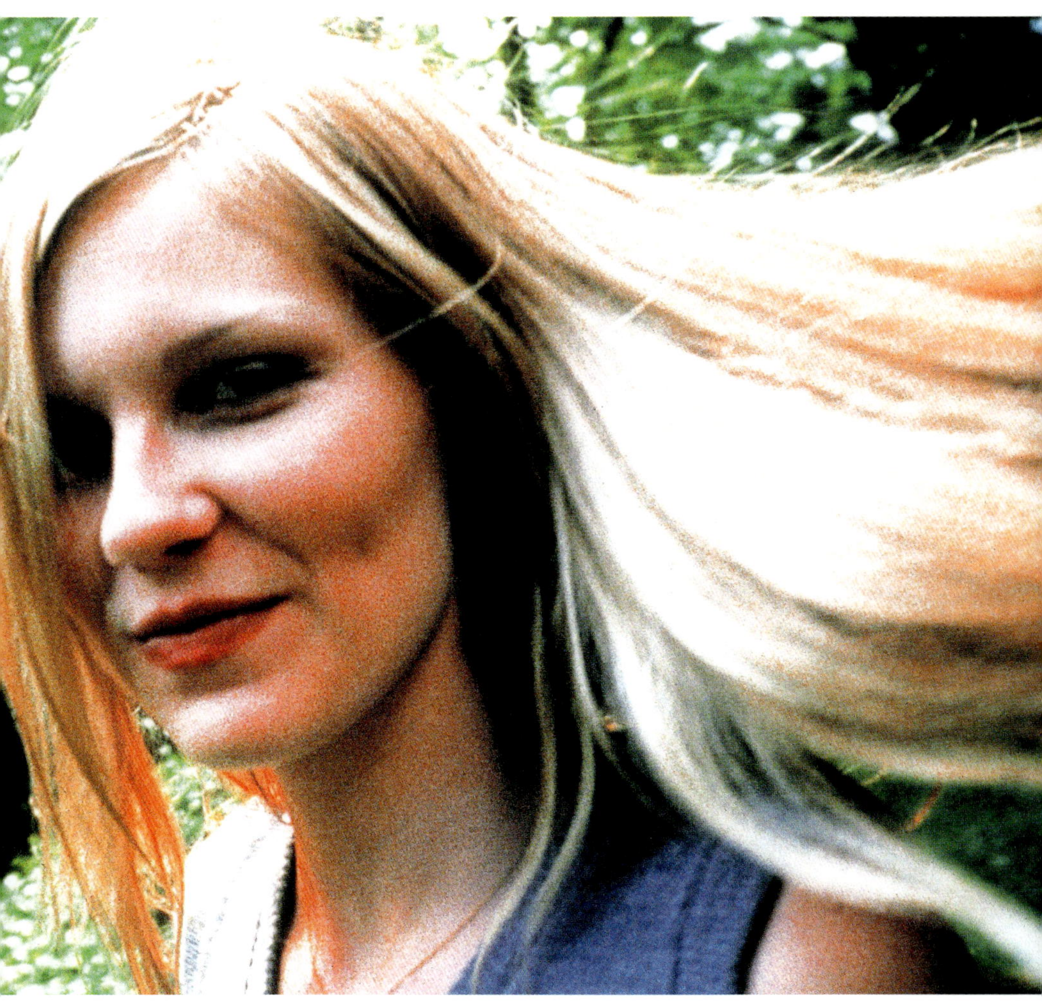

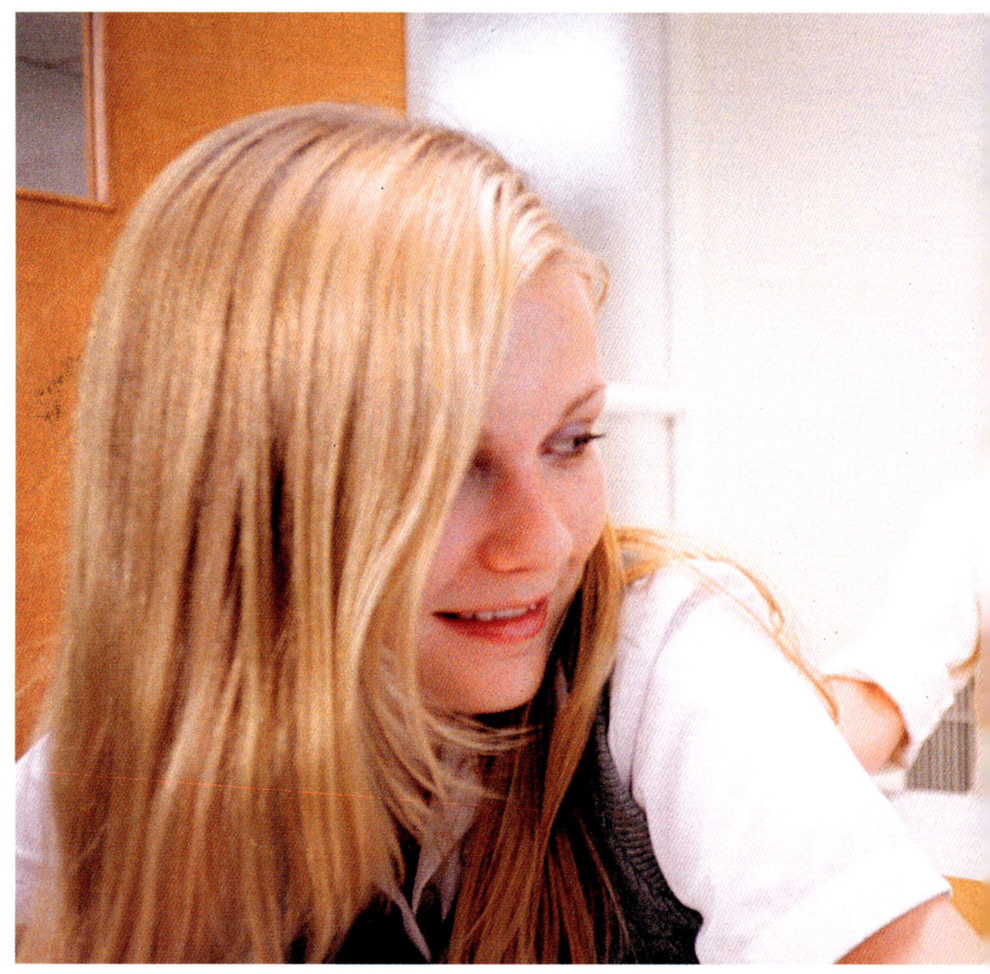

Coppola also finds a lightning rod for the female gaze in the form of Trip Fontaine, the weed-smoking jock heartthrob of the high school. Played by Josh Hartnett in a wig that was, apparently, notorious for falling off at inconvenient times, Coppola films him in intentional smitten slow-motion, tossing his pretty head back as girls stare in the high-school corridor, or an overhead shot of him topless in a swimming pool. She luxuriates in filming Hartnett

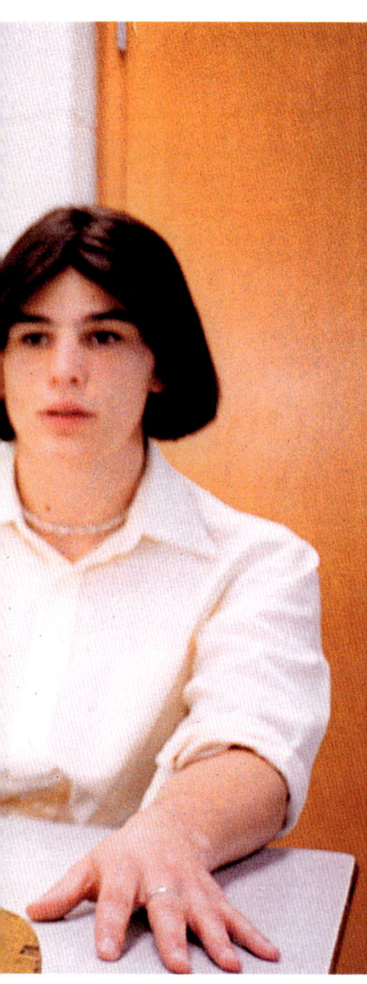

ABOVE: Lux Lisbon (Dunst) and Trip Fontaine (Hartnett) as short-lived high-school sweethearts.

with the wide-eyed, hormonal gaze of a teenage girl, even as Hartnett, apparently embarrassed by the attention, didn't quite know where to put his hands.

The other actors were a mixture of ingenues and stalwart veterans, with a cameo from Danny DeVito as a school psychologist. But the majority of the cast were teens themselves, lending a summer-camp feeling to the atmosphere on set, as Coppola later described it. She was, after all, only 29 herself, a de-facto camp counsellor to the largely teenage cast. Josh Hartnett, as one of the oldest of the youths, had his twentieth birthday on set. Onlookers like Eugenides referred to the mood during production as circumspect and carefully premeditated; apparently Coppola gave her direction quietly to individual cast and crew members, running a relaxed but disciplined set that never operated via declarative shouting. Coppola later said that her father, an important mentor, gave her advice that she ignored in favour of doing things her own – less macho – way. 'He would tell me to shout "Action!" louder so they knew I was in charge. I would say: "But Dad, this is how I do it."'

Throughout her career, Coppola would be known for maintaining controlled, quiet sets, and for taking a firm but gentle approach that contrasted with the stereotypical (read: masculine) idea of a film set. That she spent much of her childhood on her father's film sets – including on the inspiring but chaotic production of *Apocalypse Now* (1979) – seems to underline the fact that she appreciated her dad's mentorship while consciously cultivating a different atmosphere for her own work. In this cast full of mostly young women, navigating sensitive subject matter of sex and suicide, Coppola preferred to pull her actors to one side and confer with them privately. It says something about her sense of self-assurance as a young woman director, as well as her sensitivity towards her actors.

Another interesting addition to the cast was the all-important voiceover, speaking for the infatuated boys who had grown up into equally puzzled grown men, and in a sense, for Eugenides' own authorial voice. For this role, Coppola selected Giovanni Ribisi, who would go on to play the indifferent husband of her next film, *Lost in Translation*. Also key to *The Virgin Suicides* cast were, of course, the Lisbon parents, played by two acting veterans who brought plenty of authority – and other associations with past film work – to the screen. Mr Lisbon, the well-meaning maths teacher patriarch of the Lisbon family, is played by James Woods, usually a rather unctuous screen presence in films like *Salvador* (1986) and *Casino* (1996), but here supine and placid, letting his wife rule the roost.

Mrs Lisbon is a hawk-eyed helicopter mother with a strict religious bent, played by Kathleen Turner, who burst onto the screen in one of the most openly sensual, provocative erotic thrillers of the 1980s, *Body Heat* (1981). It hardly seems accidental that this hypersexual, adulterous past role might add layers to Mrs Lisbon's fixation on maintaining her daughters' purity. Her cruelty reaches a peak that's both literally and figuratively noxious when she forces Lux to burn her rock 'n' roll records as a punishment for

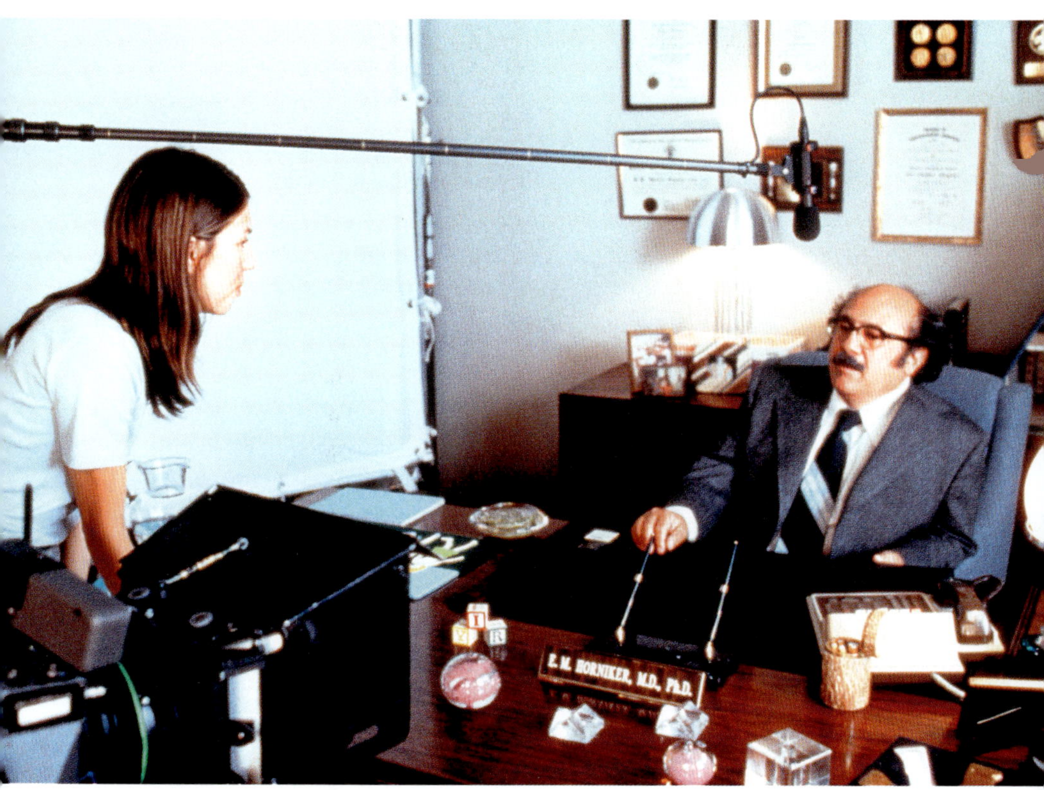

ABOVE: Coppola directs screen veteran Danny DeVito in his brief but memorable scenes as the school counsellor.

breaking curfew – and the smoking vinyl nearly chokes out the entire household.

There are shades of Brian De Palma's horror classic *Carrie* (1976) in this toxic mother-daughter dynamic, adapted from the Stephen King novel of the same name; that film, too, has an obsession with the struggles of female puberty. (Take Coppola's more subdued visual nod to tampons in a bathroom cupboard, an object key to the unforgettable opening scene of De Palma's film, where the protagonist is pelted with them in a locker room). Never was this visual and thematic reference clearer than in one of the most memorable sequences of *The Virgin Suicides*; the homecoming dance that the Lisbon girls have to beg their parents to attend, with Trip Fontaine's help. With its blinking fairy lights, chintzy polyester gowns and giant corsages, the dance can't help but to recall the climactic, hysterical prom scene in *Carrie*.

Per Coppola's subtle, elliptical style, nothing quite so theatrical occurs. Instead, the girls have a whirlwind of an evening, kiss some boys and drink some peppermint schnapps. But an underlying, creeping dread fills the atmosphere, and the turning point of the film is, ultimately, one of crossing a sexual threshold. But instead of De Palma's bloody, retributive revenge on a fickle football player, Coppola offers a different and far more realistic coda: a magical evening that descends into a disappointing one, a thrilling mutual infatuation that, for the boy, ends immediately once they have sex. Trip disappears into the night, leaving Lux alone, and soon after, the voiceover reveals that it's the last time the pair will see each other. To borrow a cliché, love's young dream has curdled. When Lux loses her virginity to Trip that night on a freezing cold football field, nothing is ever the same. The extreme punishment meted out for missing her parents' curfew – pulling the girls out of school and locking them indoors for weeks on end, cutting off all their access to the outside world – is ultimately the final catalyst for the girls' actions.

Throughout the film, Coppola uses a variety of cinematic tricks and clever stylistic choices to convey these girlish desires and the prism through which the boys view them. She and her cinematographer Lance Acord often borrow from the visual vernacular of photographers like William Eggleston and Joel Meyerowitz, with their ethereal sense of everyday Americana, and Coppola's use of low, almost bleached lighting, like an overdeveloped photograph, gives a further air of memory to proceedings.

For many of Coppola's films to follow, she would call upon the skills of the talented costume designer Stacey Battat, but on her first two projects she worked with the respected Nancy Steiner, who had designed to costumes for Todd Haynes' psychodrama *Safe* (1995), and perhaps more fascinatingly, outfitted both Nirvana and Gwen Stefani for music videos in the early 1990s. Steiner had grown up in the 1970s herself, and wanted a floaty, natural look for these rather sheltered young women, who would care about fashion trends but not be at the forefront of the era's styles.

Steiner made the Lisbon sisters white floral prom dresses – all notably similar but for a tiny colour difference in the pattern – with the intention of giving the sisters an out-of-time quality; they are not cutting-edge or hyper-trendy, and are notably covered up given their strict Catholic upbringing. Even in her filmmaking debut, Coppola was thinking very carefully about fashion and psychology (which makes sense for a woman who had interned with Chanel in Paris at the age of 15). Style, colour and costume would remain a key factor in every one of her films to date. She would also deploy her first use of the band Air in her quest for the perfect soundtrack on the movie; outside of the period-specific 1970s rock featured, their art-rock vibe fit perfectly, and she would go on to use them again in *Lost in Translation*.

The Virgin Suicides premiered at the prestigious Directors' Fortnight of Cannes Film Festival to broadly positive reviews, and would go on to have a real cult-hit impact on generations of young women; the film is often still referenced today on TikTok and Instagram, paying homage to the moody teenage aesthetics of 'bed rotting' and reading *The Bell Jar* in a white nightgown like the suburban waifs of *The Virgin Suicides* might have done. There is something ineffable and timeless about this portrayal of teen girlhood angst and the inability of outsiders to understand, while the film's wry sense of humour keeps it from sinking into total darkness.

'None of my daughters lacked for any love. I never understood why,' says Mrs Lisbon near the end of the film. But she – perhaps like everyone else, ultimately – fails to understand that love and possession are not mutually exclusive. The central enigma is never fully satisfied by Coppola's interpretation of the story, but it is hinted at in a deliciously ambiguous manner. In a microcosm of the wider world at large, the pretty and well-loved (by their parents, the school, one another) Lisbon girls seem to have it all. But the endless surveillance and policing of their bodies from the adults and the boys who confuse love for control is what drives them to despair. The only way the girls can think to reclaim themselves is through an act of strange and defiant self-annihilation, committed collectively.

RIGHT: *The Virgin Suicides* US poster, 2000.

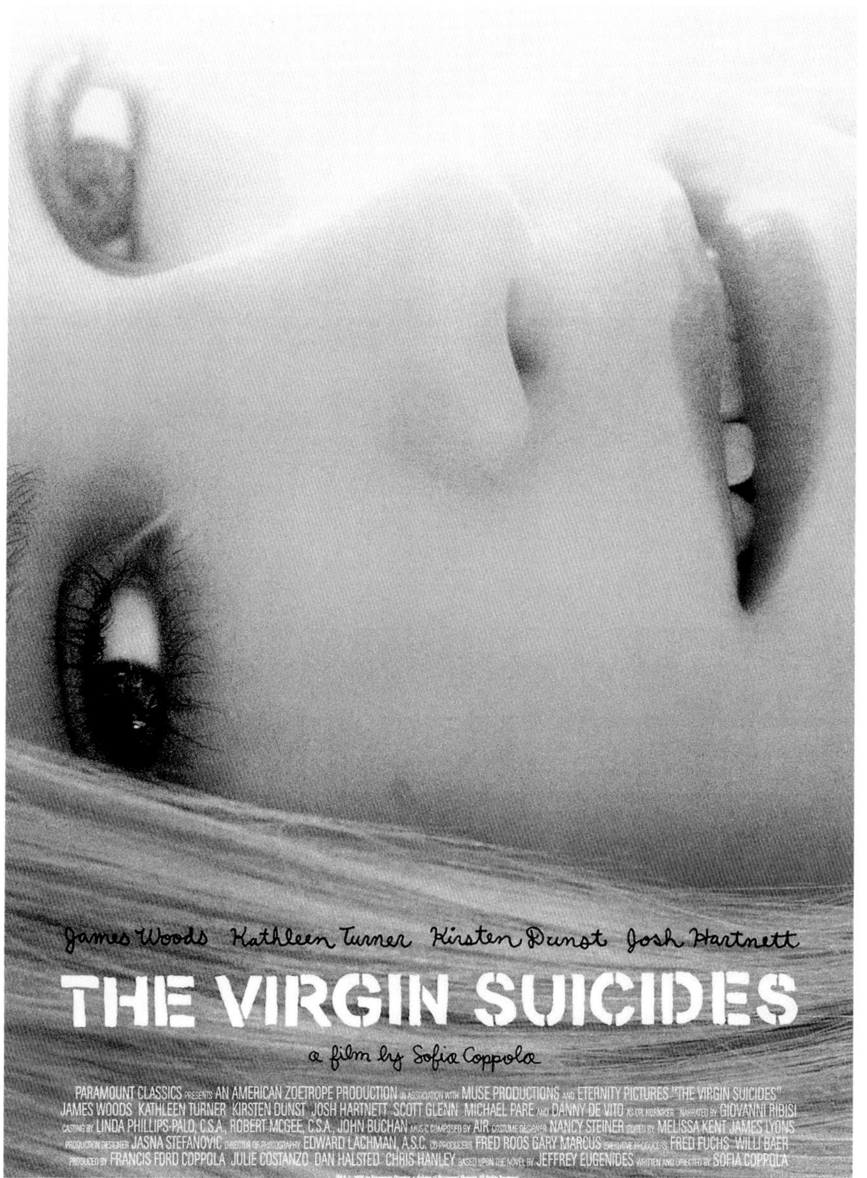

James Woods Kathleen Turner Kirsten Dunst Josh Hartnett
THE VIRGIN SUICIDES
a film by Sofia Coppola
PARAMOUNT CLASSICS PRESENTS AN AMERICAN ZOETROPE PRODUCTION IN ASSOCIATION WITH MUSE PRODUCTIONS AND ETERNITY PICTURES "THE VIRGIN SUICIDES"
JAMES WOODS KATHLEEN TURNER KIRSTEN DUNST JOSH HARTNETT SCOTT GLENN MICHAEL PARE AND DANNY DE VITO AS DR. HORNIKER NARRATED BY GIOVANNI RIBISI
CASTING BY LINDA PHILLIPS-PALO, C.S.A., ROBERT MCGEE, C.S.A., JOHN BUCHAN MUSIC COMPOSED BY AIR COSTUME DESIGNER NANCY STEINER EDITED BY MELISSA KENT JAMES LYONS
PRODUCTION DESIGNER JASNA STEFANOVIC DIRECTOR OF PHOTOGRAPHY EDWARD LACHMAN, A.S.C. CO-PRODUCERS FRED ROOS GARY MARCUS EXECUTIVE PRODUCERS FRED FUCHS WILLI BAER
PRODUCED BY FRANCIS FORD COPPOLA JULIE COSTANZO DAN HALSTED CHRIS HANLEY BASED UPON THE NOVEL BY JEFFREY EUGENIDES WRITTEN AND DIRECTED BY SOFIA COPPOLA

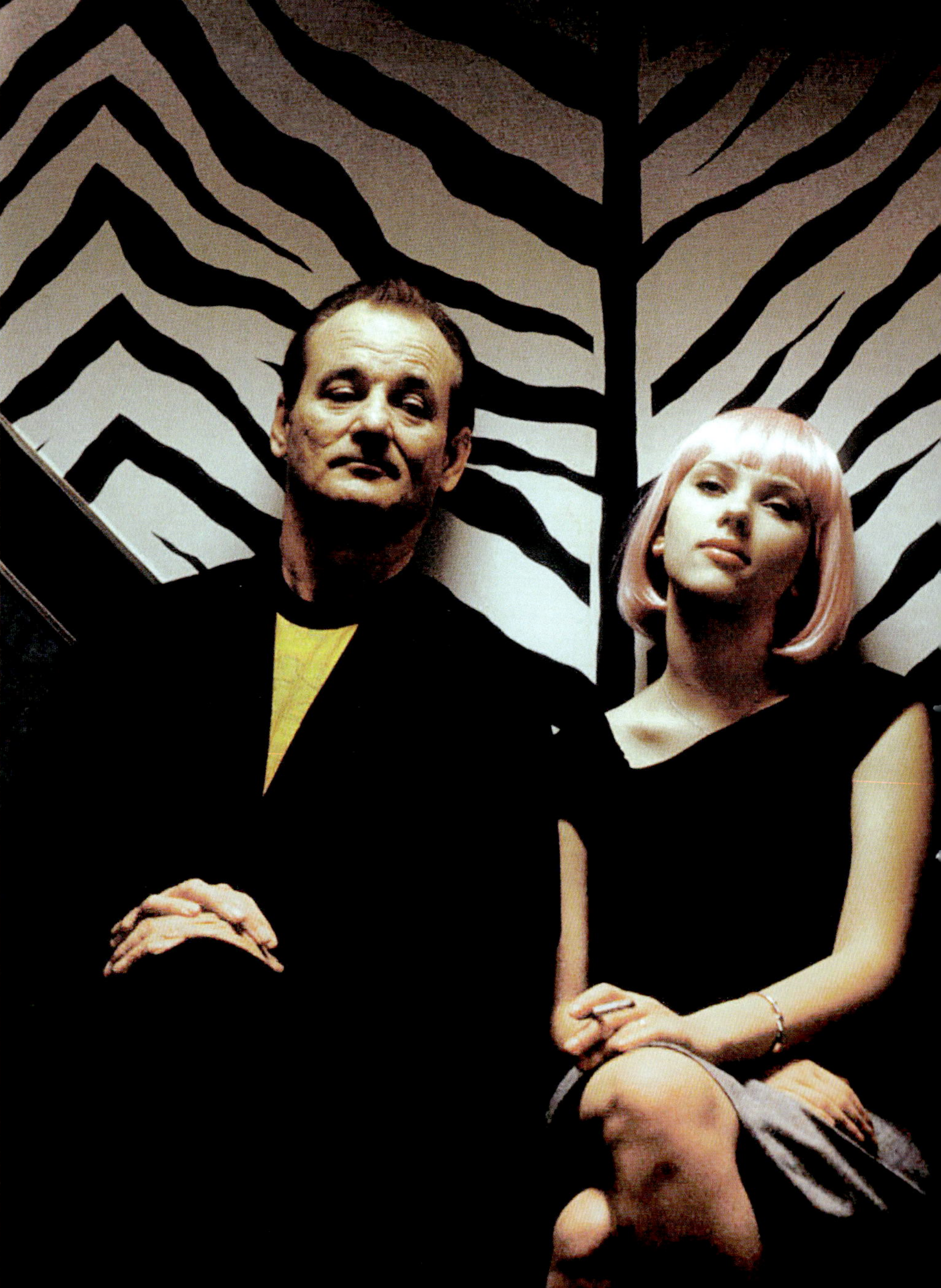

'Let's never come here again because it will never be as much fun.'

LOST IN TRANSLATION
2003

Over the course of 27 days in the sprawling city of Tokyo, a plucky crew of Americans with little of the Japanese language under their belt – along with a team of helpful local film crew – made a movie that would go on to become one of the key films of the new millennium. But *Lost in Translation* began its life in the loneliest corners of Sofia Coppola's imagination. Before Scarlett Johansson and Bill Murray, before *that* pink wig and the Roxy Music karaoke, before Suntory whisky jokes and that now-iconic opening shot of a girl laying in bed in her underwear, it was a personal story. Coppola's screenplay – which she wrote over the course of six months – was based on an amalgamation of her own experiences of travelling and working in Japan in her twenties. At the time, Coppola was married to Spike Jonze, a buzzy indie-darling director who was, at least initially, more established than her. Countless headlines and gossip columns were later dedicated to speculation around which characters in the film were based on whom and how close it was to reality. It hardly matters. The end result transcends any of Coppola's autobiographical detail, because it touches on the ache of uncertainty that runs through so many of our lives, no matter our age or circumstance.

While Coppola wrote what would become *Lost in Translation*, she bounced back and forth between another idea. She would stop to work on one screenplay when she felt stuck with the other,

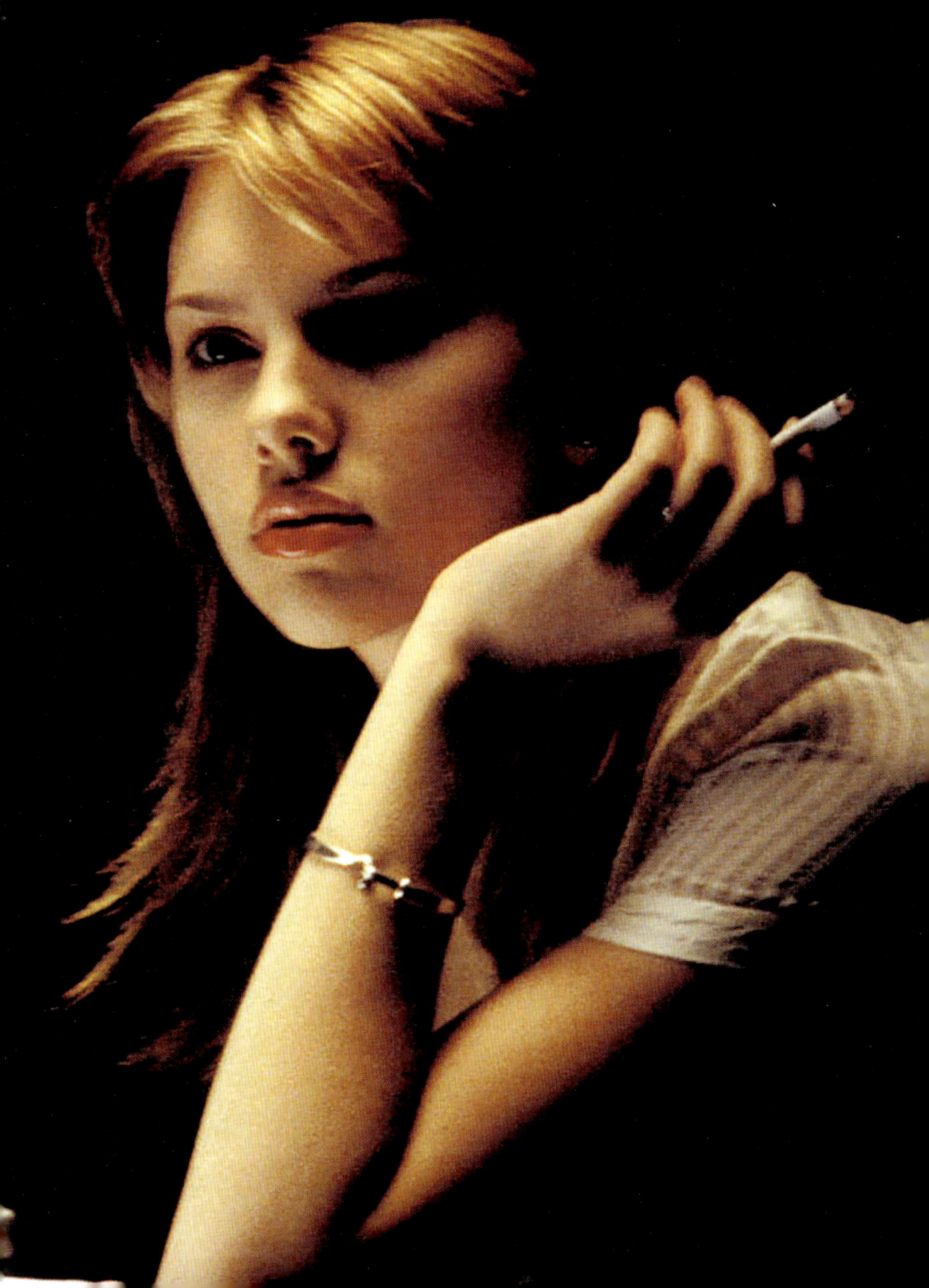

but they couldn't have been more different. What they had in common was that both screenplays were set in far-flung locations, a great distance from the suburban America of her debut film. One, a period piece about a famous historical French queen, would require serious funding to achieve. But *Lost in Translation*, a melancholy almost-romance between two lonely Americans in the sterile luxury of a foreign hotel, seemed more within reach, if nonetheless ambitious. It was written with an elusive A-lister in mind for its lead male role; it would have to be shot on location, without shooting permits, and with logistics and language barriers to rival those in the film itself. Coppola raised £4 million to do it, which even in 2003 was not exactly a huge bankroll; but she had something to say, and she was determined to say it.

To tell this tale of alienation and romance, Coppola lands on the protagonist of an unformed newlywed, 22-year-old Charlotte (played by Scarlett Johansson, who was only 17 at the time). She is in

RIGHT: Coppola's distant dream of casting Bill Murray as her jaded movie star, Bob Harris, came true.

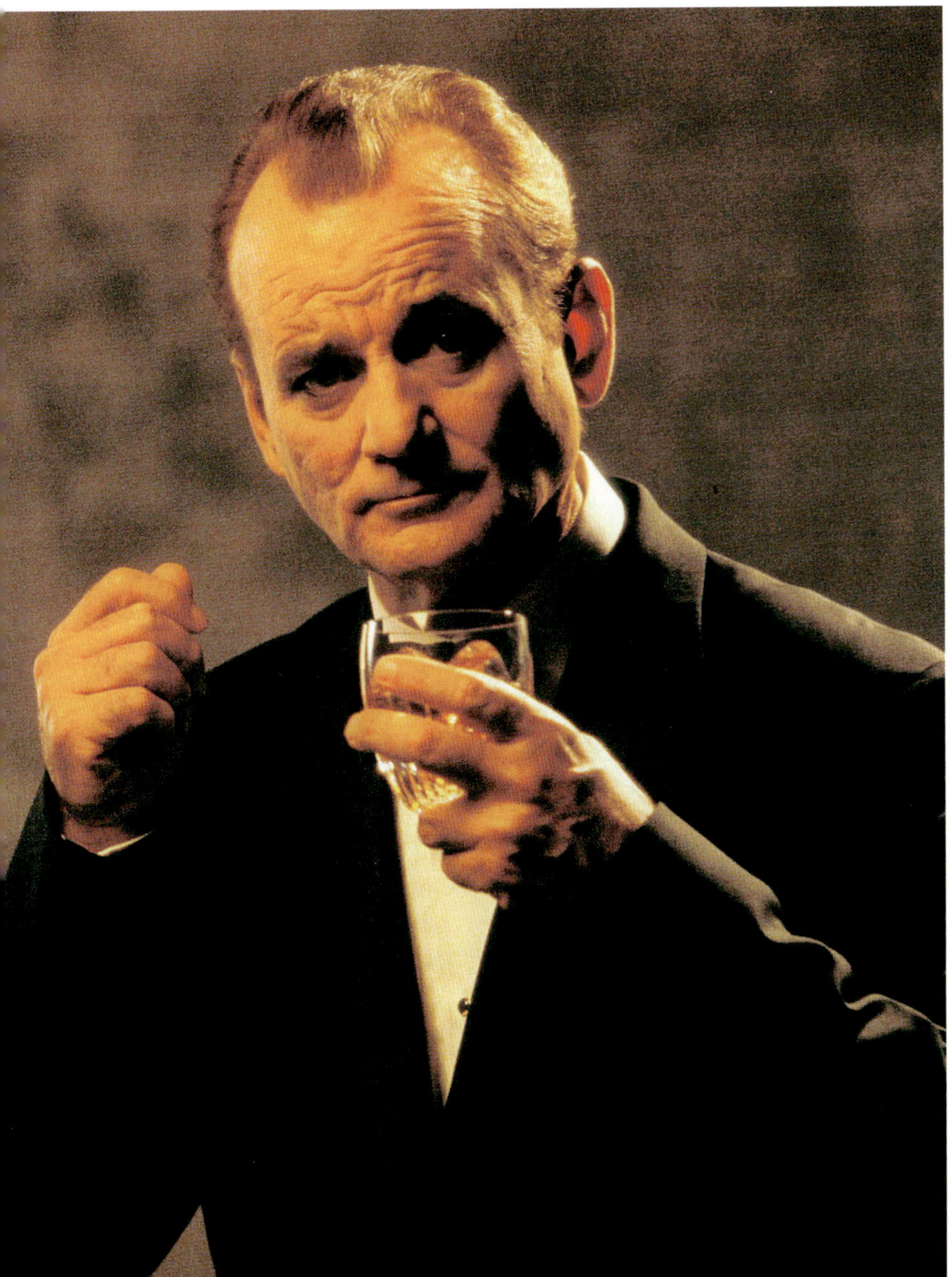

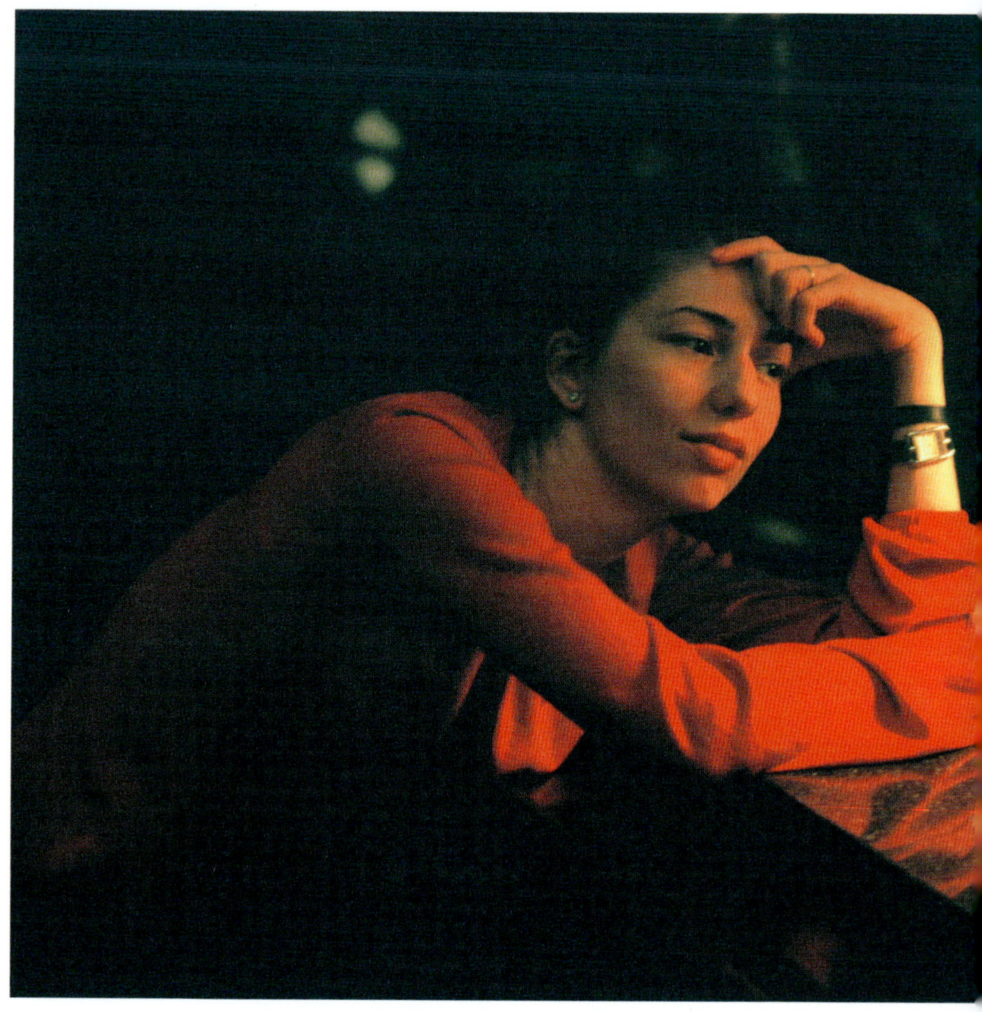

Tokyo mainly to accompany her hotshot photographer husband (Giovanni Ribisi, pretty evidently based on Coppola's own ex-husband Jonze) while he's on a fashion shoot. He works (and, you begin to imagine, plays) long hours away, leaving his wife alone for days on end. In her imposingly quiet luxury hotel room, Charlotte pads around in her underwear, insomnia-ridden and restless.

ABOVE: A pensive moment for Sofia on a busy Tokyo shoot.

OVERLEAF: Charlotte and Bob nurse drinks at their lonely hotel bar.

She doesn't know anyone, or speak any Japanese, and so she is in this liminal space, left with her thoughts and her worries about whatever her husband is up to (mainly that he is ignoring her for long stretches of time).

We learn through the course of the film that Charlotte is a Yale alumni with a degree in philosophy. We also learn that as a recent graduate, she is feeling uncertain and unmoored. At one point, she admits she has dabbled in photography, and also in writing, but worries they were phases, suffering from the all-too-common female impostor syndrome. Like the characters in *The Virgin Suicides*, she remains rather opaque to the viewer even as she shares a few scant morsels about herself. But one thing we do know is she's close to a crisis. At one point, early in the film, she makes a phone call home to a friend, tearful and lonely. She's rebuffed with casual, ignorant good cheer, as though her friend hardly notices her mood. With the kind of sweeping, disjointed train of thought reserved for someone who is, so to speak, 'going through it', she says: 'I went to this shrine today...there were these monks and they were chanting. And I didn't feel anything. You know...I don't know. I even tried ikebana. And John is using these hair products. I just, I don't know who I married.'

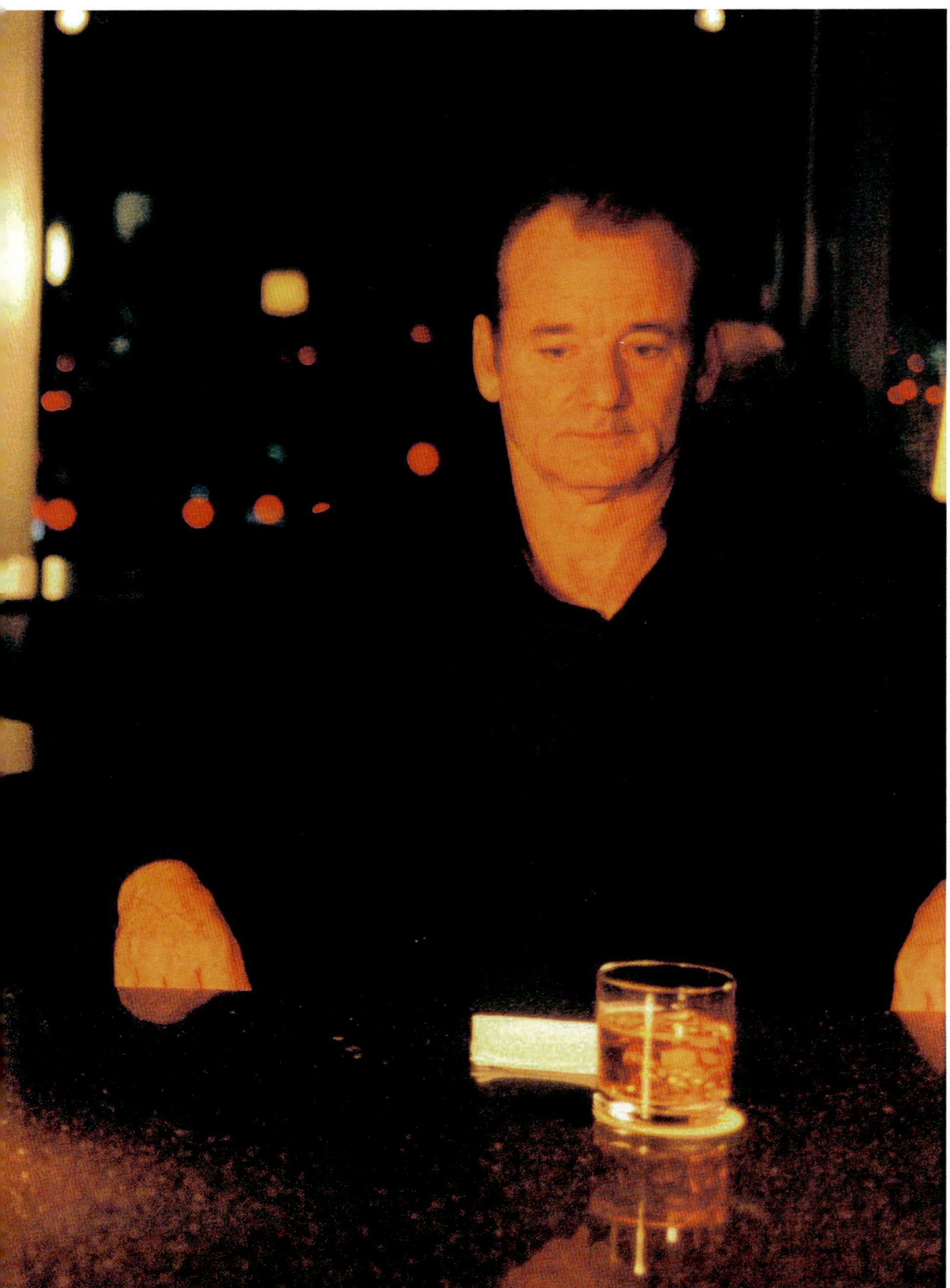

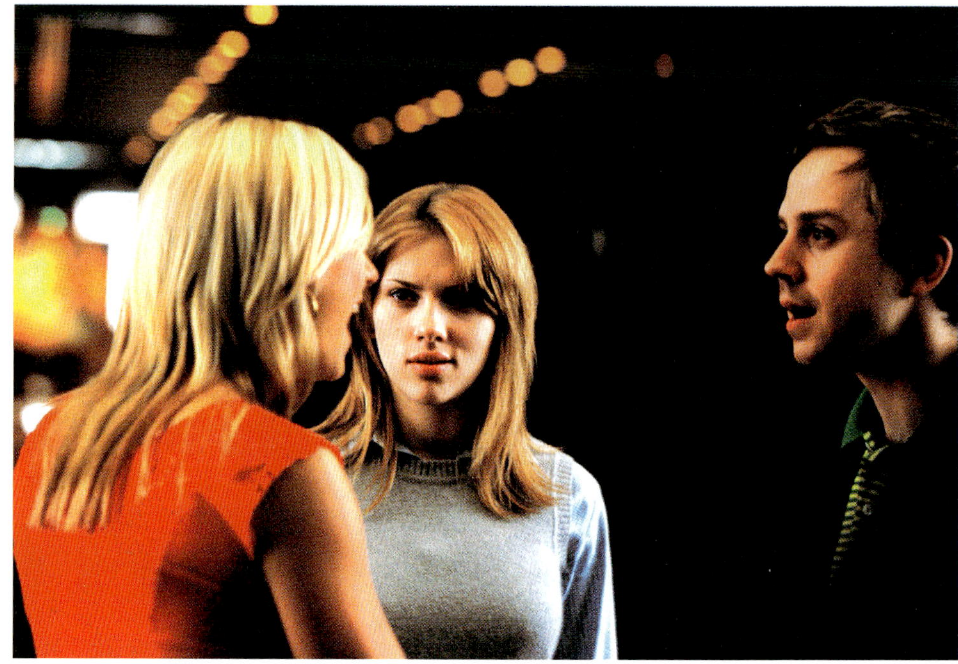

Her non sequiturs reveal a deep, implacable discomfort with what she's doing in this place and her husband's superficiality. Her attempts – and failure to – enjoy her trip only seem to compound her anxiety (ikebana, the traditional Japanese art of flower arranging, should probably be relaxing). But her friend is hardly up to the task of helping her unpick it. Scarlett Johansson, who Coppola first spotted in the 1996 indie *Manny & Lo*, had an interesting quality: a youthful baby face combined with a rather husky, low register in her voice. Coppola was reminded of 1940s siren Lauren Bacall and enjoyed this quality enough to trust the teenager with the role. For Johansson's part, it was a star-making turn, even if – as she later admitted – at the time she had no real idea how the film would come together onscreen.

For the part of Charlotte's romantic interest, Bob Harris, Coppola needed someone who could give a meta quality to the role of a disillusioned, middle-aged movie star shooting a whiskey commercial for spare cash. The director had no clue if she could obtain Bill Murray, apparently spending five months chasing the 1980s comedy legend around, writing him letters and asking friends of Hollywood friends for a contact for the then-agentless actor. Finally, she had some luck and managed to go to a dinner with Murray, but he was difficult to pin down even once he'd agreed. He never signed a contract prior to production, and right up until he appeared in Tokyo a week before the shoot began, she was still half-convinced he might not show. Her risk-taking paid off; Murray is perfect as this frustrated actor who is both accustomed to being treated as a special guest and exhausted by it. It's a unique problem only afforded to the wealthy and famous, but if anyone could understand it, it would be Bill Murray.

As Coppola herself has pointed out, very little about *Lost in Translation* could work as well as it does without the chemistry of its leads. It was a risk; she did not rehearse or test Johansson and Murray together before production. But her instinct for casting the right people worked: onscreen, the pair have an unassuming, slyly funny rapport. Their characters' natural ease and honesty with each other is unusual from the start, particularly given the gulf between their ages and experience. ('Is this your midlife crisis?' Charlotte teases Bob when she sees him in a garish designer T-shirt.) There's no desire for pretense between them.

It's a finely tuned balance to achieve when you're casting an ironclad screen veteran opposite a young relative unknown, particularly when your real protagonist is ultimately the latter of the two. It could have been easy for Murray's casual charm and familiar presence to bulldoze the teen actress, but Coppola's delicate threading of their stories ensures this is not the case.

She dedicates much of her screentime to Charlotte's interior life, and as the director later pointed out, 'My first three films all felt tied together by these themes of girlhood and womanhood.' Which is to say, this was still in many ways the locus of her interest. In *Lost in Translation*, it's the essential loneliness of Charlotte's character that we're meant to zero in on. Her fears about the future are answered, in part, by the age and experience Bob has to offer, and she sees the possible pitfalls and the reality of a lived-in, unhappy marriage. As much as anything, Charlotte can't seem to get anyone to truly *see* her, even if her husband, a photographer, and the film's own camera eye, in ironic commentary, are *looking* at her all the time.

Still, actors can only take a film so far. Coppola calibrates their scenes together – and apart – with a wry sense of physical humour (Bob unable to operate a treadmill, or standing a foot taller than everyone in a lift), staging it and her camera with perfect deadpan distance from the action. Body language and placement of actors within the frame are meaningful; perhaps never more so than in the striking shot of Bob and Charlotte in the late-night karaoke bar hallway, sitting intimately shoulder to shoulder but not looking at each other. They are close but distant, and there is seemingly an impossible gulf of experience between the two of them. Coppola and director of photography Lance Acord, inspired by compositions from the likes of Wong Kar-Wai and Jean-Luc Godard, have this carefully-choreographed quality throughout, utilizing nocturnal neon lights and elegantly removed ennui to speak in visual language alone.

RIGHT: Sofia Coppola and Bill Murray walk through Tokyo streets.

OVERLEAF: Bob calls out to Charlotte as they part ways.

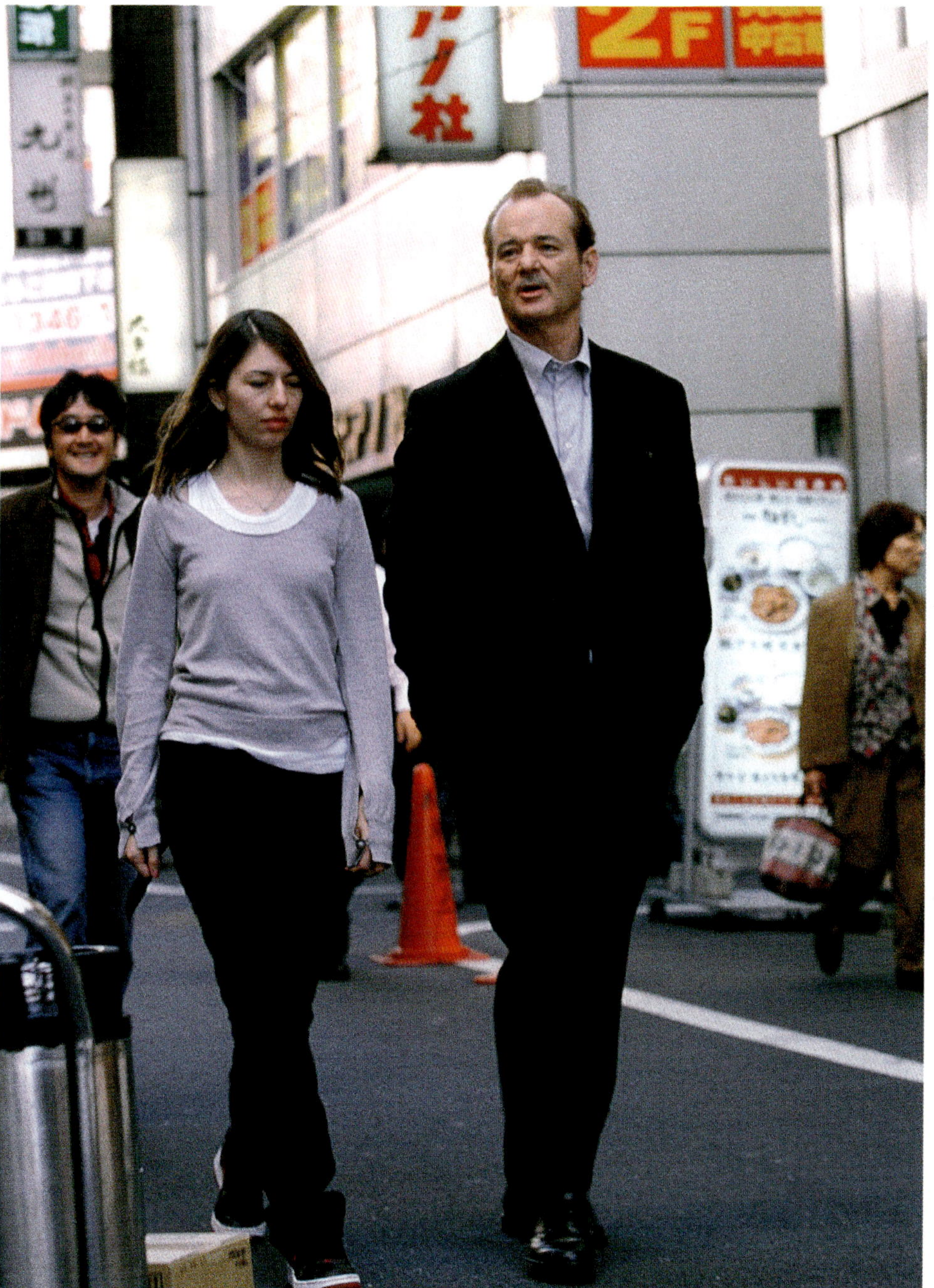

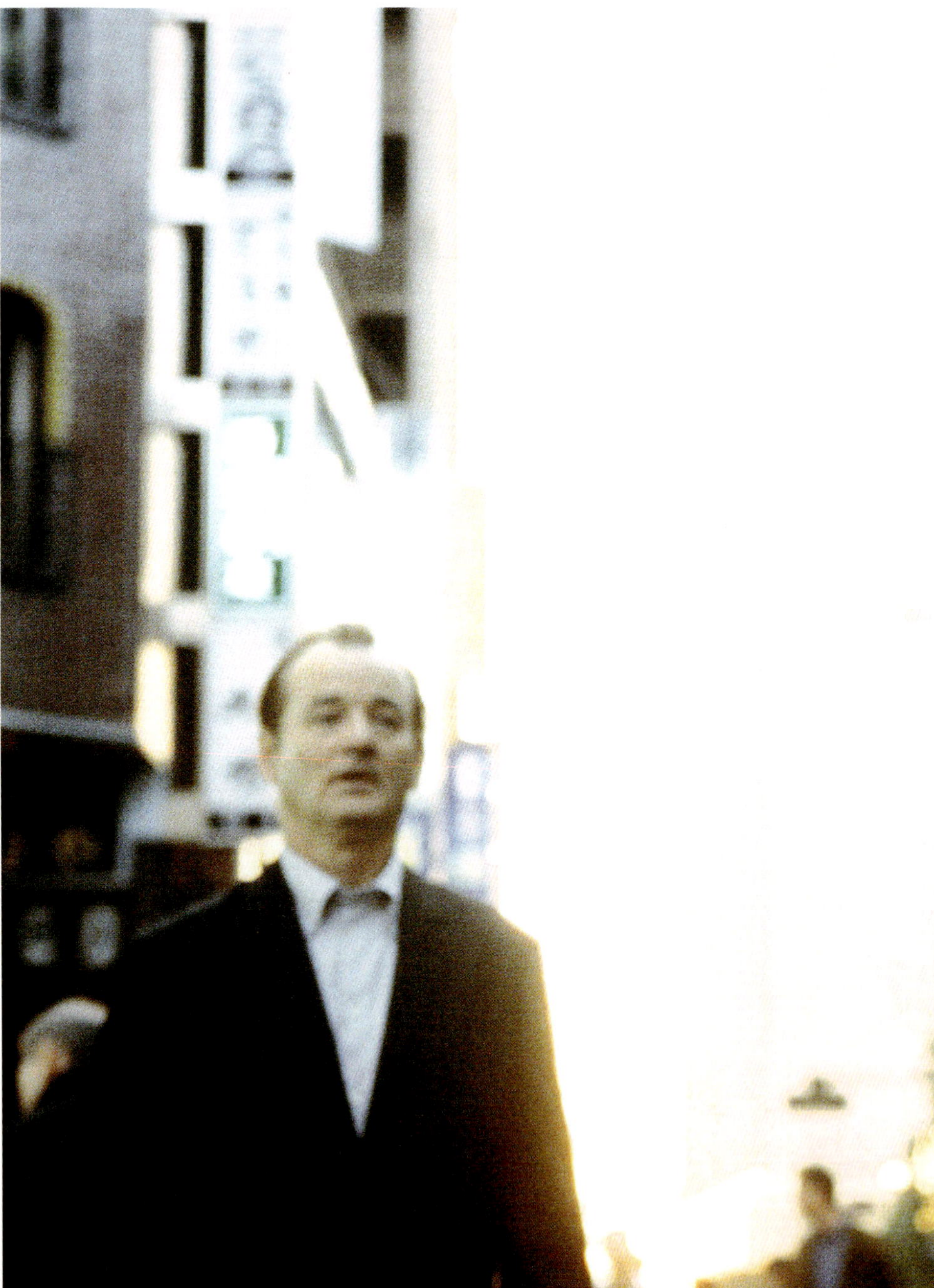

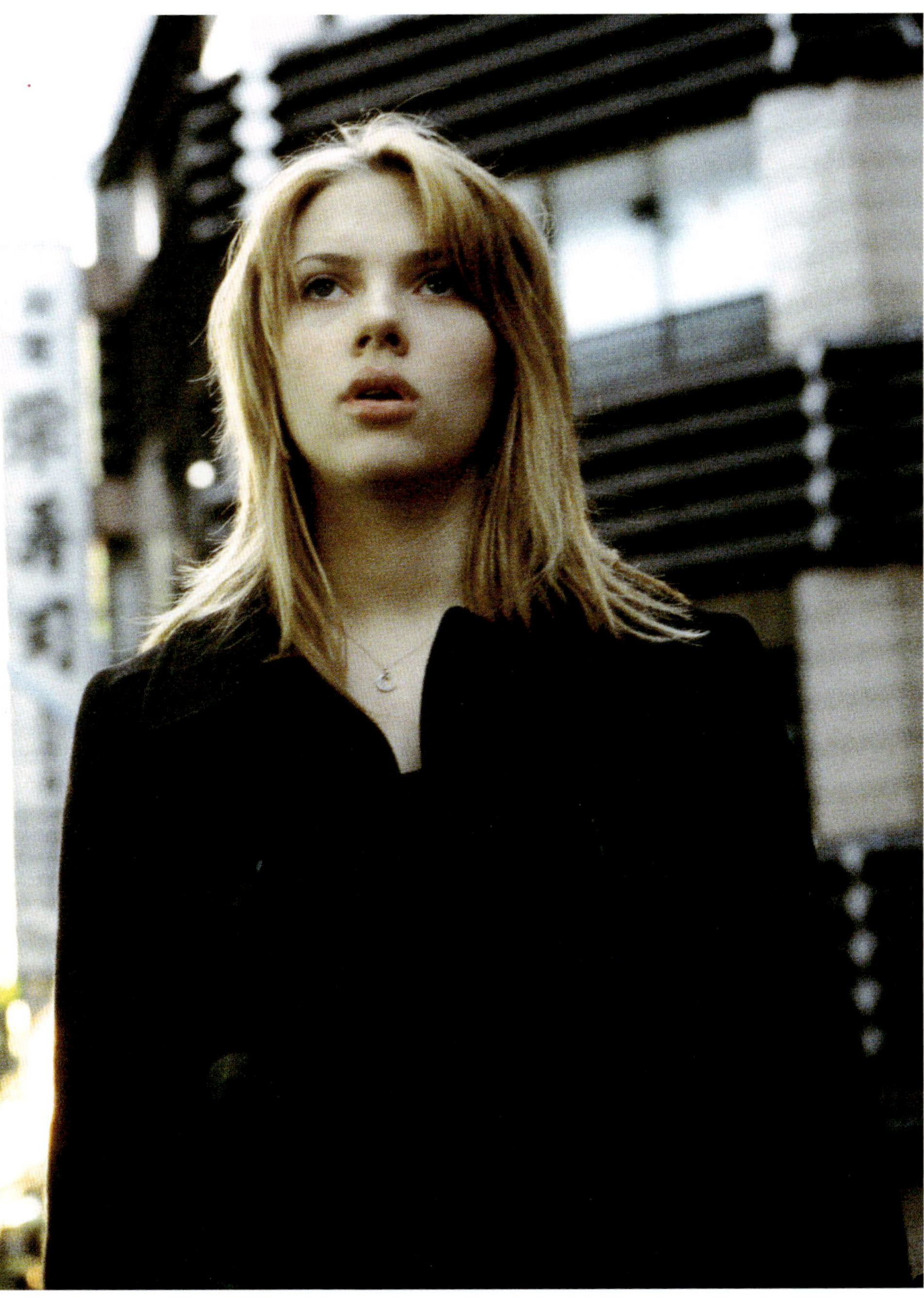

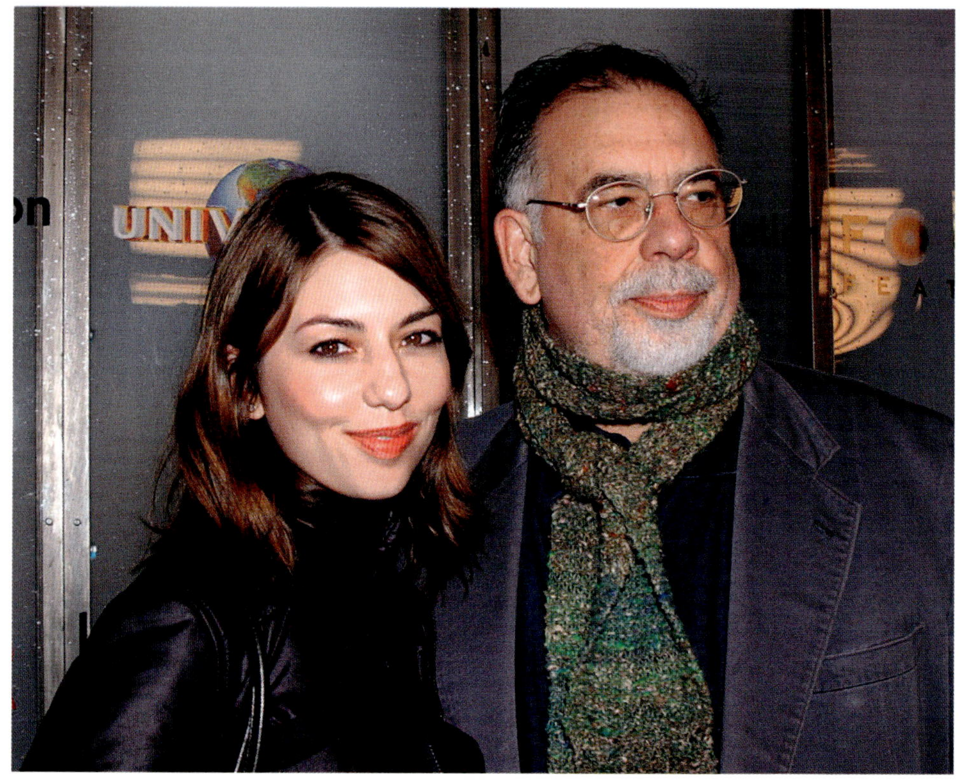

ABOVE: Coppola pictured with her father, film director Francis Ford Coppola.

Coppola's film, like many of her others, is one of relatively minimal dialogue. Her characters are not usually especially garrulous. They speak when spoken to, or are capricious, or solitary. But most of all Coppola likes to use their silences, their gaps. They are watchful, mute, sometimes almost disassociated. Potential funders balked when they first saw Coppola's rather short screenplay, only 70 pages, but her producer Ross Katz explained that relatively banal-sounding scenes on paper, like walking through Shinjuku, would be long and important visual sequences when presented onscreen. The filmmaker has said before she is less interested in dialogue than in atmosphere and music; that feels particularly true of several key scenes in *Lost in Translation.*

And if you want to know what Coppola thinks about people who talk too much, you only have to look at the chattiest (and dumbest) character in the film: an A-list actress played by the irrepressible comedian Anna Faris. She bumps into John and Charlotte in the hotel lobby and before long she is rhapsodizing tediously about diets and action-movie junkets. Rumours abound that this flirtatious, thuddingly dull-minded threat to Charlotte's marriage is loosely based on Cameron Diaz, though Coppola has always insisted the character is more of an amalgamation of a certain Hollywood 'type'.

For the all-important music in the film, Coppola leaned on a friend's boyfriend, Brian Reitzell, who had a remarkable record collection and used it to make mixtapes that would end up in the completed project. He would go on to be her music supervisor on a number of films, and he also enlisted the help of Kevin Shields, frontman of shoegaze rock band My Bloody Valentine, to write a song for the film. Looking to achieve the somnambulant, dreamy feeling of jetlag in a city full of sensory overload, Coppola sought music to fit that mood. In the all-night party/karaoke sequence, she also features partygoers dancing around a living room to French disco-rock band Phoenix's song 'Too Young'. This was a significant needle drop if ever there was one. Phoenix and their frontman Thomas Mars would go on to work on Coppola's soundtracks throughout her career, in various guises; they appear as 18th-century lutists briefly in *Marie Antoinette*, and compose a thrumming, minimal score for her later Los Angeles story *Somewhere.* (Mars and Coppola married in 2011 and have two children together.)

The film also wears its movie-buff influence on its sleeve. Sofia Coppola's childhood home was, unsurprisingly, one where she was constantly introduced to and educated about world cinema past and present; she grew up in a household where her father was always watching films like Alain Resnais' *Last Year at Marienbad* (1961), and her dog was named for the Akira Kurosawa classic *Yojimbo* (1961). *Lost in Translation* feels like a culmination of some of those influences; Coppola has mentioned films like the transitional and doomed romance of *Brief Encounter* (1945), David Lean's tale of married strangers who, for a brief time, find impossible love at their local train station. There are also degrees of Italian arthouse maverick Michelangelo Antonioni in the film's cool appraisal of urban alienation; there's an unnerving quietude and almost intimidating quality to the architecture of the city. It makes sense that Coppola would credit Antonioni's *La Notte* (1961) when listing her favourite films – and on-stage, when she would go on to win the Academy Award for Best Original Screenplay.

After a successful premiere at Venice Film Festival, *Lost in Translation* was released to increasingly positive word-of-mouth. It turned out to be a sleeper hit, ultimately earning $120 million at the box office. Nominated for four Academy Awards, including Best Picture, Best Director, Best Actor and Best Original Screenplay, its success far transcended its small budget. Coppola became the first American woman – and only the third woman ever, after Lina Wertmuller and Jane Campion – to be nominated for Best Director. Shocking as that stat is, it's quite an achievement for a sophomore filmmaker in her early thirties who made an indie film while feeling directionless and struggling within her own marriage. But it would be on Best Original Screenplay that Coppola would cement a win at the Oscars, ensuring her a powerful place in an awards-hungry industry ready to pounce on the Next Big Thing.

RIGHT: *Lost in Translation* poster, 2003.

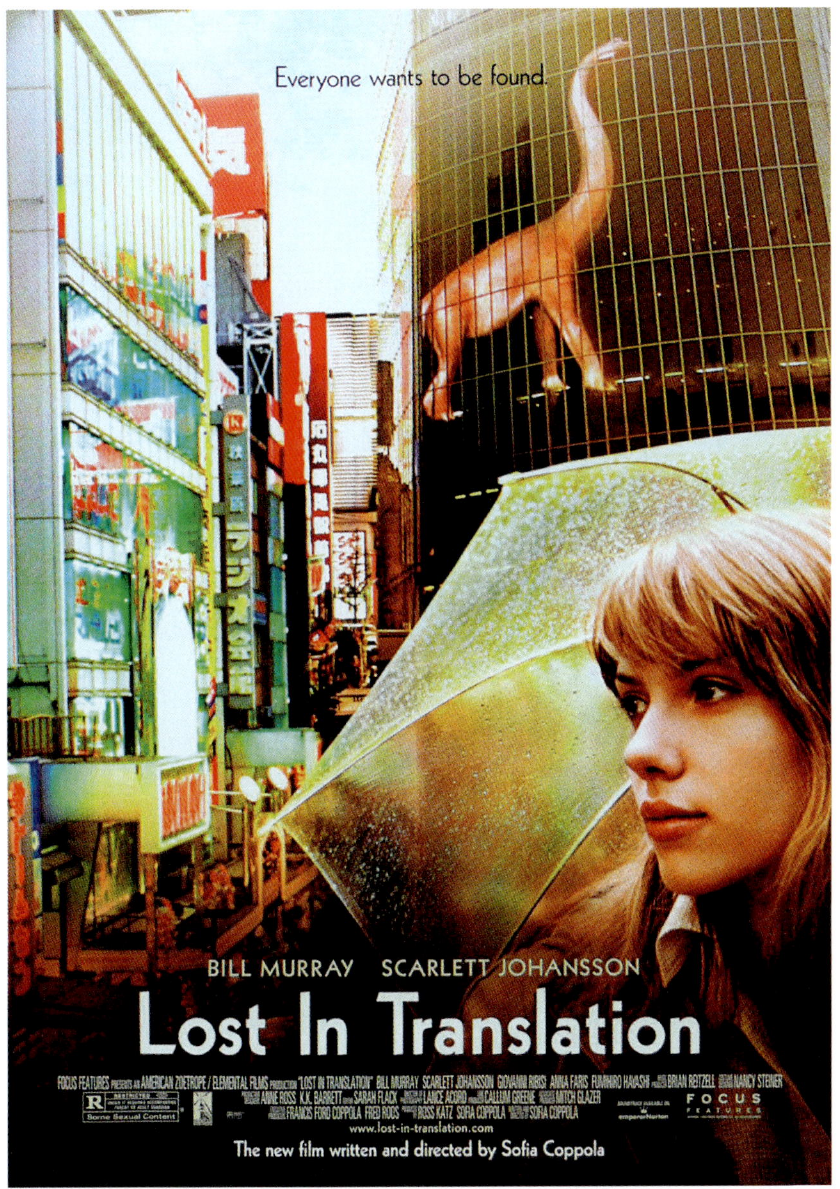

Everyone wants to be found.
BILL MURRAY   SCARLETT JOHANSSON
Lost In Translation
www.lost-in-translation.com
The new film written and directed by Sofia Coppola
FOCUS
FEATURES

Music and the soundtrack in Coppola's world

Coppola has long been a filmmaker known for minimizing dialogue and instead deploying soundscapes, or playful needle drops, to convey the spirit of her stories. From her youngest years, she has been entrenched in her musical influences as much as cinematic, in many ways, from her earliest years. From her friendships with bands like Sonic Youth and Air to her exacting taste in indie and shoegaze music (she has cited My Bloody Valentine's 'Loveless' as one of her favourite records), she has long been a part of the musical worlds she evokes onscreen, too. As something of a Gen X it-girl, she would appear in music videos for Sonic Youth and The Chemical Brothers in the 1990s, but more presciently, going on to direct those videos would be some of her first experiences behind the camera in a professional capacity. (In 1996, she directed The Flaming Lips' video for 'This Here Giraffe'.)

In her film career, Coppola has deployed her own taste – from The Strokes to The Jesus and Mary Chain – as well as relying on the shared knowledge of longtime music supervisor Brian Reitzell, whose mixtapes would help inspire Coppola as she worked on her screenplays, and then make their way into the films. When Coppola chose a song ('Too Young') from French disco-rock band Phoenix for *Lost in Translation*, she likely had no idea quite how long and meaningful that creative collaboration would turn out to be – nevermind that she and lead singer Thomas Mars would go on to marry in 2011. More to the point, Phoenix has continued to innovate and surprise in relation to Coppola's needs as a filmmaker, shifting their style and approach based on what her films require. For *The Beguiled*, a Civil War-era drama which would not seem to obviously call for the services of a band like Phoenix, the band worked to create a sonically low-key, ominous synth-based score; a few years later, they showed their remarkably chameleonic talent by tackling the back catalogue of Elvis Presley for *Priscilla*.

On paper, *Lost in Translation* is the film that cinephiles and serious movie lovers are liable to cite when they talk about Sofia Coppola's entry into the indie filmmaking canon. And rightly so: its success was undeniably a catalyst for the rest of her career. But it's also interesting to consider how the film now stands nestled between her other early work, *The Virgin Suicides* and *Marie Antoinette*. Of them, *Lost in Translation* is the only contemporary film. While her period pieces seem to have a striking timelessness, the specificity of this peak-hipster era, with its clothing and manners, seems extremely 2003. This isn't a bad thing, but it's worth acknowledging that it might be more controversial had it been released today. With an age gap of this size between its potential romantic leads, and with its jokey, baffled attitude towards the cultural and linguistic differences of the Japanese, it might not have gone down nearly as well.

But it's also true that Bob and Charlotte are ultimately the clueless Americans and the real aliens on this foreign turf. It's these two who aren't multilingual, and they who are unaware of customs and make fools of themselves as a result, as when Bob and the sex worker he unwittingly lets into his room have a total – and very amusing – communication breakdown. The film does not deny the arrogance of the well-off American abroad, but takes care to capture a side of Japan which is not mere stereotype; Coppola populated the film with Japanese fashion designer friends – like Hiroshi Fujiwara, a Nike designer – and colleagues, who shared with her the best off-the-beaten-path bars and restaurants for film locations. You can visit the real locations of the film if you find yourself in Tokyo: the multi-floor Karaoke-kan in Shibuya, or the Park Hyatt jazz bar where so much time is spent.

Another one of Coppola's major inspirations was 'girly' street photographer known as Hiromix, who appears in a tiny cameo in the film to break the fourth wall and wave at the camera from her background spot on the street. Her desire to capture the early noughties energy of a youthful artistic subculture of Tokyo is reflected in the film itself, and another testament to how closely Coppola paid attention to Japanese friends, muses and collaborators to guide her.

When Bob is finally set to leave Tokyo, he finds Charlotte in the street and leans over to offer some parting words in her ear. They are intentionally left unheard by the audience. All we hear is him finishing his statement with: 'Okay?' and her response: 'Okay.' They embrace, and finally, kiss; a look of meditative happiness and affection crosses the young woman's tear-streaked face. After weeks of companionship and the frisson of unspoken romance, they are unlikely to see each other again. Both, unhappily married though they are, will return to their spouses for the time being, at least. The beautiful, poised ambiguity of this conclusion is not only in the question of what Bob whispers to Charlotte; it's also in the question of what these two people will do with the rest of their lives. Will this fleeting experience jar something loose in them? Will that feeling of potential joy, of not wasting life feeling small and lonely, facilitate them to seek change?

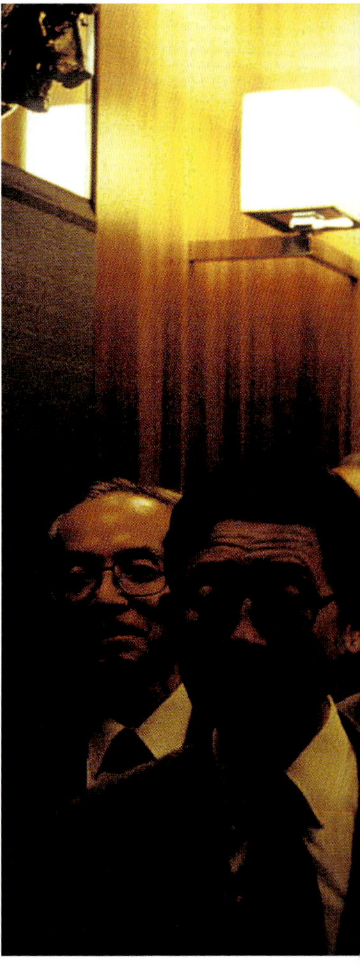

ABOVE: Bob Harris (Murray) stands tall in a Tokyo lift.

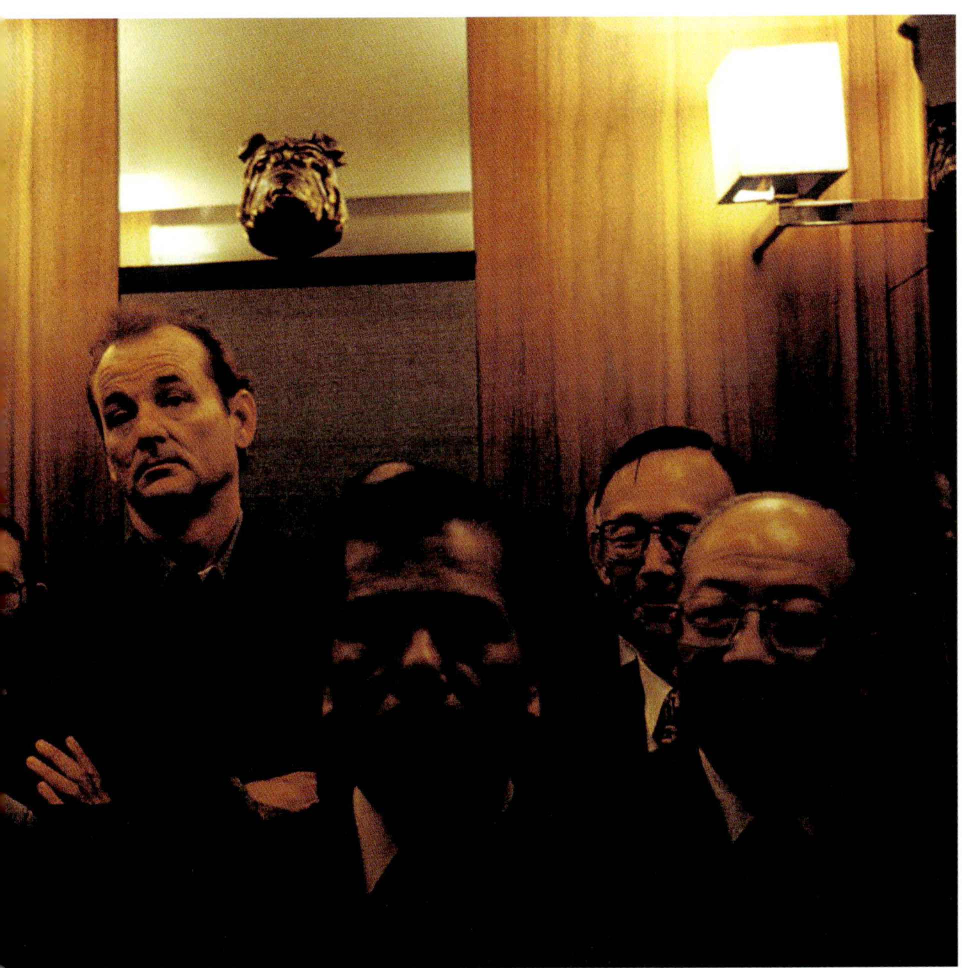

Maybe the question on everyone's lips – the abiding mystery – about the film is: what does he whisper in her ear at the end? 'People always ask me what's said,' Coppola told *Little White Lies* in 2018. 'I always like Bill's answer: that it's between lovers – so I'll leave it at that.'

A film of looming melancholy and brief connection in a lonely nocturnal Tokyo, *Lost in Translation* contains more than this specific mystery. It's also a film about the mystery and transformation of travel, of foreignness not only in location but also to one's self. Of growing estranged from who you used to be or might become in a strange place, without the usual markers of routine and familiarity to ground you. There's a reason there are so many stereotypes and clichés about the restorative nature of solo travel, after all. *Lost in Translation* is hardly *Eat Pray Love*, but it does locate some essential and universal truth in the fact that being alone in a new country and relearning how to orient yourself tends to teach you a few things about the way you live.

For a film which lingers on the Americanness of her protagonists, and how they are as alien to their Japanese hosts as their hosts are to them, Coppola avoids a particularly 'American' ending for her film. She isn't interested in giving us any clear answers or traditional narrative closure here, and the film's strength is in that very ambiguity. Her influences in cinema have always had a strong European arthouse flavour, and her characters' ambivalence feels more aligned to that than to any mainstream Hollywood imperative for a neat or explicable conclusion. The age gap is ultimately not one that's being measured for power dynamics, but for two people who are presenting a version of the future – and of the past – to each other. They are both vessels to teach the another something about their lives that is missing.

As a brief and unexpected smile crosses Charlotte's face, and the shoegaze strains of The Jesus and Mary Chain's 'Just Like Honey' kick in to close the film, Coppola leaves us with a sense that there's optimism and room for more intimacy in the future for both of these people – that they are newly open to the world and its connective tissue. In spite of loneliness and separation,

RIGHT: Coppola in 2004, holding the *Lost in Translation* Golden Globe for Best Musical or Comedy.

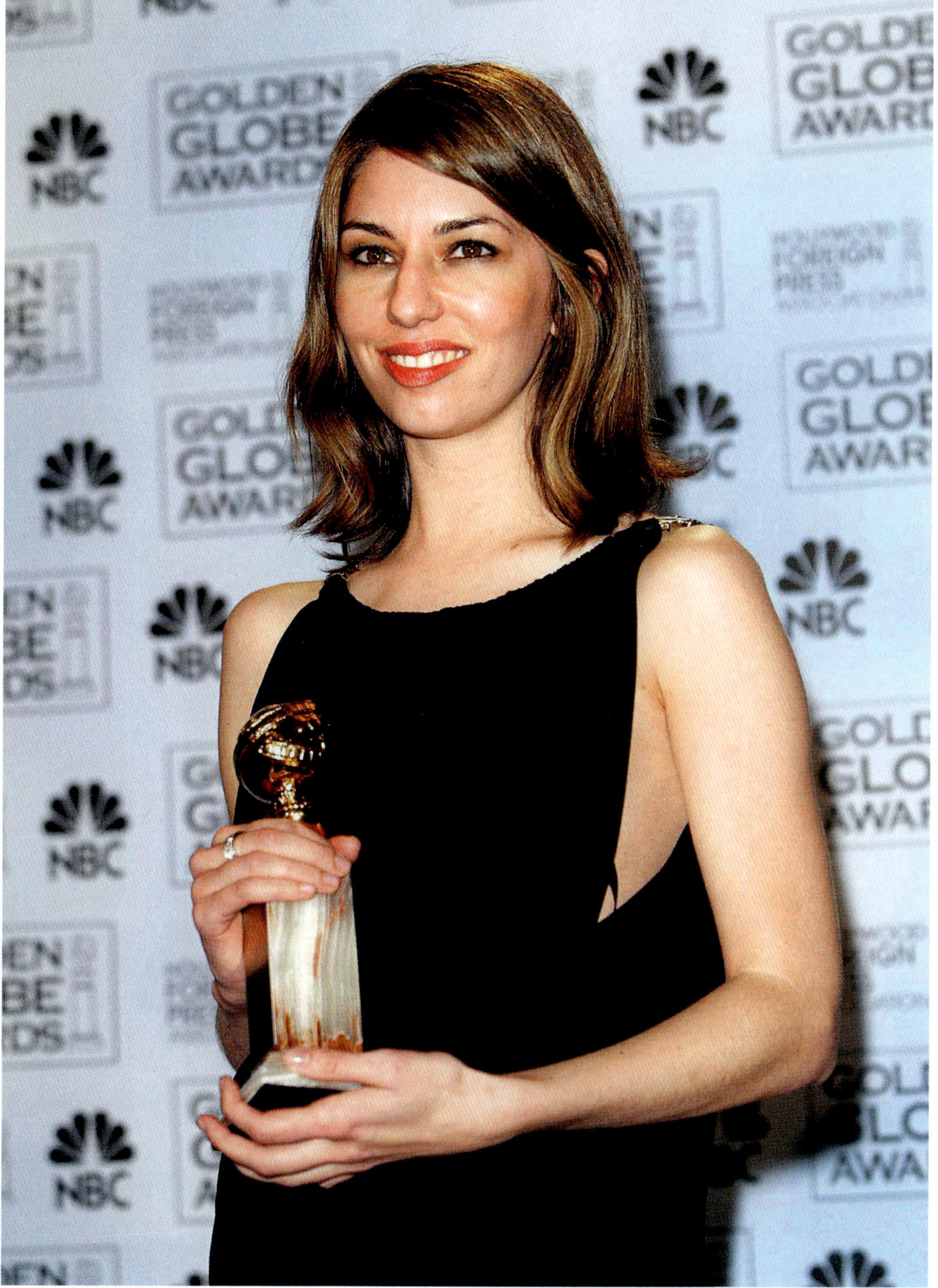

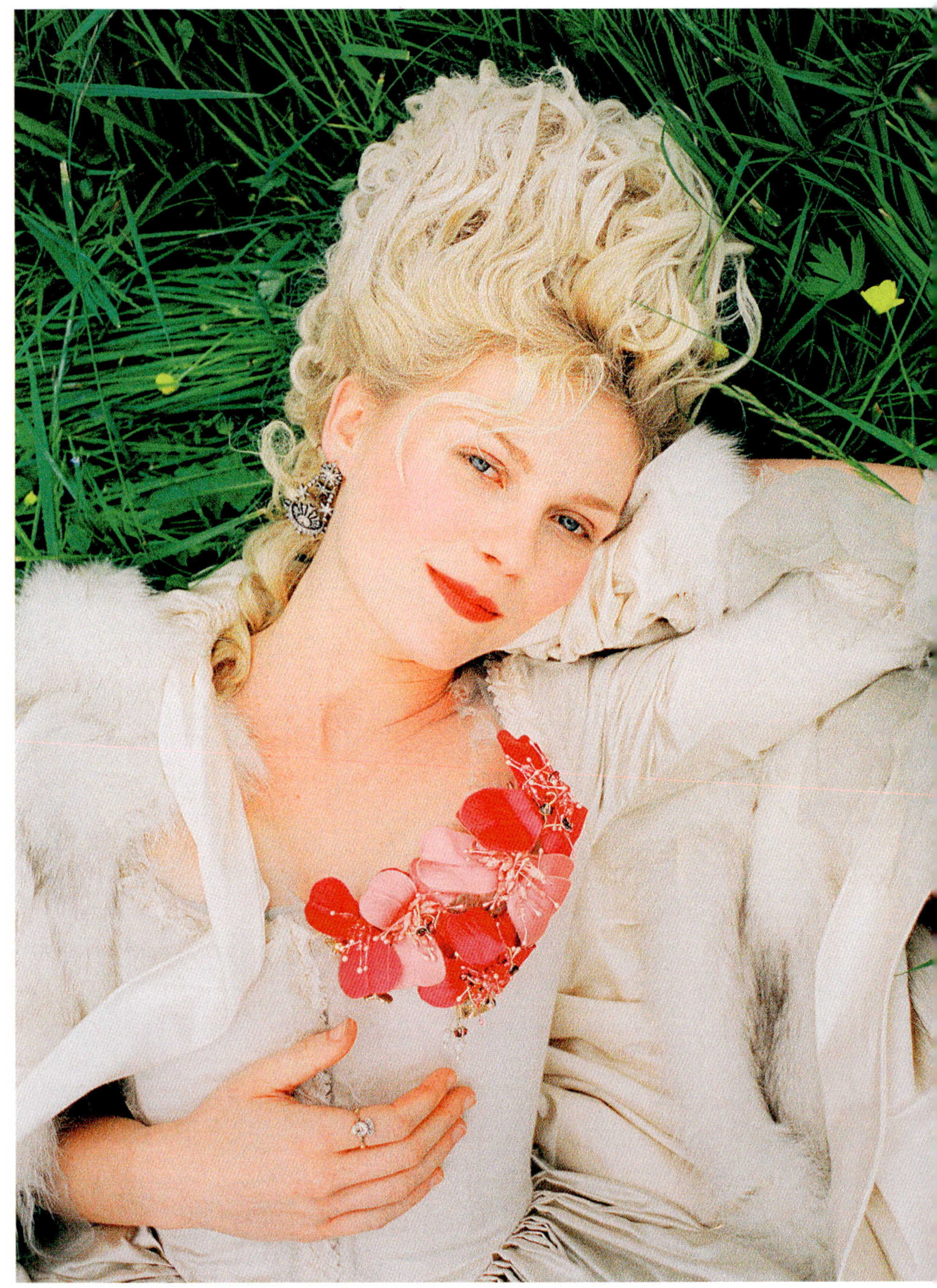

'Letting everyone down would be my greatest unhappiness.'

MARIE ANTOINETTE
2006

A glittering jewel in the crown of Sofia Coppola's career, *Marie Antoinette* marks the arrival of one of her most self-assured, spiky and deliriously enjoyable pieces of filmmaking. Her most ambitious (and expensive) work to date, picking up from the critical and commercial momentum of *Lost in Translation*'s success, Coppola tackled a big historical subject with equally big historical scale: the infamous, fickle Queen of France, known for her excess, beauty and, of course, losing her finely-wigged head on the guillotine at the start of the French Revolution. Vilified for centuries as a cruel and out-of-touch monarch and misattributed with the notorious 'let them eat cake' quote (reportedly in response to news of a bread shortage causing starvation), Marie Antoinette's was a story everyone thought they knew. But not the way Coppola tells it.

Amy Pascal, producer at Sony Pictures, apparently became obsessed by Sofia's work in the wake of *Lost of Translation*. Determined to collaborate with the auteur on whatever her next film would be, Pascal learned about Sofia's passion project: an impressionistic, dreamy exploration of the life of France's most notorious and glamorous queen, killed at only 37. It would be Coppola's priciest production thus far, costing some $40 million, with Coppola's insistence upon filming in French locations. The jewellery budget alone would rival the entire cost of *Lost in*

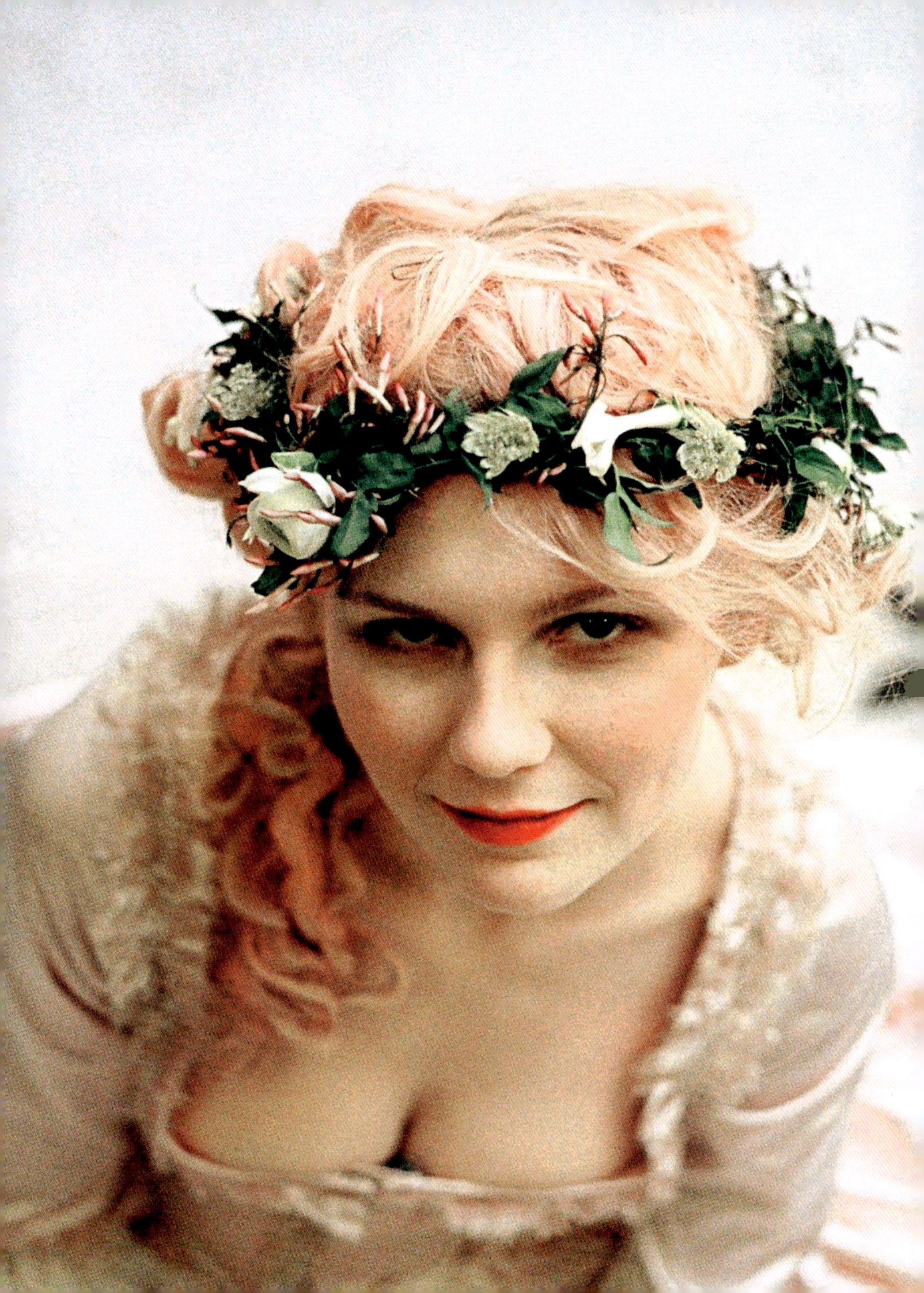

Translation, with real diamonds and priceless antiques brought in by jeweller Fred Leighton for Kirsten Dunst and her co-stars to wear on set.

The film announces its radical intent from the start, with acid-pink opening credits and the dissonant guitar of Gang of Four song 'Natural's Not In It' (a song about the relation between sex, power and capitalism: hardly a mistake). The opening is a static image of the queen in her full splendour, reclining on a chaise lounge with a servant at her feet. Coppola makes a clever visual nod to that so-called quotation, with a towering cherry-festooned layer-cake in

BELOW: Dunst and co-star Jason Schwartzman as Louis XVI, attending the opera.

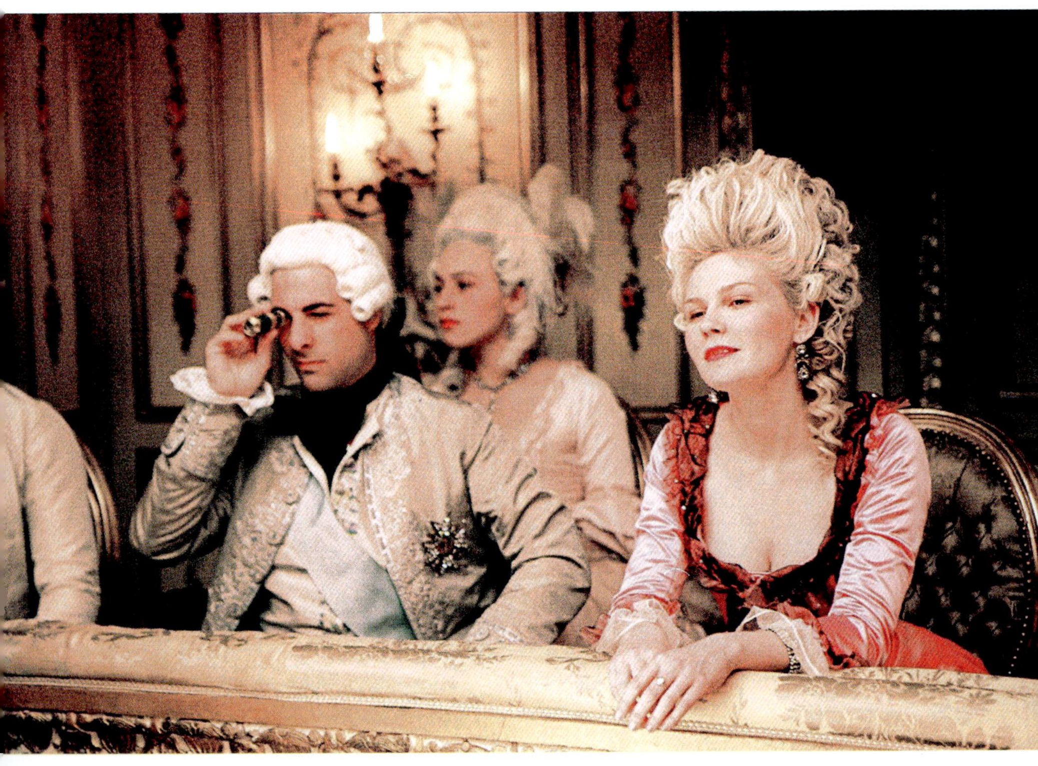

the corner of the shot. Then we're off to the beginning in what will otherwise be a chronological story: a 14-year-old Antoinette is sent off by her mother (Marianne Faithfull in a fun, small supporting role) to an advantageous marriage to unite the Austrian and French empires, as was the wont of the 18th-century royals. Sent away from her home and family and set to marry a young man she has never met – in a country she's never been to – we are immediately wrong-footed by the sight of this young, uncertain slip of a girl, nothing like the intimidating and glamorous image we are first presented with (and which is closer to the historical stereotype).

By casting the all-American Kirsten Dunst as the lead (though Coppola thought Dunst's German extraction gave her the right look for the Austrian-born protagonist), Coppola also set the tone of the film to follow. Innocent yet mischievous, Dunst gives a stellar central performance. But the largely American-based casting for a very French story also showed that strict historical accuracy was never Coppola's goal. Feeling that the spirit of the characters hanging around the Sun King's court were always rather eccentric, Coppola decided to cast the ensemble with an equally ragtag attitude. Rip Torn, a Texan, plays the old King of France, while his bawdy mistress, Madame Du Barry, is played by Italian Asia Argento. And for the all-important role of Antoinette's own timid husband and eventually King Louis XVI, Coppola cast her cousin, actor Jason Schwartzman, in the role.

If Coppola's interest had always been on reclaiming the feminine point of view onscreen, she owns it more fully than ever in her reimagining of the teen royalty's much-discussed life. Basing the story loosely on Antonia Fraser's book *Marie Antoinette: The Journey* (2001), the intention was to offer what Coppola called a 'more impressionistic' vision of the woman's experiences, from her own point of view rather than from a so-called objective

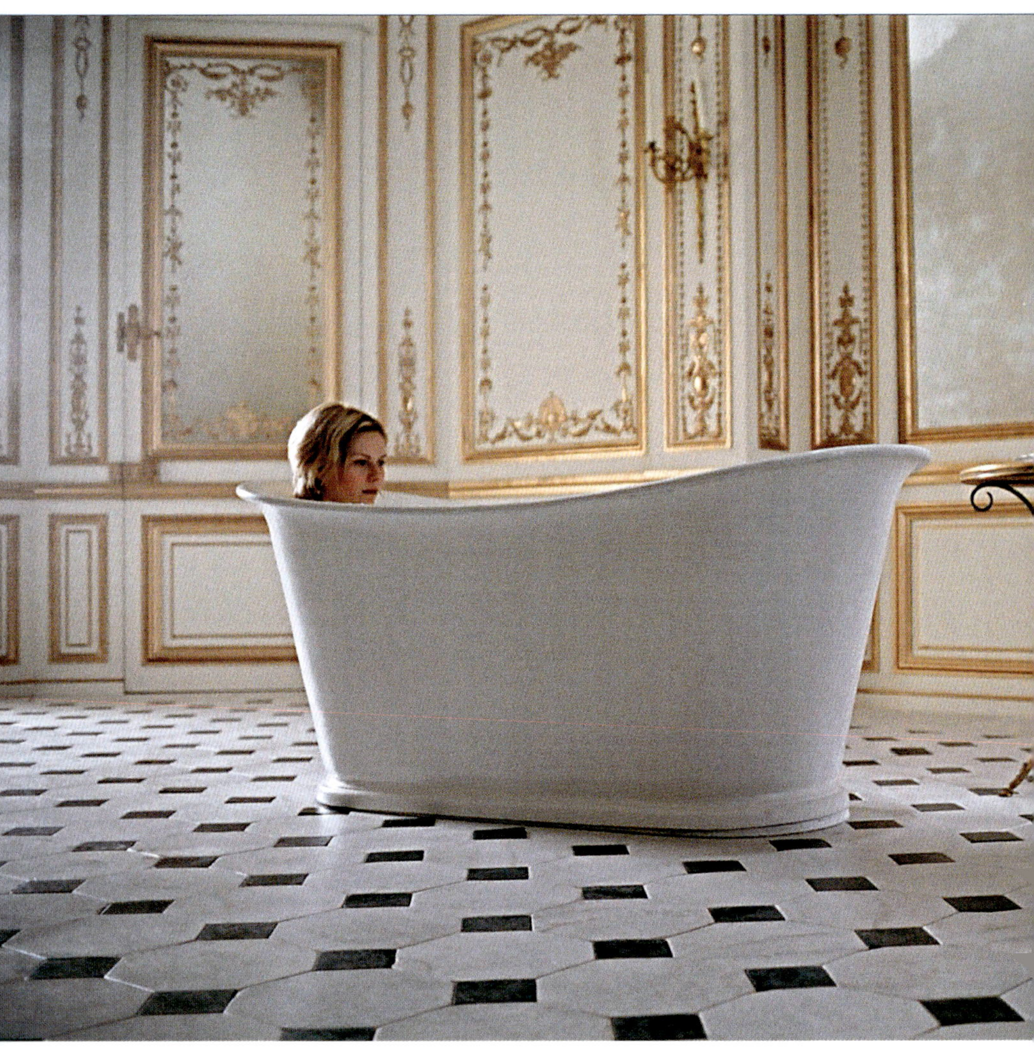

ABOVE: Coppola received special permission to film in the Palace of Versailles, seen here.

OVERLEAF: Antoinette finally produces an heir to the French throne, much to everyone's relief.

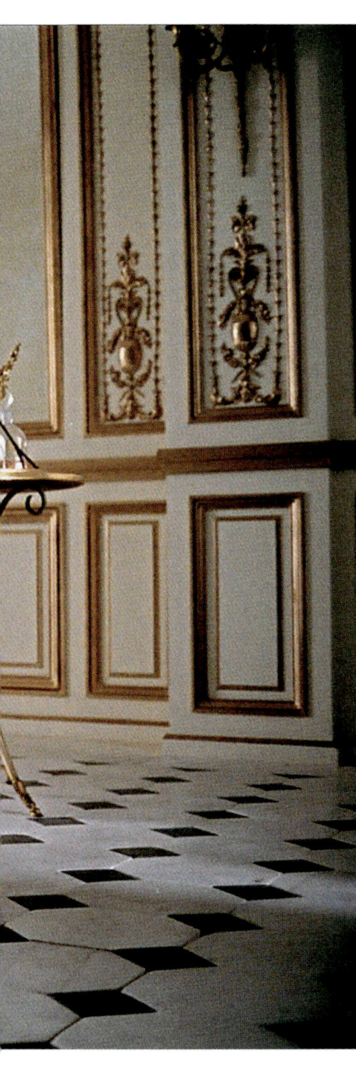

exterior. And rather than deviate from reality entirely, Coppola cleverly chooses to outline the reasons why the teen queen's personality would paint her into so much of a corner in this male-dominated and corrupt era: society desperately needed someone to blame.

Crucially, these are people who essentially behave like they are modern, in spite of differences in social ritual, propriety and gender; the absurdly rigid rules of the French court notwithstanding, we recognize their behaviour. This is particularly true of Antoinette, who by an 18th-century understanding would have been considered very rebellious. We are told she has an 'artistic temperament' by way of explanation. But the panopticon of her life at Versailles, where bedsheets were analysed for signs of marital consummation and a descending list of hawk-eyed aristocratic women had the right to dress you every morning, feels utterly insane by contemporary standards. Coppola pokes fun at it in a scene where the pecking order of the lady who has first dibs on dressing Antoinette with her chemise keeps switching, leaving the girl shivering in the nude while the clothing changes hands. It hardly seems like coincidence that, regardless of the storytelling or framing device, Sofia

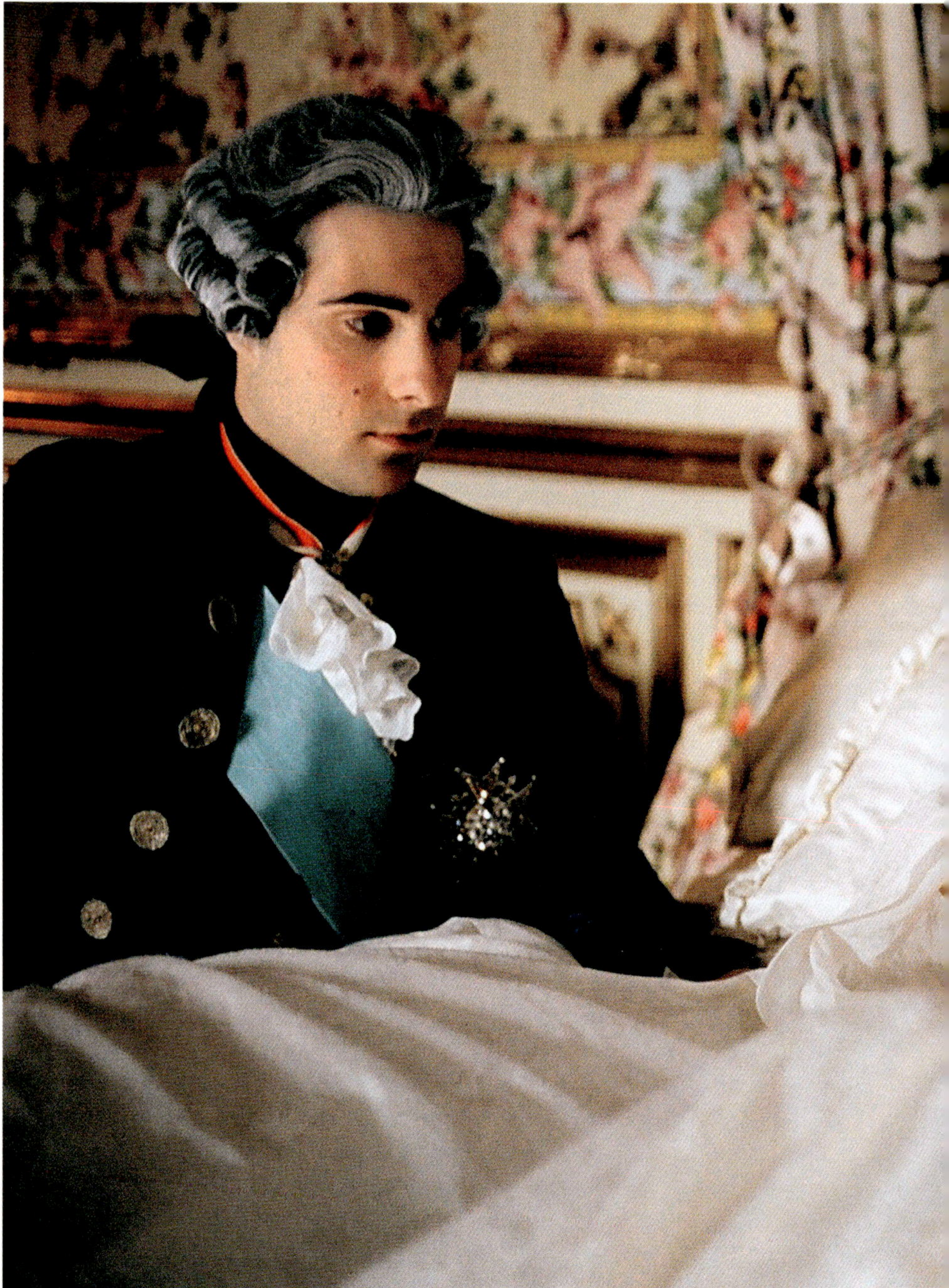

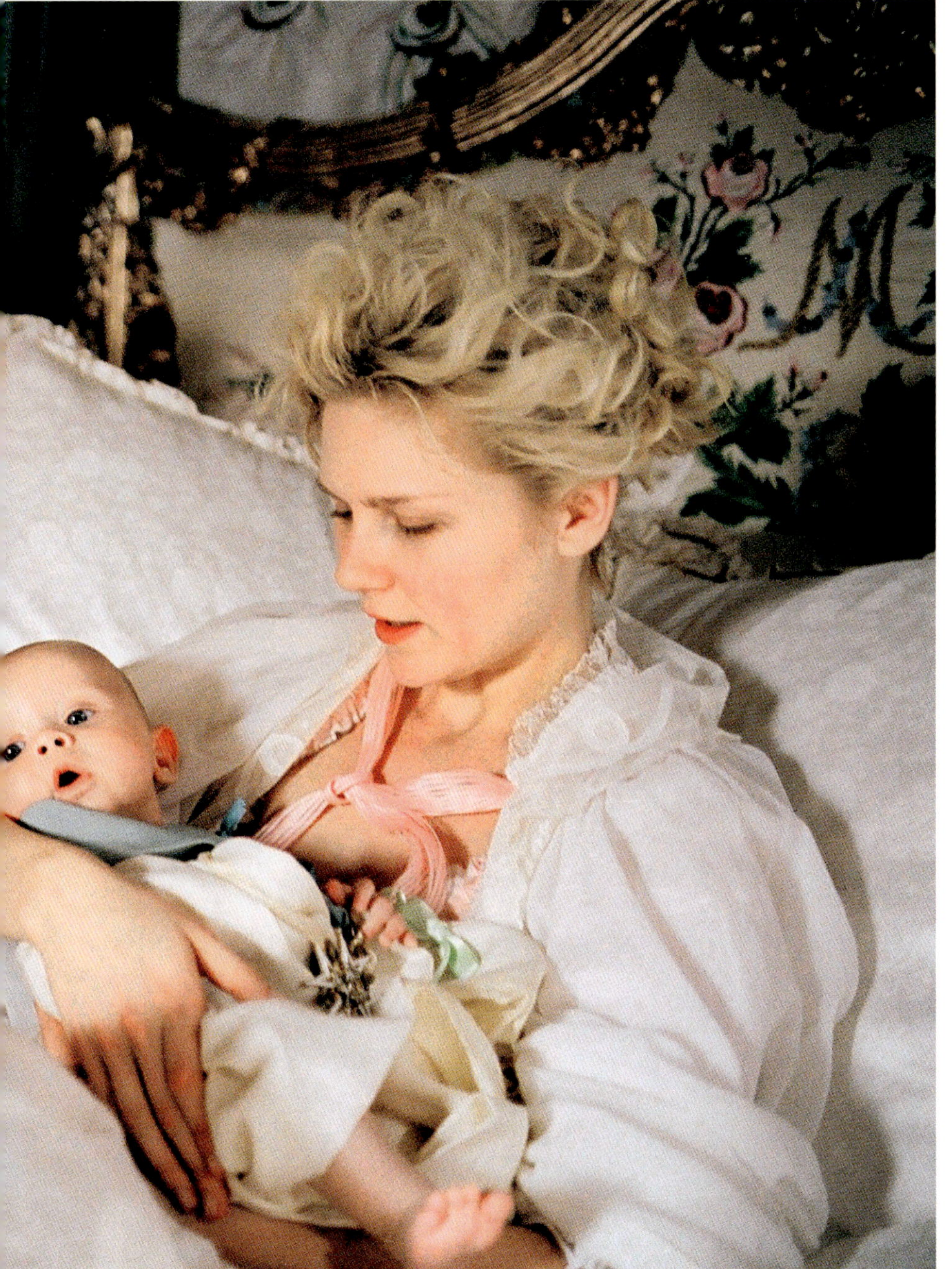

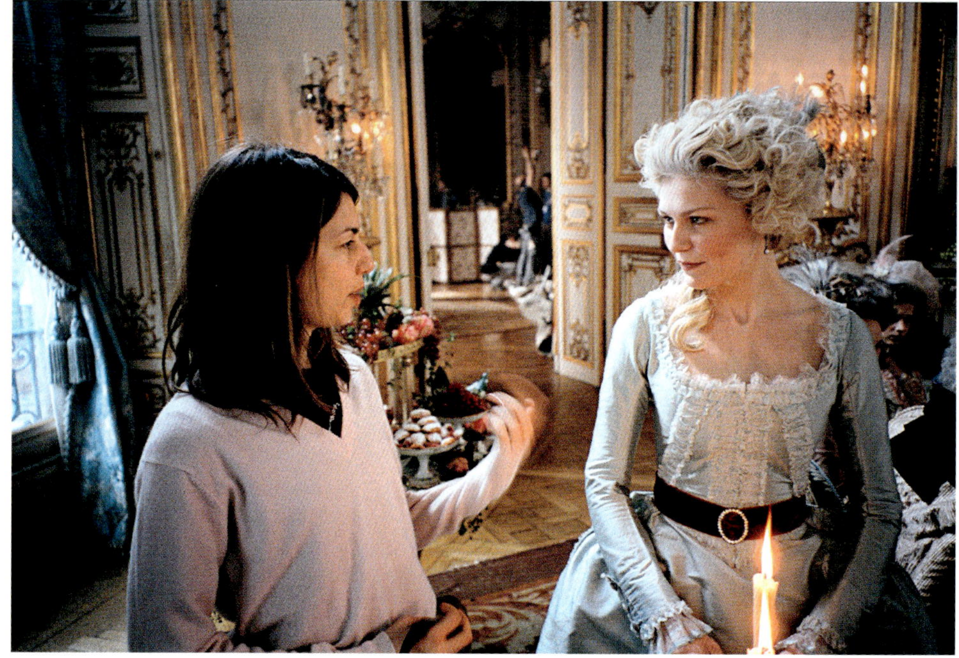

ABOVE: Coppola and Dunst on set in Versailles.

Coppola's films so frequently involve women who are unwillingly in the limelight or prone to being gawked at for one reason or another. It's not difficult to map her own upbringing, her father's fame and her often challenging time as a teen actress onto the feelings of some of her female protagonists.

If Marie Antoinette might have hoped for some comfort or companionship in the arms of her new husband, she finds little consolation there, either. The pair have a chalk-and-cheese energy, and Antoinette always seems vaguely, sardonically amused by Louis XVI's nerdy shyness. After a prolonged refusal to consummate their marriage, the awkwardness between the pair grows. It takes years for a vague affection to build between them, particularly after they finally do have children and the public pressure on

Antoinette eases somewhat. But these two, customary to the realities of marriage at their time, were never a match made in heaven.

Wishing to avoid any echoes of the usual, staid historical biopic, Coppola dispenses with long title cards for historical context and simplifies the ongoing financial and political turmoil of France down to a few simple exchanges between advisers; those wishing to get a full factual picture of pre-Revolution French sovereignty are unlikely to be satisfied. It's reflective of Antoinette's own relative disinterest in public matters; she's a teenager, more interested in choosing between the ruffles on the sleeves of her dress than the international affairs between Poland and France, as Coppola wryly shows in one scene with Dunst opposite her loyal ambassador Florimond Claude (Steve Coogan). Crucially, Coppola does not deny the queen's so-called frivolity; she simply asks: why *wouldn't* a trapped, bored and sexually stifled young woman end up escaping into what enjoyment she could?

For Antoinette, that enjoyment was derived from the immense wealth at her disposal, and taking pleasure from shopping, gambling and other frippery. That shoes and champagne and pretty Ladurée cakes might be her downfall seems to build into the common, frankly misogynistic narrative about the queen: she was characterized as a superficial person whose extravagance became a symbol for the corruption of the entire regime, therefore she essentially deserved her fate on the guillotine. What Coppola does, with her intoxicating camera work and focus on the aesthetic beauty of this world, is to revel in those luxuries in the way that Antoinette does, knowing that the party will indeed come to an end. Ultimately, it's clear that the queen's spending or perceived indulgence was ultimately only a product of an environment full of people – most especially men – who did the very same thing, unchecked, for centuries. That she should be permanently separated from her mother, expected to toe the line and breed male heirs at will in the very harsh glare of her royal rivals and onlookers only makes you sympathize with her desire to have a little fun.

A pivotal part of that fun comes in the form of the handsome Count Fersen (a debut role for a young Jamie Dornan), a Swedish military man who Antoinette meets at a masked ball in Paris. He, unlike her husband, seems more than up to the task of making love. Sex – and more importantly, a lack thereof – is interwoven through much of Coppola's work, however oblique. Her films often are about a failure to consummate, or to do so satisfactorily. In *The Virgin Suicides*, either protecting or stealing the sisters' 'purity' seems to be the simmering motivator beneath the surface of everyone's behaviour. In *Lost in Translation*, nothing sexual happens between the besotted protagonists; they don't even kiss on the lips until the final moments of the film, and that's when they're parting.

For Marie Antoinette, she comes of age and goes through the bulk of her teenage years as a bride to a sexually incompetent husband; the inference is that she remains a virgin for years and has the additional humiliation of taking all the blame for his disinterest simply because of the misogyny of the era. (As a letter from her mother, Maria Theresa, insists, she must calibrate her attractiveness and personality to her husband's tastes to appeal to him. It never seems to occur to anyone that her husband may be the problem.)

As such, when the couple finally do have sex, Coppola luxuriates in Antoinette's response. The screen goes black but Dunst releases a sharp sound of surprised delight and pleasure and a giggle, followed by a cut to the queen later on, laying happily on the grass and beaming. It's a good little visual and aural joke, but it's not exactly enough to keep the young woman busy for the

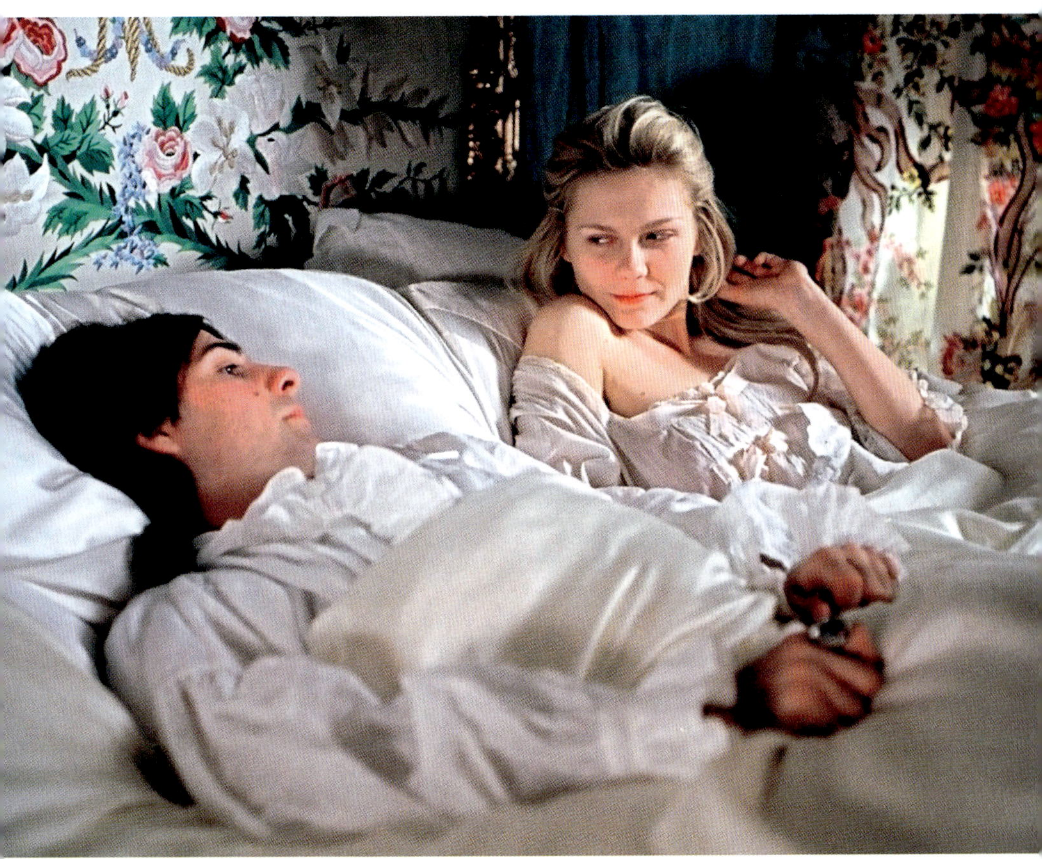

ABOVE: The film depicts the lack of sexual chemistry between the historic couple.

OVERLEAF: The iconic opening shot of a lounging Dunst. Note the pastel pink Manolo Blahnik mules.

years to come. Thus, on Count Fersen's return from fighting in the American revolutionary war, the two fall into a far more passionate affair, beginning in heated exchanged glances and culminating in a scene of Antoinette alone which is far more tantalizing and suggestive than any of her actual moments of lovemaking. Once Fersen has left and Antoinette is forced back to the dull normality

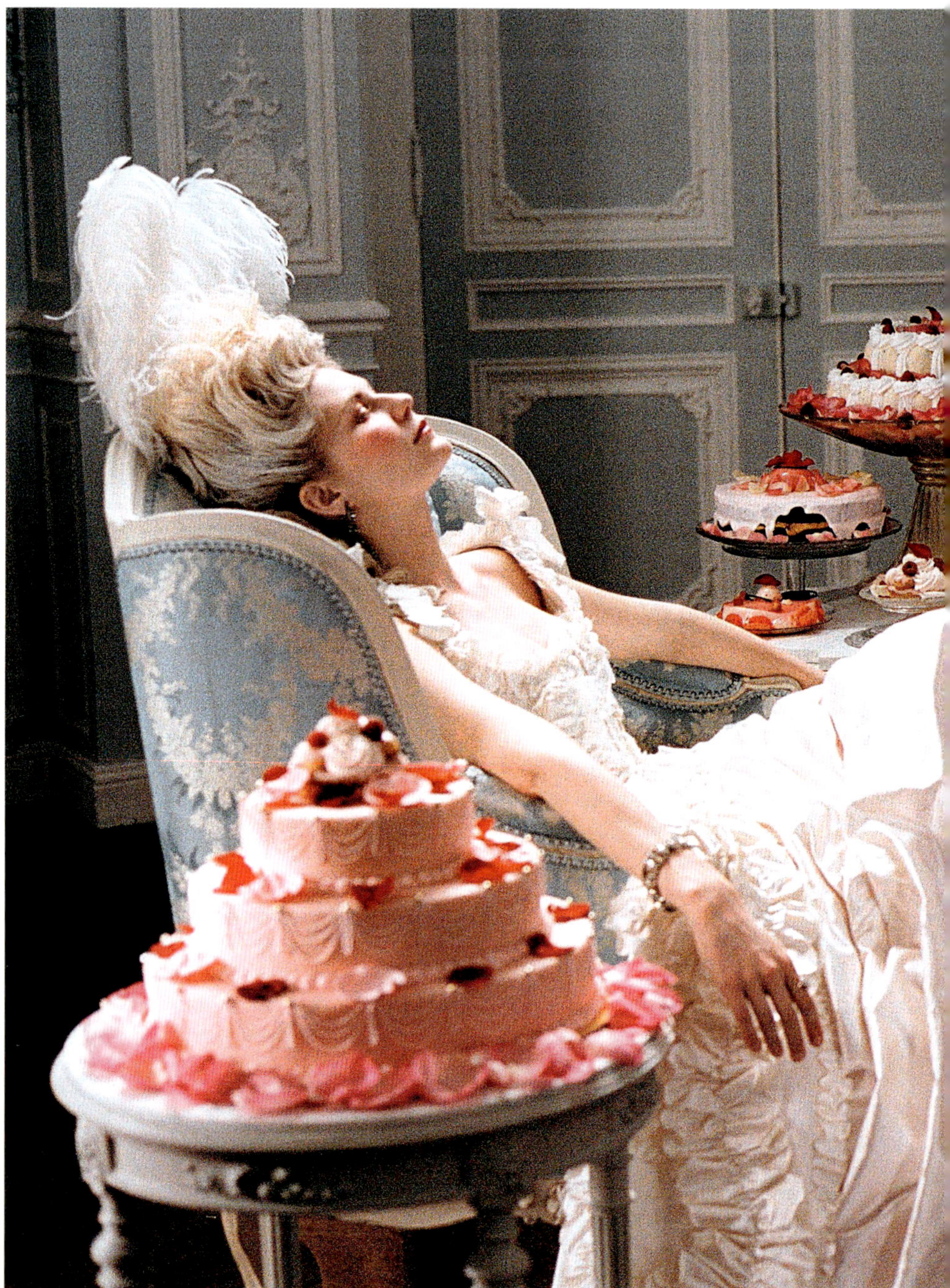

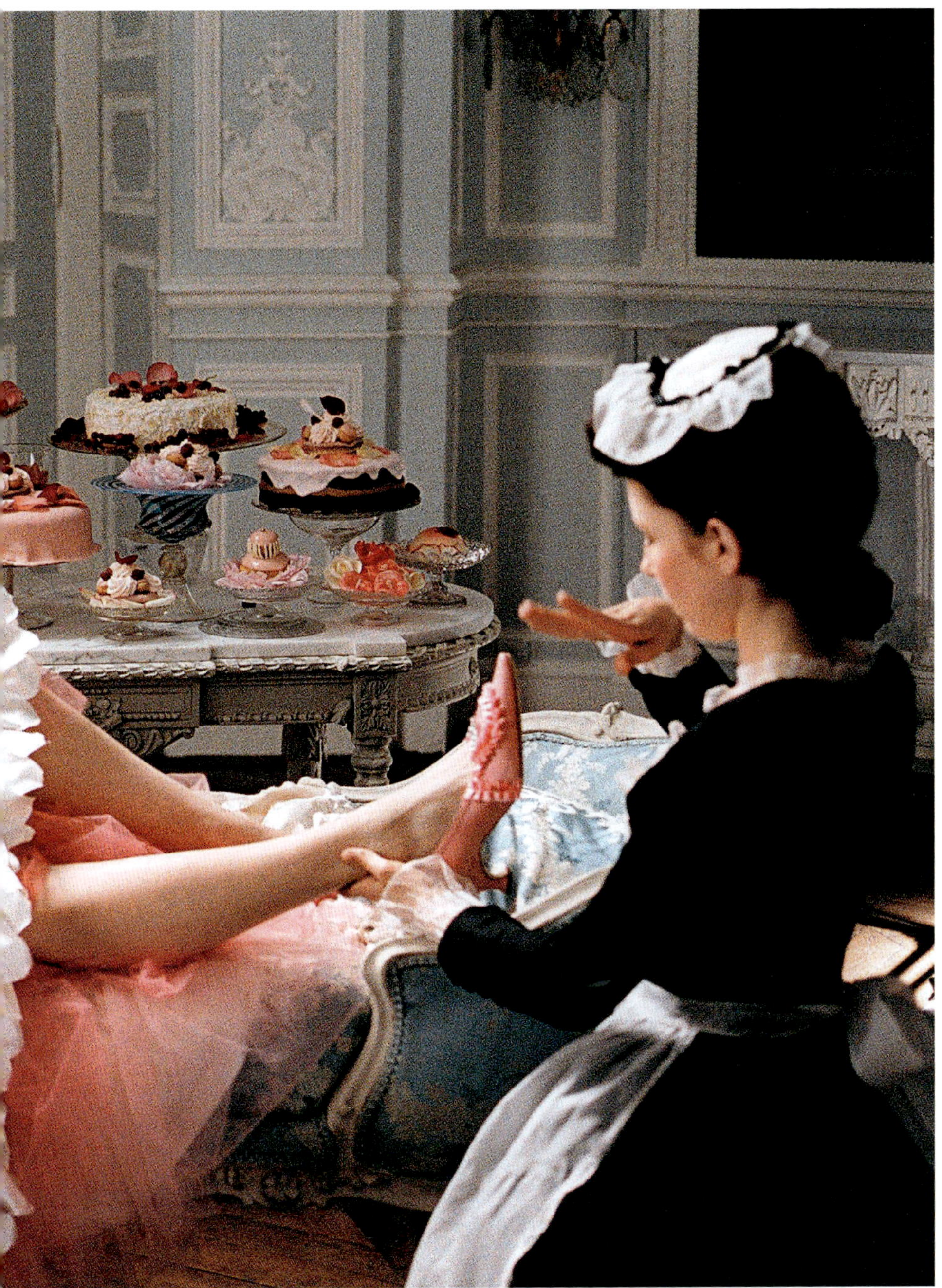

of the court, her fevered daydreaming about their tryst leads her to excuse herself from her husband's card game. She dashes back to her quarters, The Strokes, pulsating guitar on 'Whatever Happened' soundtracking her quaking desire. Cheeks flushed, she throws herself onto her bed; we don't need Coppola to show us what's probably going to happen next.

In reality, there's no concrete evidence that the real Count Fersen and Marie Antoinette had a physical affair, though many rumours abounded on the paternity of her third child, and the film leaves that question open to the viewer too. Ultimately, Coppola admits that when she asked biographer Antonia Fraser if she thought the pair had slept together, Fraser simply said: 'I hope so.' And that was enough.

In Coppola's view, it seems that there are enough films for people interested in simple, cut-and-dried history. This is a story which also has allegorical qualities; about a cosseted young woman, far from home and afforded the trappings of immense luxury even while her actions, behaviour and marital sex life were being obsessively monitored by the French court. When you view the film through this lens, it mirrors so much of Coppola's interest as an artist. She just couldn't seem to get away from her preoccupation with the gilded cage, and what the young women within them do to survive (in this instance, one of those things is to sleep with Count Fersen).

This rebellious streak is evidenced in Coppola's brilliantly anachronistic use of music, which is largely taken from late 1970s and early 1980s New Wave as well as sprinkles of oh-so-2006 earworms by The Strokes and other indie rockers. The spiky modernity of the music feels knowing in a couple of ways. For one thing, Coppola was heavily influenced by both the sound and the look of the New Romantics, particularly Adam Ant for the dashing young Count Fersen who seduces Antoinette. There's also something notable about how the film echoes the hazy cool-kid hedonism of the 2000s' indie rock scene, peopled by models and musicians who read 18th-century poetry for kicks; this, after all, was a scene Coppola was entrenched in herself, with her pals in Sonic Youth and the like. For the music, Coppola turned to longtime collaborator and music supervisor Brian Reitzell, who incorporated bands from Sofia's own teen years – The Cure, New Order, Bow Wow Wow – into two mixtapes that she listened to while she worked on the screenplay.

In her delightfully pretty 'I Want Candy' montage, Antoinette responds instinctively to the continued public humiliation in court (due to her 'failure' to provide an heir to the throne) by going on a spending spree. The montage of outrageously ribbon-festooned,

BELOW: Manolo Blahnik designed an entire Marie Antoinette line for use in the film.

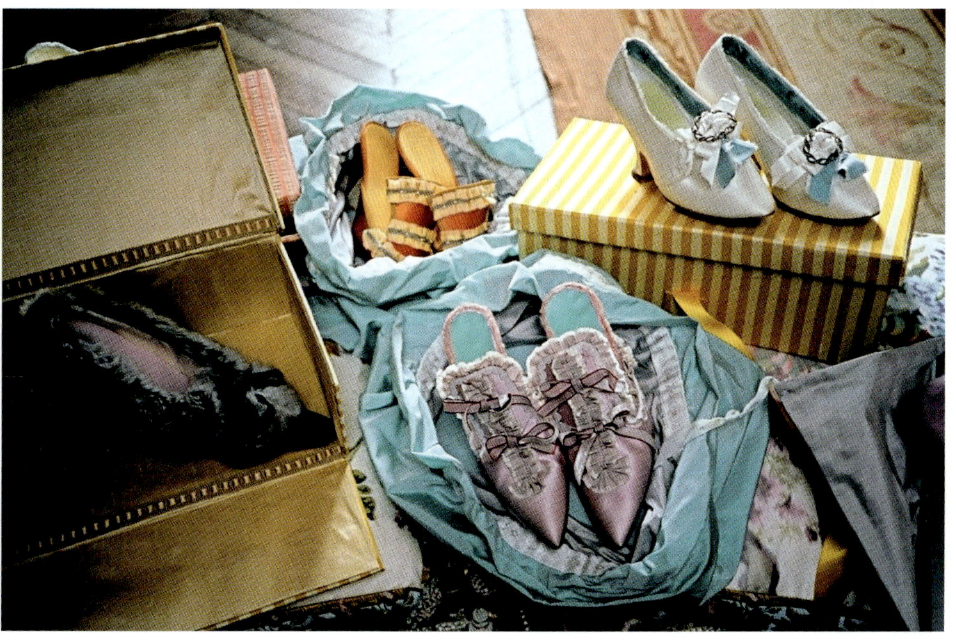

brocade-adorned, striped, floral and polka-dotted shoes and accessories – all in beautiful pastels – are swoon-worthy enough, and that's before you get to the exquisitely decorated cakes. It's a veritable feast for the eyes, and Coppola knowingly smudges the pink icing on your nose; you're bound to understand the exhilaration, whether you're a girly-girl with a penchant for shopping or not. This is retail therapy to the nth degree, and of course, the keen-eyed will notice a pair of aqua blue Converse All Stars tucked under the furniture in this sequence; another playful nod to the relatability of this teenage girl regardless of her place of historical significance.

To capture a sherbert-coloured wonderland that evoked baroque 17th-century Versailles without slavishly copycatting it, Coppola insisted to her production designer K K Barrett and to her costume designer Milena Canonero that she didn't want any brown, beige or sepia tints in the film. In other words, nothing which felt like a burnished past or an old photograph, and nothing which felt intentionally old. Instead, Coppola's instructions to her creative team were inspired by Ladurée macarons and other unnatural colours for the era; in reality, you would have been far more likely to see deep reds, navy blues and rich yellows than you would the bubblegum pinks and baby blues of the film. And even when wearing the period-correct silhouettes and undergarments, there was a psychological or symbolic purpose for the costuming; constricting corsets, for instance, were only worn at court in Versailles but never in Antoinette's country cottage, where she could, quite literally, breathe more freely. 'The corset helped. It was like she was a little bird trying to get out,' Kirsten Dunst noted.

Milena Canonero was an Academy Award-winning costume designer for her work on Stanley Kubrick's period masterpiece *Barry Lyndon* (1975); the designer made over 70 outfits for Dunst alone, with hundreds more for the rest of the cast. Rose Byrne,

Sofia and fashion

Coppola's appreciation for fashion and costuming is colourfully evidenced throughout her film work. She joined the team at Chanel in Paris as an intern at the tender age of 15, and the French couturier would go on to make the unforgettable 1960s wedding dress for *Priscilla*. Coppola used to horde fashion magazines and make her own collages, moodboards and zines as a teenager – something which still guides her as a filmmaker today, heavily moodboarding her movies in advance. This approach extends to her collaborations with designers from Manolo Blahnik on *Marie Antoinette* through to the more au courant 2008-esque looks from Roberto Cavalli and Ugg in *The Bling Ring*. Coppola has also shot fashion ads for Dior, Marc Jacobs and Louis Vuitton.

While Coppola herself favours wearing clean feminine lines – crisp cotton shirts and boyfriend jeans with a dainty ballet flat or softly retro A-line dresses for red-carpet events – her friends in the fashion world include the likes of Marc Jacobs and Anna Sui, and her costuming for her feature films are often characterized by a fussier look, with a super-femme, pastel-driven 'bow girl' aesthetic. Whether it be alongside costume designer Nancy Steiner on her early films, Milena Canonero on *Marie Antoinette* or Stacey Battat, who has costumed six of Sofia's films, including *Priscilla*, detail is key. They often source their materials and textiles from authentic sources and redesign them from the ground up, injecting historical pieces with unexpected influence – 1980s New Wave music, or 1990s fashion campaigns, for instance. Symbolism is key in Coppola's approach to costuming, too, with colour often signifying the moods of her character or the direction a scene may take. Nothing is an accident when it comes to fashion and costume in the work of Sofia Coppola, be it the near-uniformity of the homecoming gowns in *The Virgin Suicides* or the too-short courtroom dresses of *The Bling Ring*.

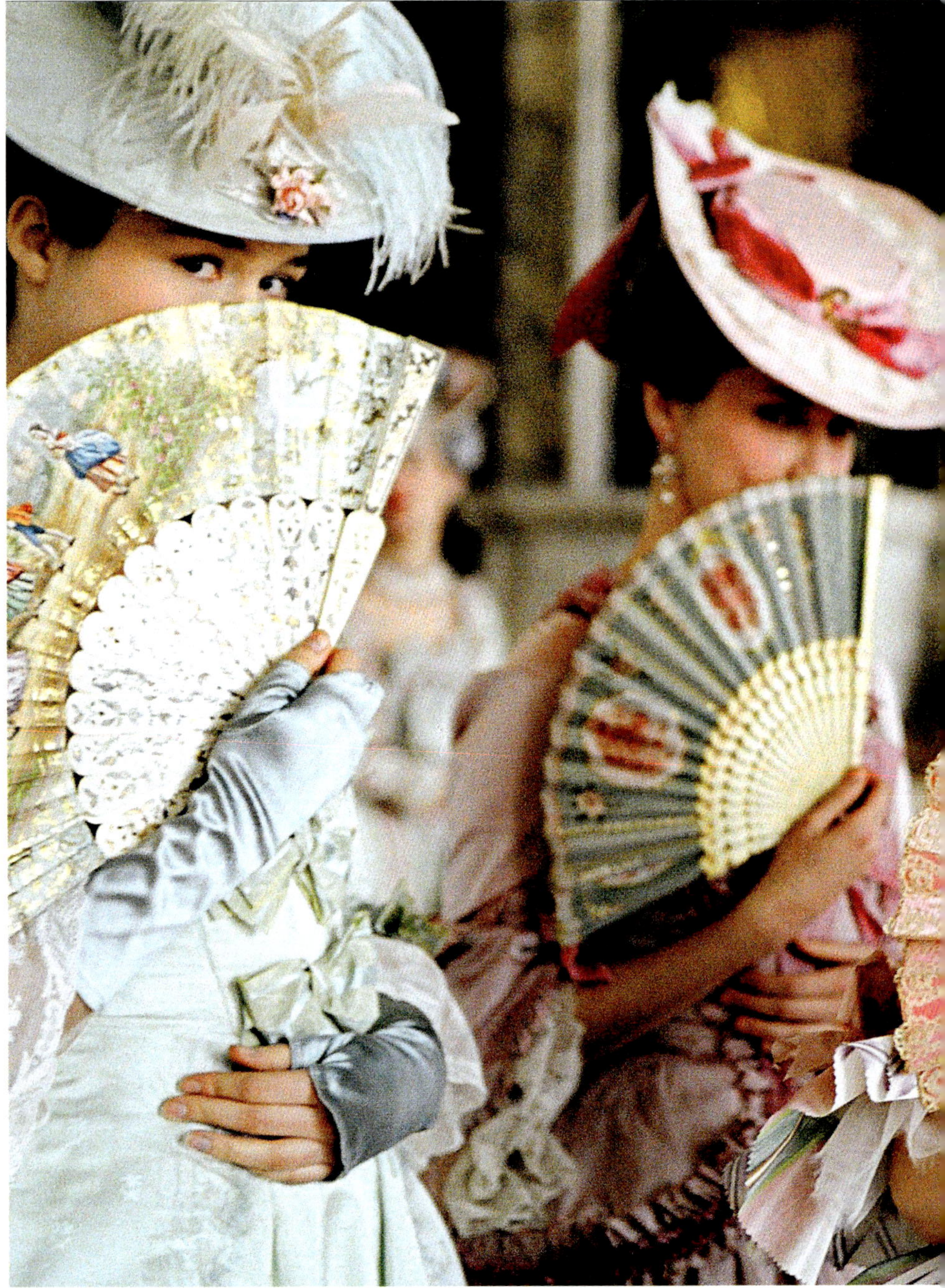

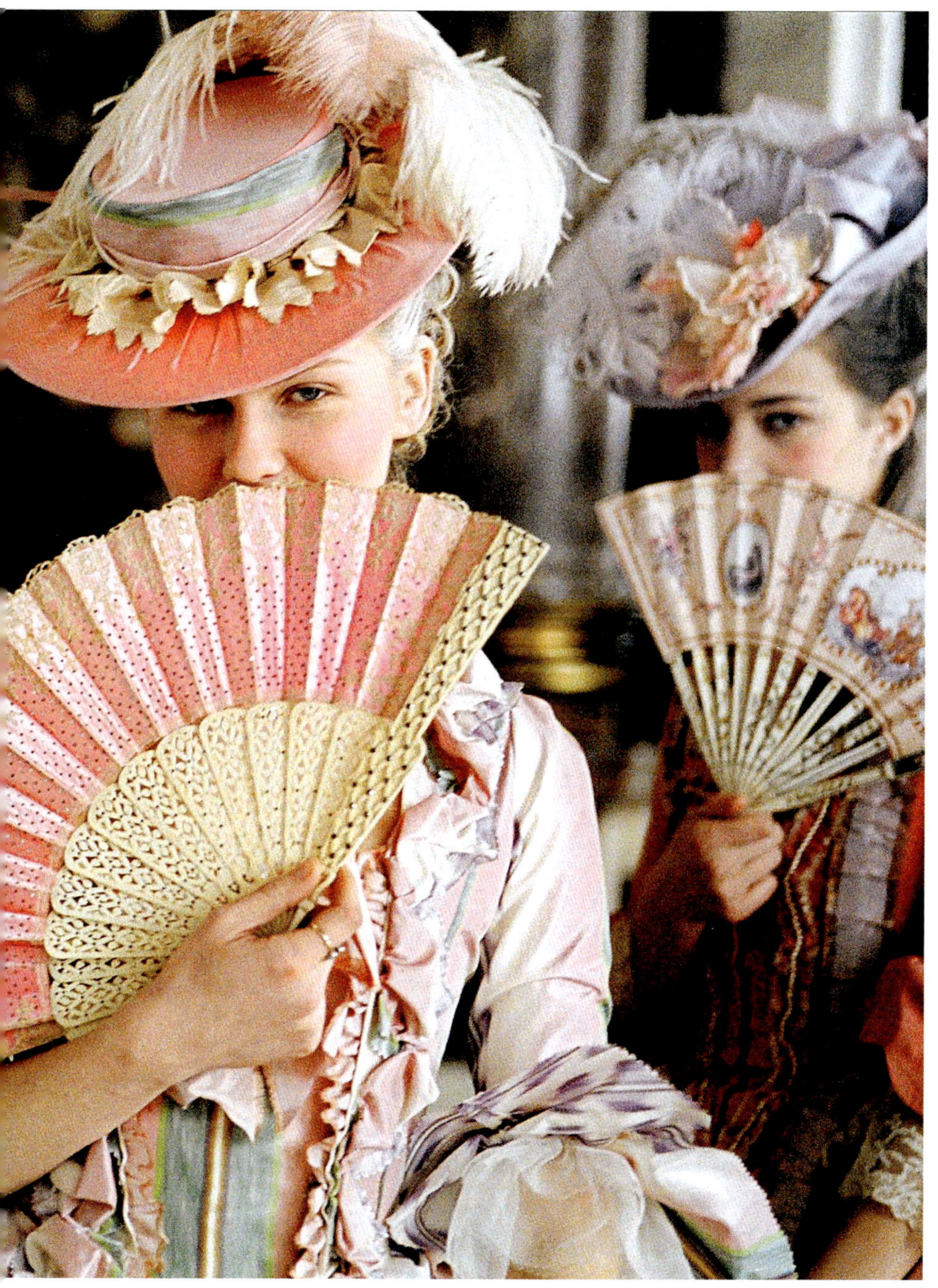

who played Duchess de Polignac – a witty, gossipy friend of Antoinette's – was even given some of the dresses worn by Marisa Berenson in *Barry Lyndon* to wear; both were 'it girls' of their eras, so Canonero felt it made sense. She went on to win another Academy Award for Best Costume Design for *Marie Antoinette*, aided by the special collection of shoes for the film designed by Manolo Blahnik.

Another major coup for the team was getting to film on location in Versailles' various rooms, including its renowned Hall of Mirrors. This was unprecedented access to such a valuable and fragile piece of history, and the crew were only allowed to film there once per week, using other palatial historical homes and châteaux around France in order to stand in for the location. Carefully reconstructing textiles and rooms based on period-correct construction methods, these rich mise en scène was then brought to life onscreen with compositions inspired by the likes of Kubrick and Luchino Visconti, paintings of Francisco Goya and the photography of Guy Bourdin.

Meanwhile, the atmosphere on set has been described as a relaxed, 'party' atmosphere, especially on the days shooting at Versailles. As truckloads of Belgian flowers and expensive French jewels were carted in, the cast were occasionally encouraged to drink a little champagne and eat macarons between scenes. Visitors to the set at Versailles included Pedro Almodóvar and Wes Anderson, who became onlookers curious to see Coppola's unprecedented access to the palace and its history. Over the course of four months between January and April, locations were

PREVIOUS: The women of the court of Versailles show off their Milena Canonero-designed wares.

RIGHT: Dunst, dressed simply in her French cottagecore phase, and the dashing Count Fersen, her lover (played by Jamie Dornan).

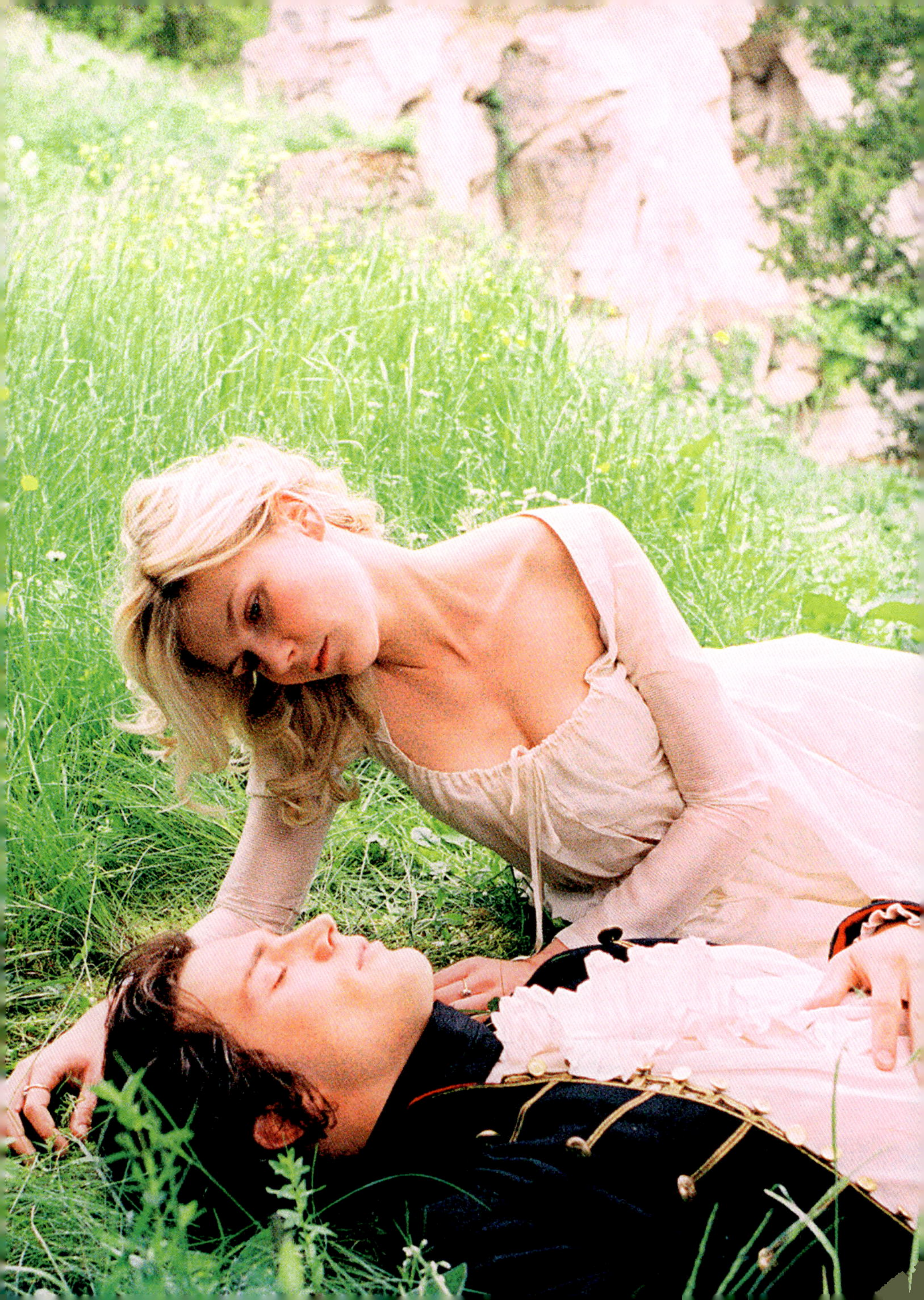

transformed and the 18th century was brought vividly back to life, albeit with an impressionistic slant.

On release, unfortunately, the film was something of a disappointment for Coppola. At its premiere at the Cannes Film Festival, where the crowds are notoriously vocal, it was booed by the audience. It was an eventual moderate box office success, earning some $60 million after a $40 million budget, but largely, it disappeared from view soon after release (with the notable exception of its Costume Design Academy Award). In 2021, Coppola told *Vogue*: 'I'm so happy it has an audience now because at the time it was not successful. People didn't go see it; they didn't really know what to make of it.'

Today, the film is often recognized as among Coppola's finest. And *Marie Antoinette*'s approach has proved deeply influential. From Autumn de Wilde's recent tongue-in-cheek adaptation of Jane Austen's *Emma* (2020), starring Anya Taylor-Joy, to Marie Kreutzer's festival favourite *Corsage* (2022), featuring Vicky Krieps as the rebellious Empress Sissi of Austria, many women directors who've chosen to take on period pieces have put a defiant female POV – and an irreverent one – front and centre. No doubt this owes something to Coppola's boldness. Quirky, Oscar-nominated Greek filmmaker Yorgos Lanthimos also seems to borrow from Coppola's influence. The clever and femme-focused subversion of *The Favourite* (2018) and even of *Poor Things* (2023), to an extent, takes some of Coppola's aura and runs further with it, pushing the sexuality to the fore. But even for the more casual viewer, *Marie Antoinette* clearly prefigures the fun wardrobe anachronisms of hit period series like *Bridgerton* or *Dickinson*, along with their wink-and-nod nudges towards contemporary social and sexual mores.

Ultimately, *Marie Antoinette*'s critical reception in some quarters – particularly those who saw the project as all music-

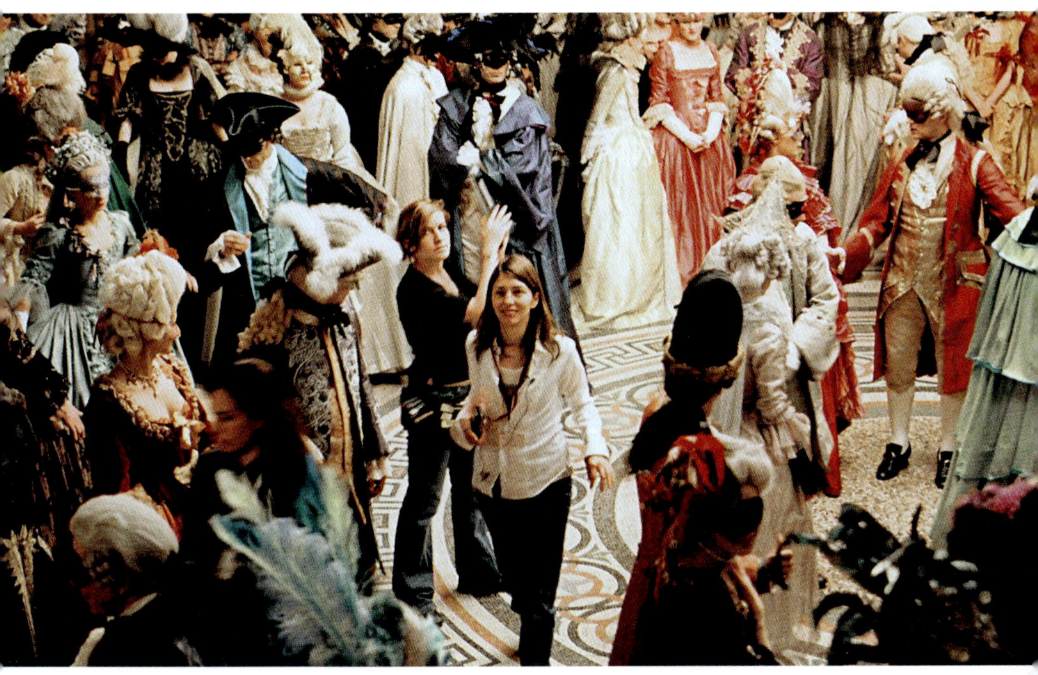

ABOVE: Coppola orchestrates the complexity of the ballroom sequence.

video-lite aesthetic, or simply as gauzy style over substance – seemed to underline the fact that many male critics did not get the point. (Legendary *Observer* critic Philip French called it 'tedious vacuity', comparing it scornfully with teen chick flick *The Princess Diaries*, 2001, while others referred to it as 'fluffy' and full of 'gimmicks'.) The film, like much of Coppola's work, gently subverts male-dominated hypocrisies around womanhood: that women are forever being scapegoated for leaning into or getting pleasure from the things they have been forced to enjoy (i.e. 'beautifying', shopping, gossip). Ahead of its time in its celebration of the more disdained or 'unserious' aspects of femininity – as well as its playful, bold, postmodern approach to capturing history onscreen – *Marie Antoinette* proved to be prophetic in more ways than one.

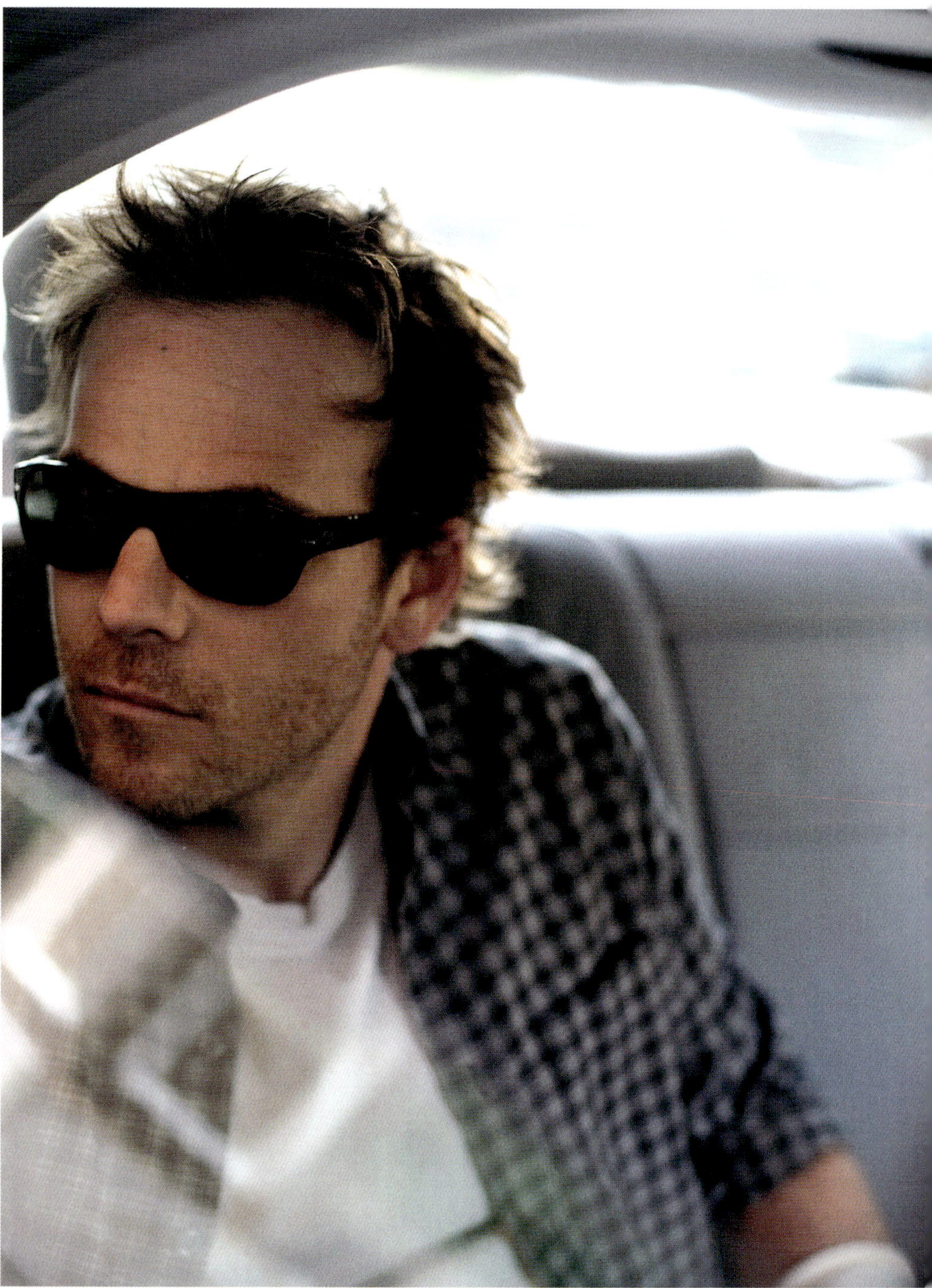

'*You think you're hot shit.*'

SOMEWHERE
2010

When you think of films set in Los Angeles, it's hard not to think of noirish crime dramas like *L.A. Confidential* (1997) or *Heat* (1995), or perhaps the shiny glamour of *Sunset Boulevard* (1950). But in 2011, Sofia Coppola offered a remarkable, poignant entry to the canon of great LA movies; one that offers none of the artificial glamour nor the thrills and spills of a genre flick. *Somewhere*, her minor key story of a few weeks in the life of a part-time movie-star dad and his young daughter, is inextricable from its California environment and is potentially Sofia Coppola's most close-to-home film to date. She referred to it as the start of a new body of work in her filmmaking career – with her first three films as part of one chapter, *Somewhere* was the beginning of the next.

The story itself is simple. A famous film star in his late thirties, known as Johnny Marco (Stephen Dorff) is doing press for a new movie, although the film itself is barely mentioned outside of his occasional work commitment. Otherwise, he seems to spend his time carousing, drinking and drugging himself into a rather unhappy haze in the hotel where he lives. He's forced to rethink things when he is tasked with spending more time than usual looking after his 11-year-old daughter, Cleo (Elle Fanning). The film follows their relationship, pinging from estrangement to affection and back again, as Cleo tries to understand and connect with a

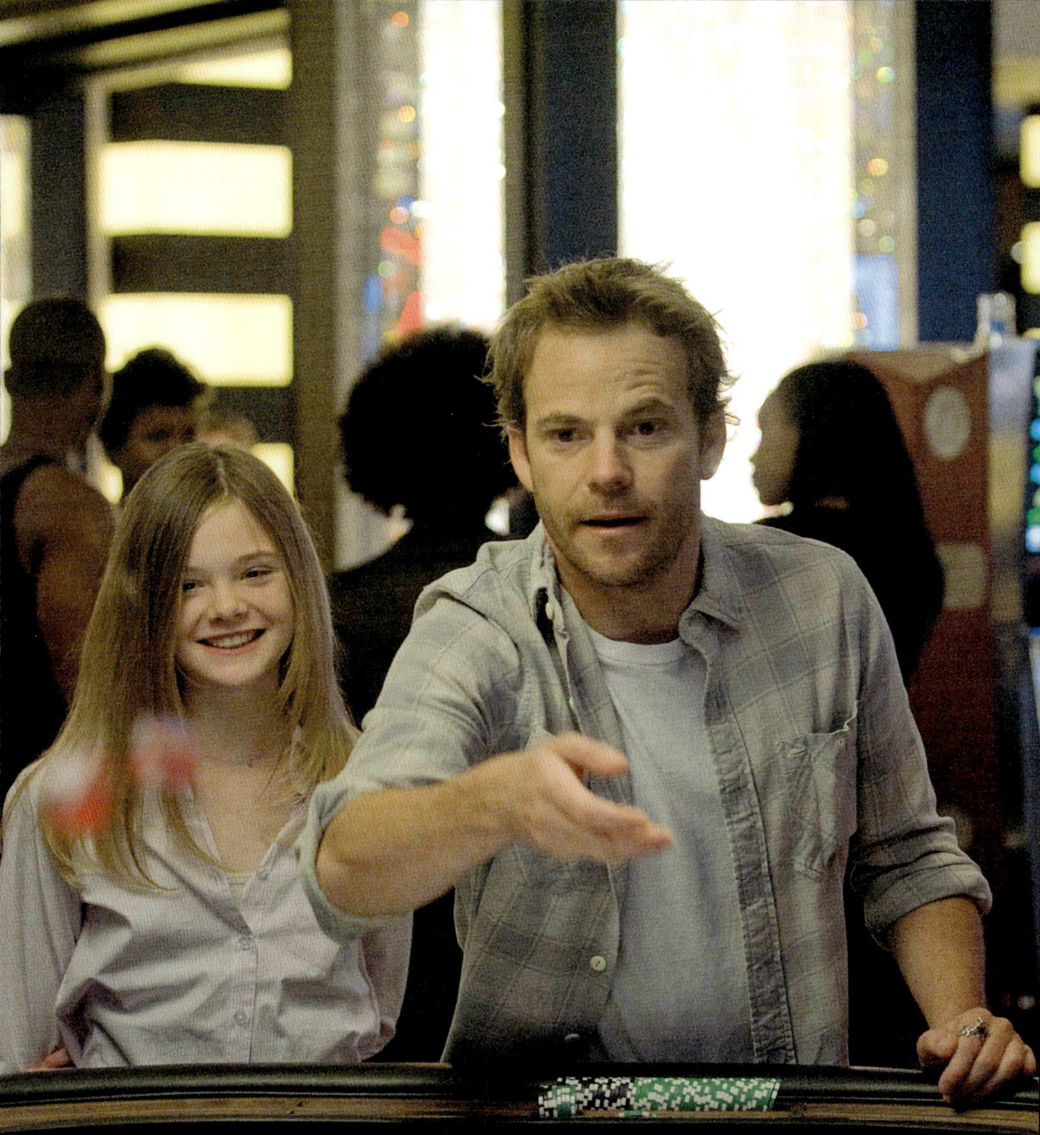

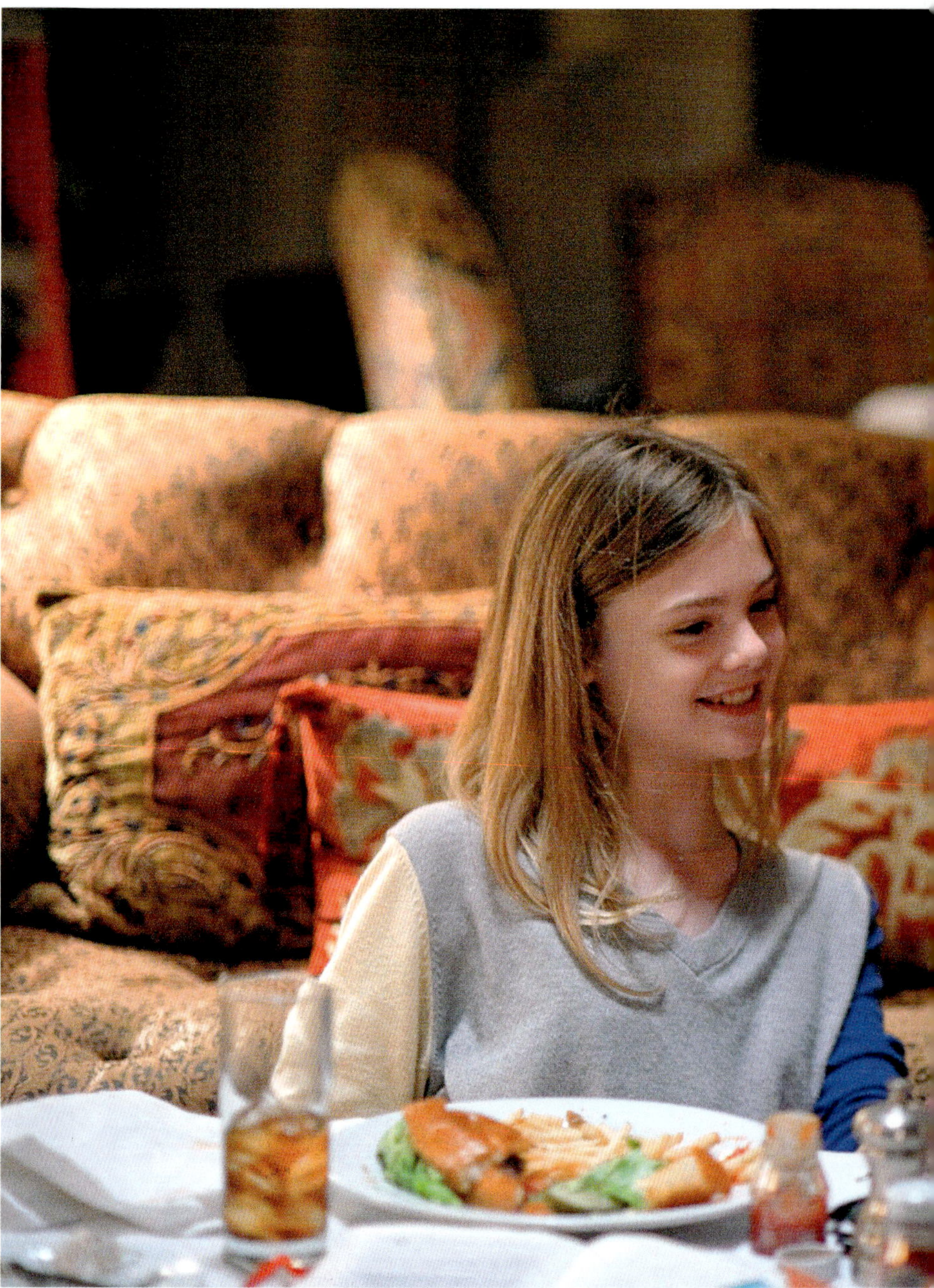

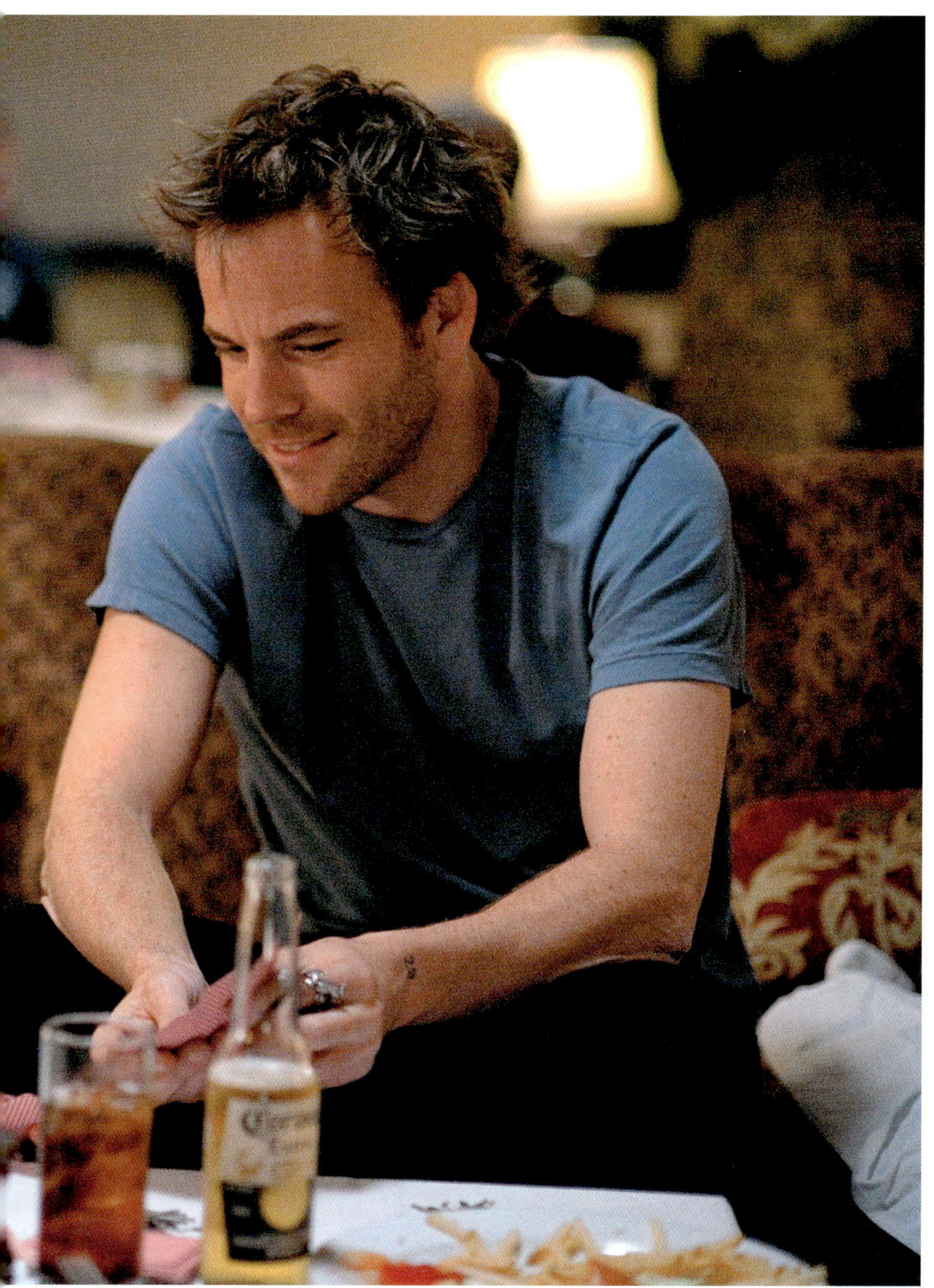

father who seems far away in more ways than one. They go on a press tour to Italy briefly, staying in a luxurious suite, but Cleo is happiest swimming laps in her father's private pool or eating French fries in the hotel lobby. They spend quality time together, and then they part ways again, with Cleo presumably returning to her mother's care. Johnny drives his slick black Porsche into the desert.

So many films suffer from being overwritten, stuffing their scenes with expository dialogue or voiceover. Coppola is assured enough in her ability to convey meaning and mood through her visual skill to dispense with this. There are no explosive fights or dramatic confrontations between father and child, as such; no explanatory backstory about previous relationships or Johnny's path to stardom. Clichés about ex-wives, alimony or rehab are dispensed with. Some might struggle with the lack of explanation provided, but the ambiguity is clearly intentional: Coppola fine-tunes her scenes so that you *know* – or at least intuitively understand – how to fill in the gaps provided. Johnny's self-evident hedonism – not to mention the endless stream of attractive women – seems pretty clearly to have been the source of a marriage gone south. And Cleo's feeling about it – his absence, his wildness – is conveyed mainly through her sideways glances, curious and guarded, as if her father were a kind of puzzle she was trying to solve. In one outburst late in the film, where she worries about her mother, she glancingly mentions that her father is never around either; that's about as direct as the film ever gets, but by this point, we already know all about it.

Coppola thought of the film as something of an experiment; a way for her to work as minimally as possible. After the ambition,

RIGHT: Coppola at work, shooting on location at Los Angeles' iconic Chateau Marmont hotel.

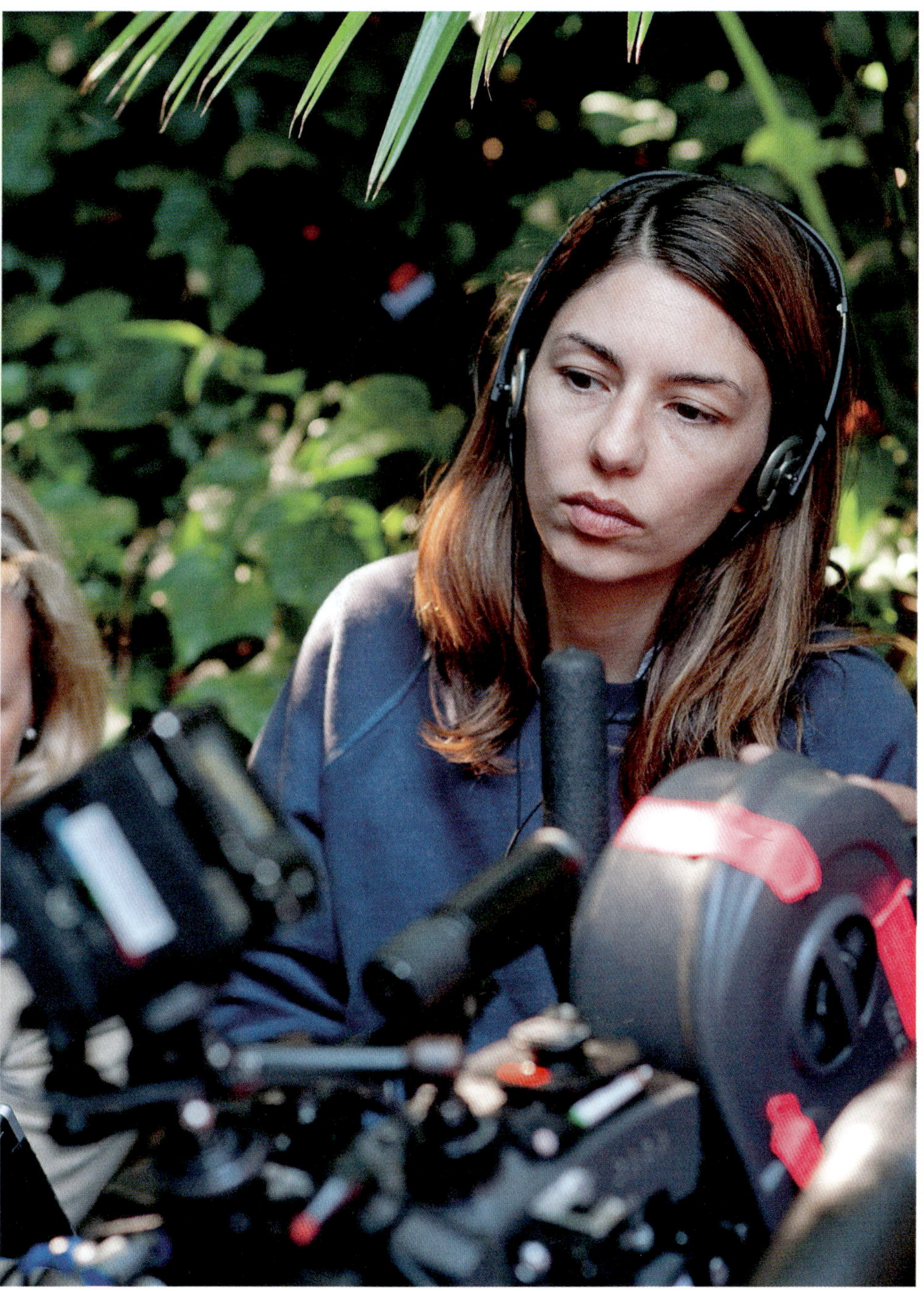

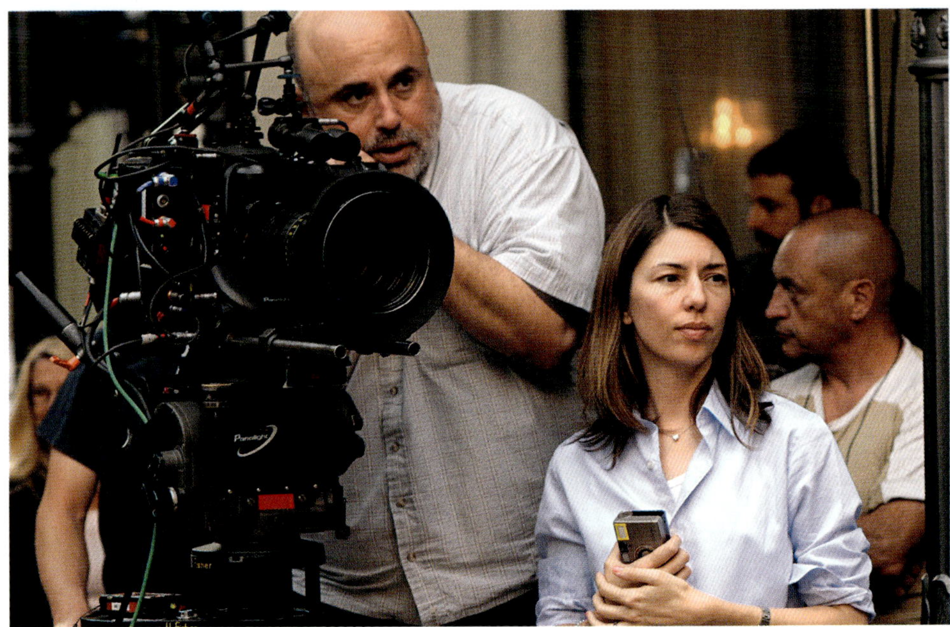

ABOVE: Coppola and veteran cinematographer Harris Savides on set.

OVERLEAF: Johnny and Cleo have a rare moment of peace by the Chateau swimming pool.

scope and detail of a film like *Marie Antoinette*, she wanted to pare down her approach. Rather than capturing an entire epoch or the narrative of a life, Coppola could focus on something she had long specialized in: creating a mood and an atmosphere. As star Stephen Dorff said, the shoot was characterized by an attitude of 'let's go in with as few people as we have to and let's limit the apparatus'. Coppola liked the fact that it was a return to the more simple, almost student-esque filmmaking of something like *Lost in Translation*.

Somewhere is a 'mood piece' if ever there was one; loose on plotting, characterized by stretches of unstructured time playing video games or smoking cigarettes in the dark or aimlessly driving around. Some may call it dreamy or oblique or even a bit meandering: its unhurried pace might not be to everyone's personal taste. But something about it lingers, seems to capture the lackadaisical malaise of Los Angeles life, and it remains one of Coppola's very finest films. It combines her usual elegant compositions, lightness of touch and skill for depicting loneliness, orchestrated together to powerful effect.

This was the first time Coppola tackled her hometown for the big screen, not only basing the story in her native Los Angeles, but also in a place she was very familiar with: Chateau Marmont. Perhaps one of the most legendary hotels in the world, this institution on Sunset Boulevard was the original haunt of everyone from Errol Flynn and Clark Gable through to Led Zeppelin and writers like Eve Babitz; a hangout for the dissolute stars and rock 'n' rollers of Hollywood past and present. It was the tragic site of the overdose of John Belushi in 1982 and the bohemian and sexy location of endless parties and trysts over the decades. The general manager of the Marmont knew Coppola and her family. After all, her father Francis spent much of his time there while she was growing up, and she herself had birthday parties organized and thrown by the staff. Everyone in Hollywood seemed to have a Chateau Marmont story; why wouldn't it be the perfect backdrop for the tale of a movie star struggling with the emptiness of his privileged existence?

Coppola had admitted that she accompanied her father and saw many 'weird, grown-up things' while staying at the Chateau. Young Cleo's experience in this world certainly seems to mirror Coppola's own childhood memories in numerous ways, from the gelato-tasting she does with her dad to the suite in Milan she actually stayed in with her father as a kid. But Coppola insists that she only coloured the story with some personal connections, borrowing instead from the experiences of a Hollywood friend's

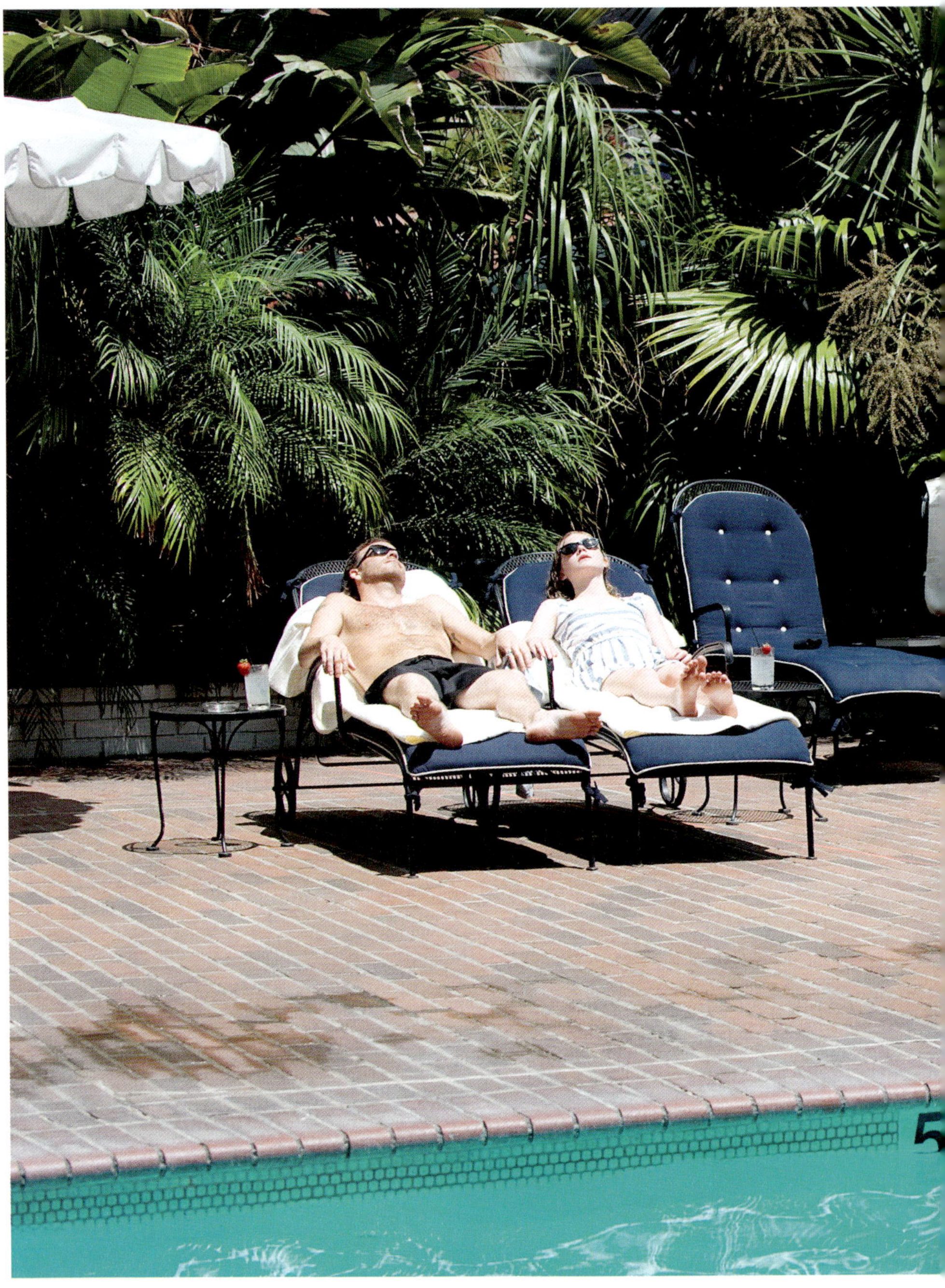
5

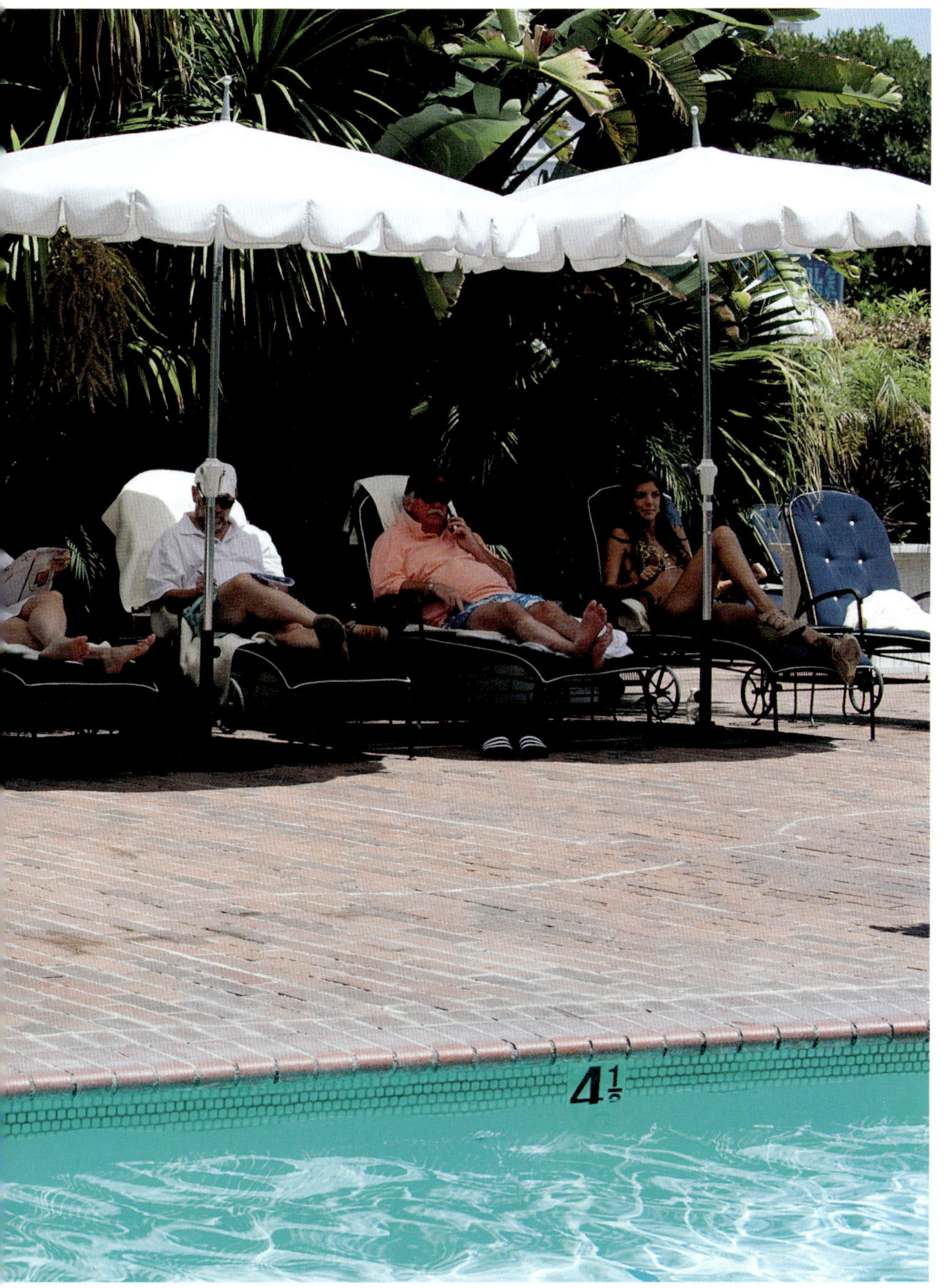

4 1/2

Sofia Coppola's Los Angeles

'There are so many different sides of Los Angeles,' Coppola mused in an interview after making *The Bling Ring*, her second consecutive film set in the City of Angels. And she would know: she spent much of her childhood there, albeit growing up in California's Napa Valley, where her parents had a family home. Like many of her artistic compatriots, she has a love-hate relationship with LA and has spent her time living in New York and Paris for periods throughout her life. But she also has something few other LA filmmakers can boast; via her family, a deep, instinctive understanding of how the city operates and looks for its most privileged and respected hometown heroes. Her depiction of the Chateau Marmont is of course derived from her own time spent there growing up, and going on to even have birthday parties there as she got older; the general manager permitted her to film there so extensively because he knew her so well.

But beyond her personal connections, Coppola has an eye for the various levels of LA life and culture, from the high- to the low-brow. Frequently casting reality television stars or Playboy models in *Somewhere*, or giving the likes of Paris Hilton a cameo in *The Bling Ring*, she knows how to mine the glitzy environment for every manner of celebrity. None appear by accident or simply as authentic background flavour – they tend to have something to tell us about the LA we're entering into and which our protagonists occupy. Whether it's the seemingly endless driving of living in the notoriously traffic-laden city or the bland McMansion suburbia of its less trendy neighbourhoods, Coppola and her team have a penchant for capturing the hazy contradictions of the West Coast spirit with authenticity and style.

child and inflecting it with cinematic influences like Peter Bogdanovich's *Paper Moon* (1973). But even if there's not much literal autobiography in *Somewhere*, there's a spirit of familiarity here. In a more overarching sense, there's a feeling that everybody *wants* something from Johnny; women, agents, press, hangers-on. It's very difficult for the father and daughter to actually be alone, uninterrupted, for long, and you can sense the yearning for it just beneath the surface. It's not difficult to imagine this was a feeling Coppola might relate to. 'My dad was excited to let me be in worlds that kids don't usually go to. My parents always took us out to the Academy Awards starting when I was probably eight,' Coppola says.

For the lead role, Coppola cast a friend, Stephen Dorff, an actor previously best known for his role as the 'fifth Beatle' in *Backbeat* (1994). Dorff had been a sensation in an era of scruffy, rebellious pretty-boy roles of the mid-to-late 1990s, but had since been relegated to work in B movies and supporting roles. He'd appeared in a few interesting parts for John Waters and Michael Mann but never seemed to be cast in anything as minimal and honest as *Somewhere*. Dorff had lived at the Chateau Marmont for a time in his youth – around the time he co-starred with Alicia Silverstone in the sensual Aerosmith music video for 'Cryin''. Coppola asked Dorff to go back and live at the Chateau again in preparation for his role as Johnny Marco.

As Dorff shared in an interview with *New York* magazine at the time: 'Ultimately, she knew that by living here, that things would happen to me as Stephen the way they probably would for Johnny. Sofia would come in the morning and say, "Any gossip from last night?" I'd say, "Funny enough, I had a dry rehearsal of our elevator scene. I was in the elevator with that actor Olivier Martinez, and I didn't know him all that well – I'd just met him once. We were riding in the elevator and he had scripts under his arm and he said, "What room are you in?" And I said, "69". He said, "Oh yeah? I had a party in 69 once…"'

That anecdote, of course, would become the basis for Johnny Marco's awkward encounter with Benicio del Toro in the hotel lift. Coppola's films are often left open to small moments of chance, inspiration or improv, although her idea of what will happen on camera is nonetheless steadfast and carefully planned. Still, there's a playful quality that does allow for some flexibility, as with the above; or in moments where her famously minimal screenplays allow for performers to come up with ideas in the moment. (In the scene where Fanning and Dorff play *Guitar Hero* and their pal watches, that's basically all of the instructions in the screenplay; they just played video games until they found organic elements to make the moment real.)

Dorff is perfect for the part, not only because of apparent parallels with the character. As Coppola has said, his real-life warmth and sincerity seems to bleed through what might otherwise be a fairly remote or unlikeable protagonist. It's hard not to like this deadbeat dad, or not to feel his heart is ultimately in the right place, even as he makes some frankly questionable parenting decisions. At one point, Johnny cluelessly drapes himself at the hotel breakfast table next to his daughter and the chatty stranger that he's just had a one-night stand with. Even as Cleo tries to catch Johnny's eye and make clear her annoyance, Coppola keeps her father's reaction out of shot; *we* see her discomfort, but *he* clearly does not. As Coppola's longtime film editor Stacey Flack pointed out, 'I love being able to, with the director, tell a story where there's no dialogue. That scene, with all the looks – his looks, her looks – I loved it.'

RIGHT: German theatrical poster for *Somewhere*, 2011.

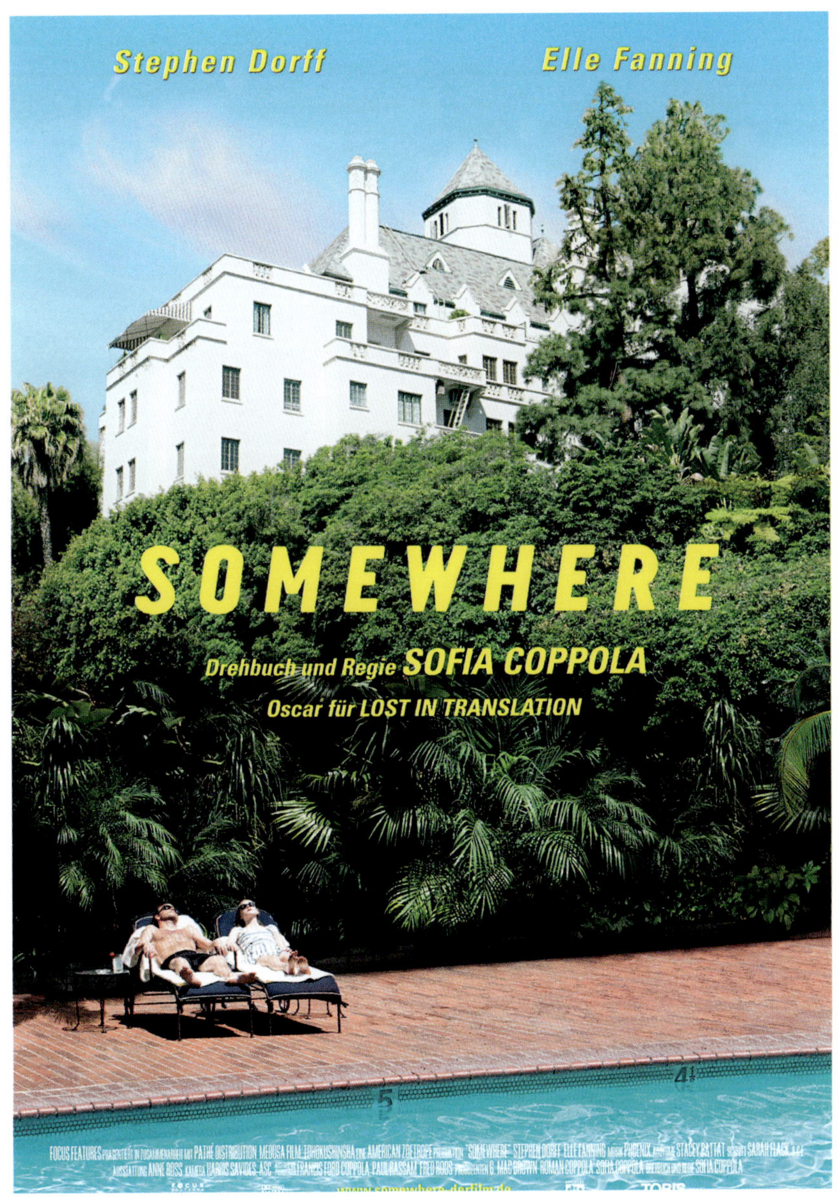

Stephen Dorff
Elle Fanning
SOMEWHERE
Drehbuch und Regie SOFIA COPPOLA
Oscar für LOST IN TRANSLATION

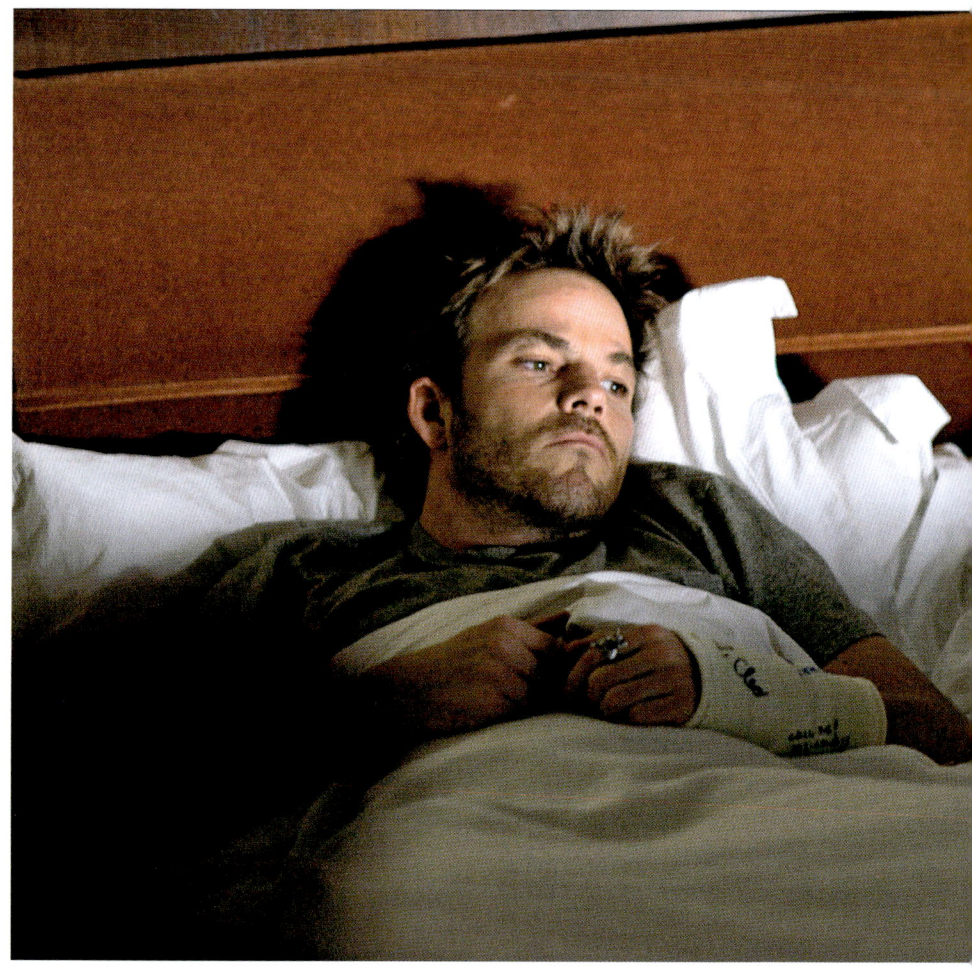

It's a stunning performance from Dorff. His slightly wolfish, worn-in handsomeness gives him the look of a man who has been no stranger to debauchery. He emanates a bone-weary solitude, a kind of remote and unreachable core, even as he slaps shoulders at parties and tips booze down his throat without tasting it. Superficiality and self-indulgence entertain him, but can't seem to satisfy him for long. He looks perennially tired in a way that

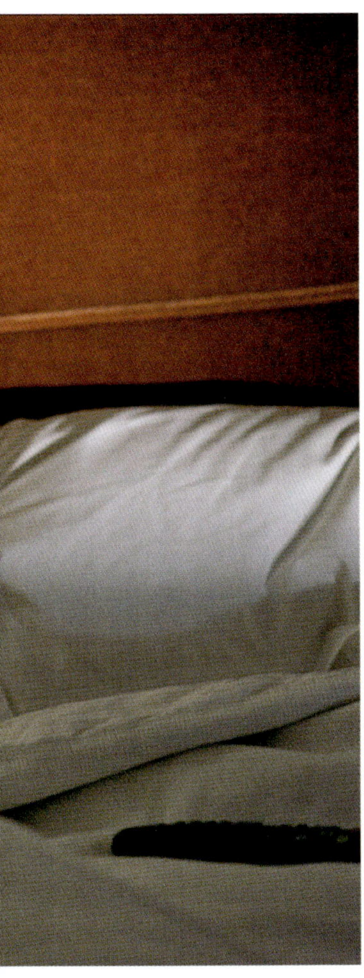

suggests more than a mere hangover. But he has a boyish playfulness too; clearly he's a man who's never really fully grown up, and his ability to have so much fun with his kid comes hand-in-hand with that very quality.

His relationship with his daughter is coloured by his regular absences – he reveals he doesn't know Cleo has been ice-skating for three years, for instance – but he is an affectionate father, mostly trying to protect his kid from too-adult situations and plying her with gelato from the room-service menu. There's a warmth between the pair that sometimes belies what should probably be a distance between them, and Coppola highlights this with her minimal, synthy soundtrack by Phoenix.

Cleo, meanwhile, has an almost ethereal sophistication for such a young girl. Elle Fanning, with her long blonde hair redolent of a lost Lisbon sister from *The Virgin Suicides*, is the girlhood figure of Coppola's film this time. It marks a shift that the filmmaker's focus is on Cleo's father – for once, a male protagonist. But Fanning is still the beating heart of the film, softening her father's persona before our very eyes, and allowing us to see him through the prism of his child's love and acceptance of him. Even as he proves imperfect indeed, it's Cleo who is our

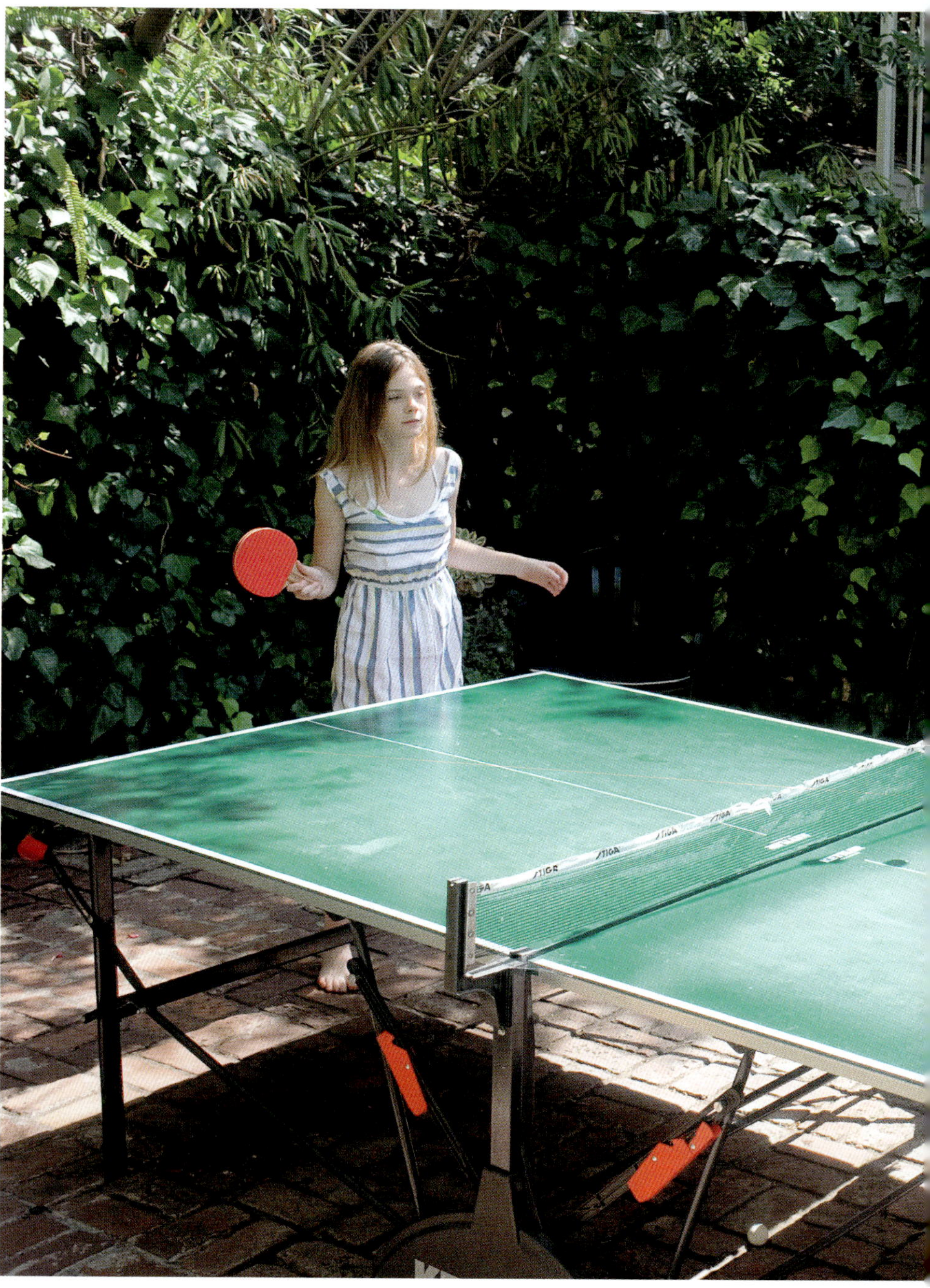

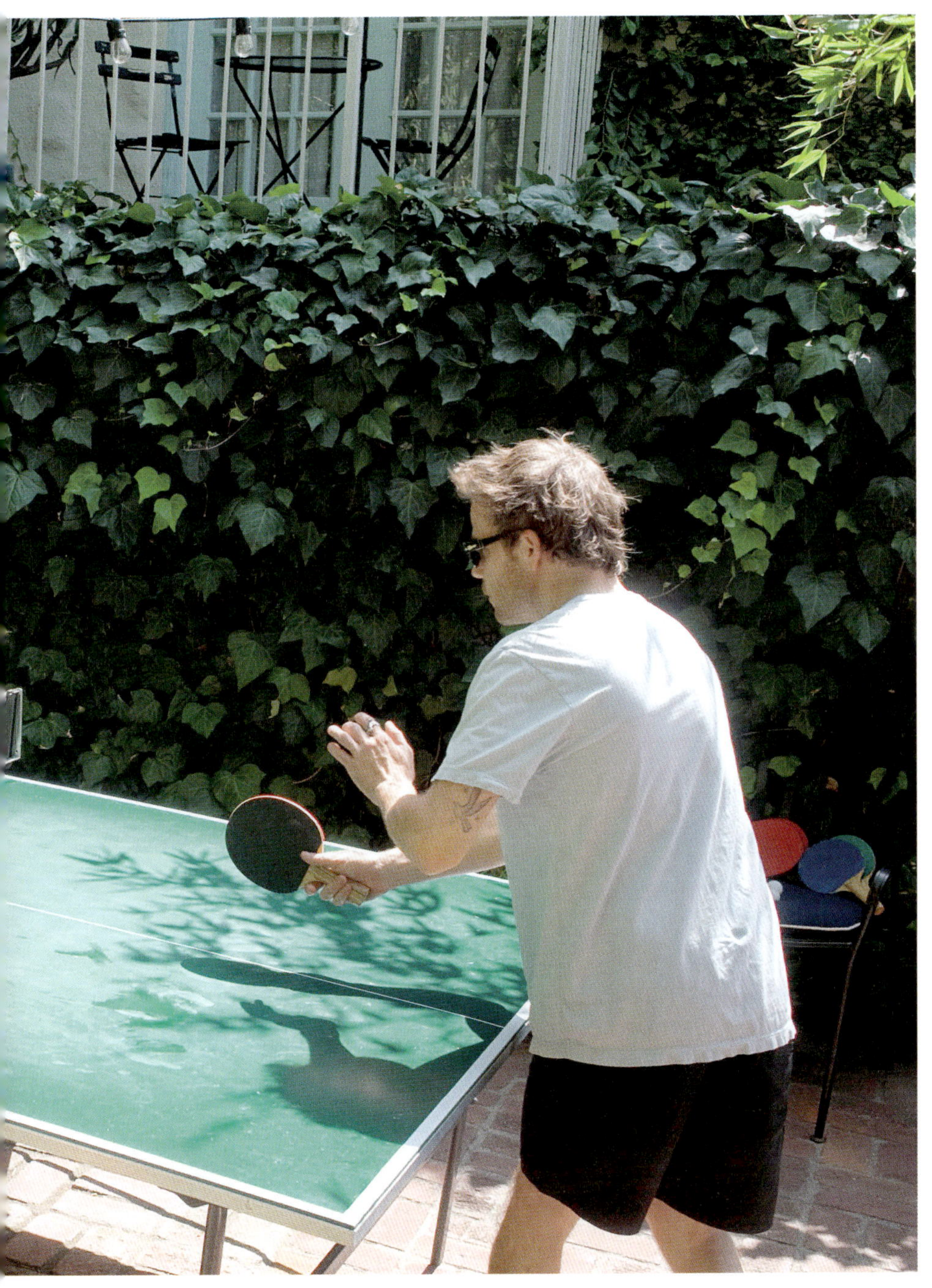

entrée into this heady, cynical Los Angeles world, standing in for our own bafflement at this world of inane press conferences and a constant army of entourage.

For the supporting cast, Coppola went meta, as she often had in the past with her casting of people like Bill Murray as a movie star, or with giving cameos to those who had inspired her. But here was a real opportunity for her to go to her little black book, given the milieu of *Somewhere* and her extensive background in shooting music videos and fashion ads. Everyone from indie-rock girl band Rooney to runway model Erin Wasson make small cameos hanging out at the Chateau. And for the part of Johnny's jocular party pal Sammy, Coppola pulled in one of the Jackass crew, Chris Pontius, more well-known for his skateboarding daredevilry than for acting in serious independent film. Coppola invoked further sleazy, tabloid-inflected 2010 vibes by casting former Playboy playmates Karissa and Kristina Shannon – even visiting Hugh Hefner at the Playboy Mansion in her quest to do so. It seems she wanted to people *Somewhere* with a supporting cast that not only felt true to the moment in LA, but also to its less-than-glossy party scene and all its gaudiness. (In many ways, this looks ahead to Coppola's interest in the very tabloid-oriented LA story of *The Bling Ring*.)

It's worth pointing out, though, that the Shannons' roles are used for more than a bit of background flashiness. There's real statement-making in how Coppola frames them. These two blonde, radioactively tanned women, dressed alike in revealing costumes and dancing around twin portable stripper poles in awkward synchronization, swivel around for the benefit of an audience of one. That audience is Johnny, sitting in his hotel room bed with a broken arm and eyes half-lidded on painkillers. It's a striptease by name, but it's curiously PG, with no nudity and certainly no real sexuality being exuded. It's all spectacle, sound

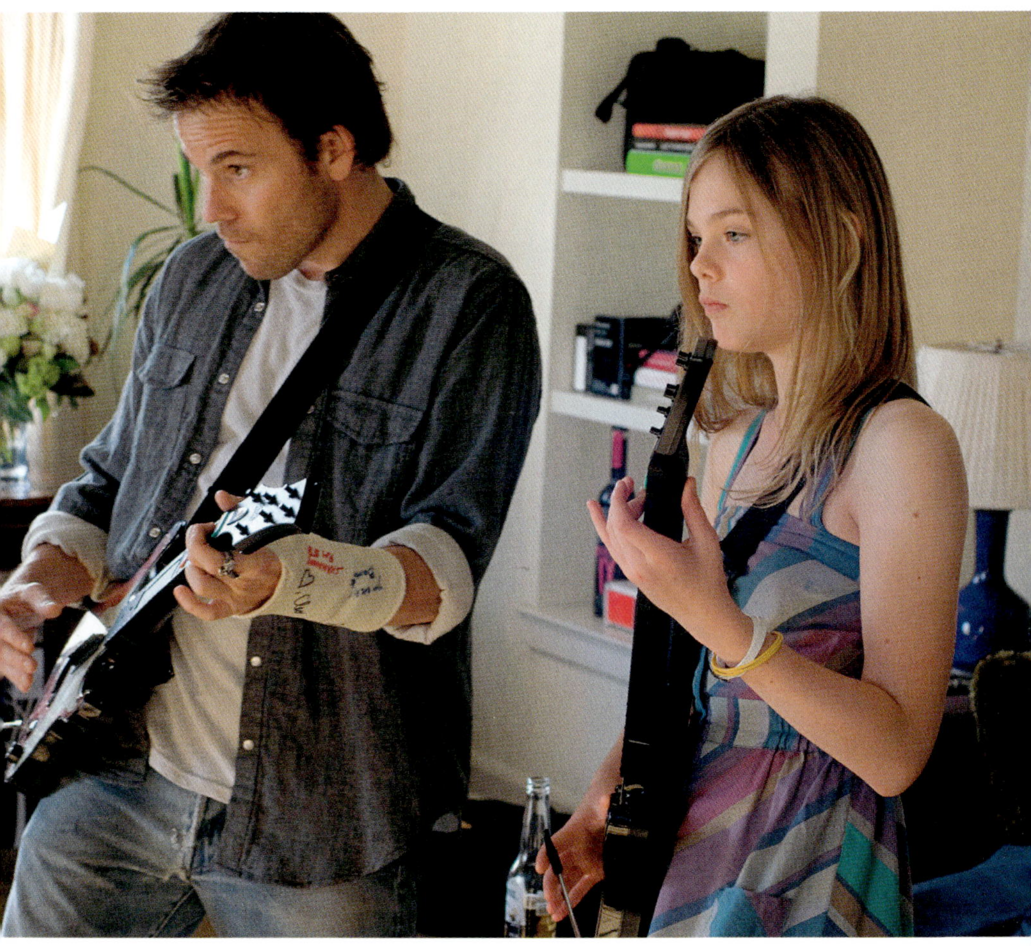

ABOVE: *Guitar Hero* is a father-daughter favourite.

and fury, signifying nothing. It's a jarring, garish sight, indicating the kind of unnatural and artificial exchange of human emotion – desire, in this case – invented by a place like LA.

Then, in his medicinal haze, Johnny drifts off and wakes up again to see Cleo hovering over him in bed, signing the cast on his

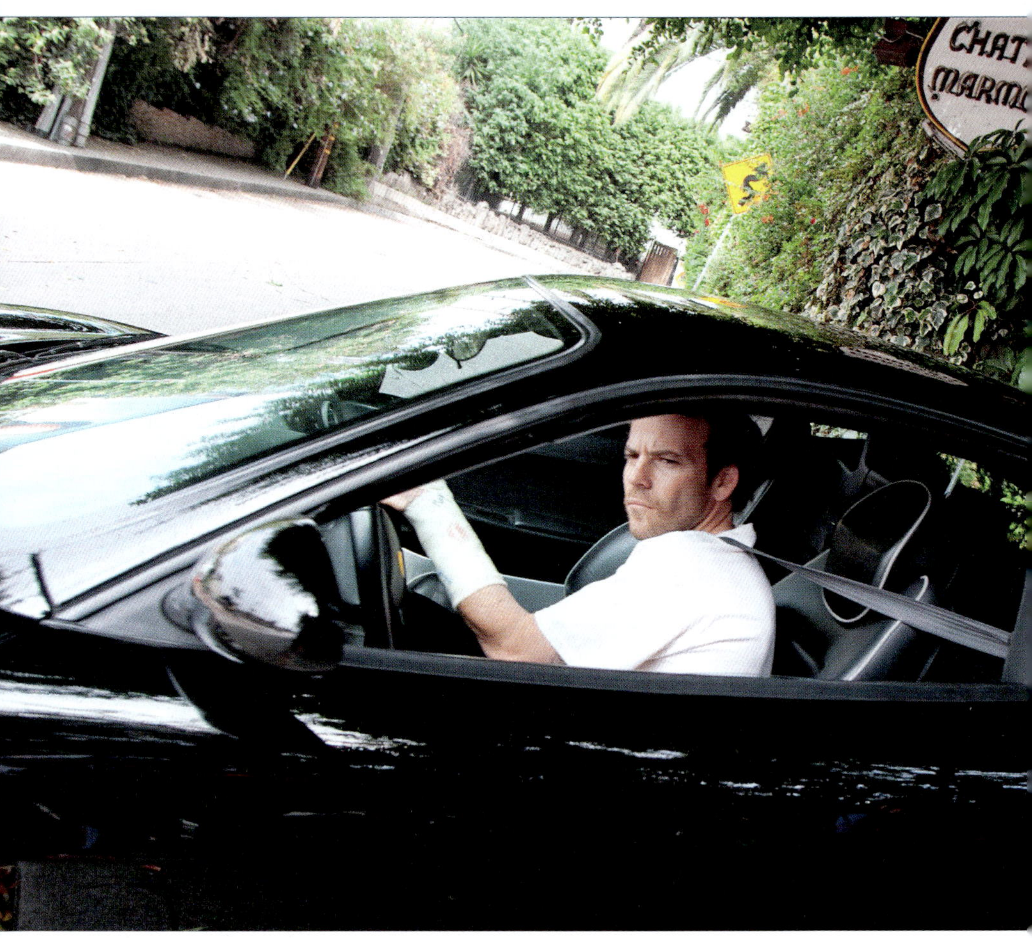

ABOVE: Johnny is continually seen driving aimlessly in his Porsche; a real Los Angeles activity.

arm with a marker pen, a curtain of blonde hair hanging over her face. It hardly seems like an accident that this would be our introduction to her character; seemingly a visual non sequitur between the hard, cynical blondeness of LA womanhood with the childish innocence of Johnny's young daughter. There's something unpleasant – and as ever with Coppola, very subtle – about this comparison and its inference about show business and its attitude towards women. But the film never lingers long enough for it to feel pointed – it's something to chew on for a viewer, a brief spark of queasy parallelism that is easy to miss or even interpret differently. Stacey Flack, Coppola's aforementioned editor, has a talent for this elliptical style. Flack had also edited films like Steven Soderbergh's *The Limey* (1999), and could clearly work in both the kinetic energy of that lively crime thriller and the lazier, long, more suggestive rhythms of a film like *Somewhere*. As Flack said in an interview at the time, 'The length of the shots brought with it a wonderful sense of realism. So there were decisions about how long or how short some shots would remain on camera, such as the opening shot of the car going around the track, or Johnny smoking a cigarette alone in his hotel room. That was a new thing for me, and I really liked it.'

To achieve the look Coppola wanted for the film, she relied on a number of influences. Borrowing from photographers like Bruce Weber and filmmakers like Chantal Akerman for her imagery – wanting to invoke a certain stillness and negative space within the frame, casting her striking human figures in overwhelming or imposing interior space. Yet for the open-air scenes of LA highways, she also leaned into some of the classic films about showbiz, exploitation and, frankly, aimless driving around: Hal Ashby's madcap *Shampoo* (1975) and Paul Schrader's stylish *American Gigolo* (1980). Finally, Coppola took influence from her own father's remarkable body of work, finding the old camera lenses Francis Ford Coppola used to make his film *Rumble Fish* in 1983. 'I feel like it has a softness, or it doesn't look like most movies,' she explained.

Rumble Fish, an expressionistic black and white film about tender juvenile delinquents and a teen misfit motorcycle gang, is very much about youth and adolescence. It's not surprising

Coppola has listed it as her favourite of her father's films, given her own preoccupation with teenage years. Although her work shifts to an interest in girlhood rather than boyhood, the hyperbole and loneliness of pubescent years are a shared family interest in this respect. And ultimately, while Johnny Marco is hardly as terrible a father as *Rumble Fish*'s alcoholic patriarch played by Dennis Hopper, there is a reckoning when it comes to his role in his daughter's life and the way he is spending his own time.

When the quiet parting of ways between Johnny and Cleo finally does occur, with Cleo off to summer camp, the pair's relationship seems to have both been bolstered by their time together and thrown into sharp relief for all the time lost between them. Again, though, there are no monologues or tearful reunions. Only an awkward late-night phone call as Johnny seems to have an emotional meltdown. 'I'm nothing,' he says to his ex-wife on the phone, who treats his apparent breakdown brusquely, as though she doesn't care very much about him at all. It's a rather heartbreaking indication of how few people this apparently beloved actor has to rely on in his personal life.

The next morning, Johnny checks out of the Chateau Marmont for what seems to be an extended period of time, and drives out into the desert in his Porsche, which we see he often does when feeling lost or thoughtful. Coppola trains her camera on the taillights of the car as it drives for an interminable period of time. Finally, with no sign of civilization around him whatsoever, Johnny pulls over onto the side of the road, gets out and strides confidently away from his car. We don't know why he's stopped, what he's walking towards, or why, indeed, the final image is of a liberated half-smile on his face. But it seems some kind of meaningful change has occurred within this man. It's up to us as viewers, ultimately, to parse what that means, both in this specific instance and in Johnny's future.

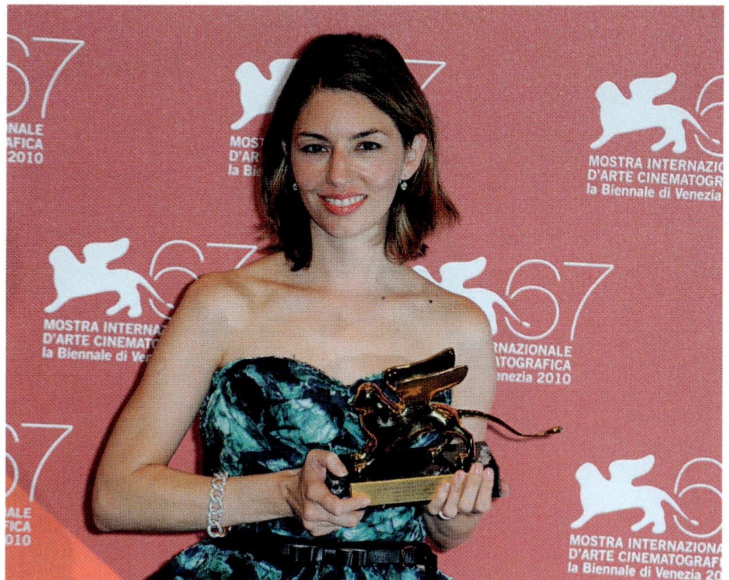

ABOVE: Coppola, pictured with her Golden Lion at the Venice Film Festival, 2010.

'There are moments in your life when you have to confront yourself, and grow up,' Coppola remarked on the film's ambiguous ending. 'It was important to see his expression. I wanted the ending to be hopeful and optimistic, that he was starting a positive phase.'

Somewhere premiered at the 67th Venice Film Festival in 2011, but Coppola and Dorff had already returned home to the States when they heard news that the film had, in fact, won the Golden Lion – the top prize of the prodigious fest. They rushed to return and accept it, where jury president Quentin Tarantino heaped the film with praise. In her acceptance speech, Coppola thanked her father.

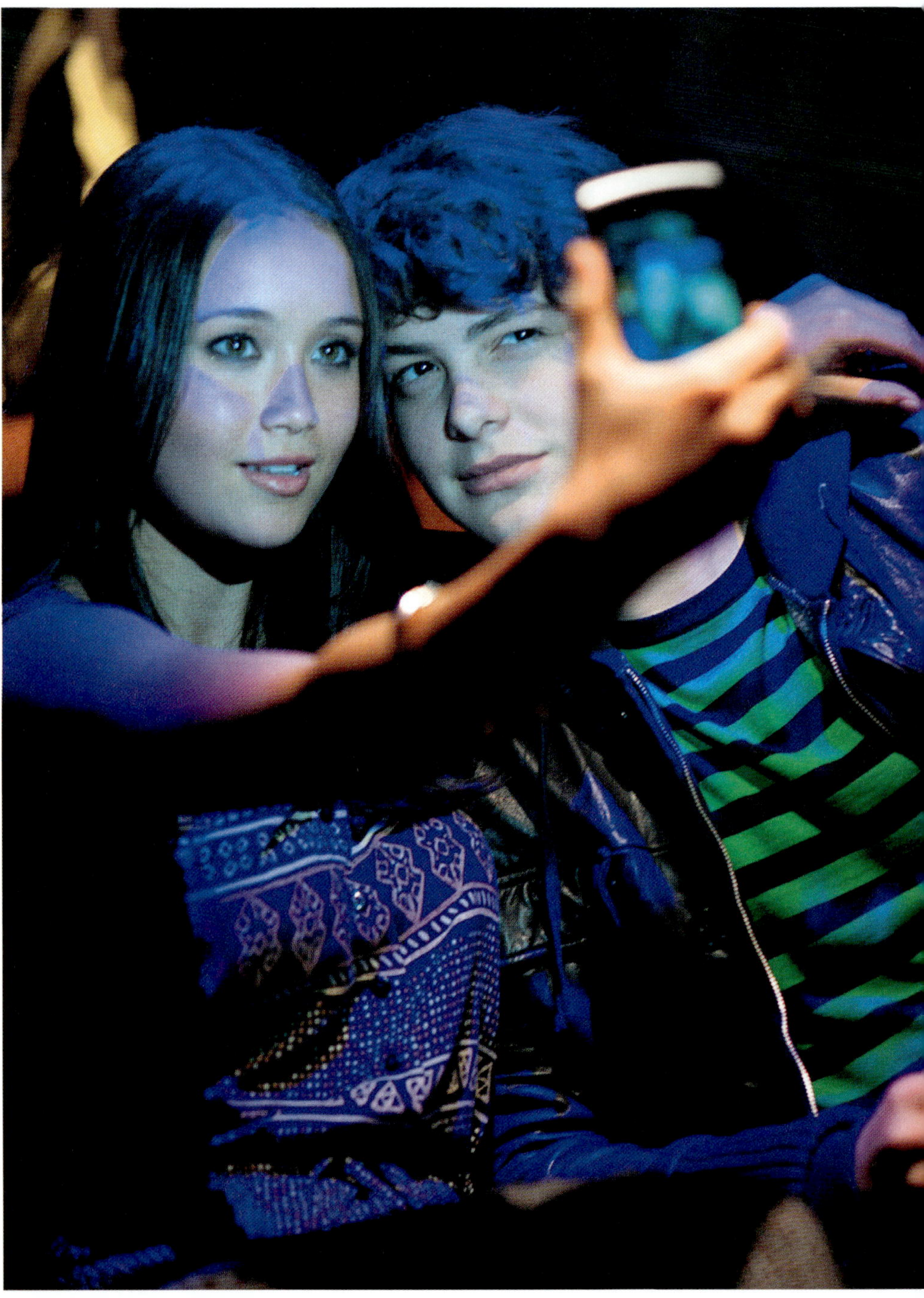

*'If I wasn't your friend anymore,
would you rob me?'*

THE
BLING
RING
2013

In 2010, Sofia Coppola was on a long-haul flight and picked up a copy of *Vanity Fair* to flip through. A longform investigative piece called 'The Suspects Wore Louboutins', written by Nancy Jo Sales, grabbed her attention. She had heard about its headline-making California teenagers, who had successfully planned and burgled a handful of A-list celeb mansions in her home city, making off with millions of dollars in luxury items. The story was so wild and topical that she assumed someone had long-ago gobbled up options to make a film about it, but after some discussion with her team, she realized the rights were available. For the first time, Coppola was going to make a film based on a contemporary true story. It would become *The Bling Ring*.

In a period between 2008 and 2009, a clutch of Calabasas teens committed a spate of high-profile crimes, using social media and gossip sites like TMZ to track the movements of their favourite celebs. Realizing when Paris Hilton was hosting a party out of town or Orlando Bloom and Victoria's Secret model Miranda Kerr might be out of their house, they often were able to find spare keys or even let themselves right into unlocked luxury homes. Fuelled by boredom, an obsession with fame and a love of fashion, the crew specifically knew how to zero in not only on the usual targets for robbery, but also on designer goods from Hermès handbags and Chanel minidresses to the ubiquitous red-bottom

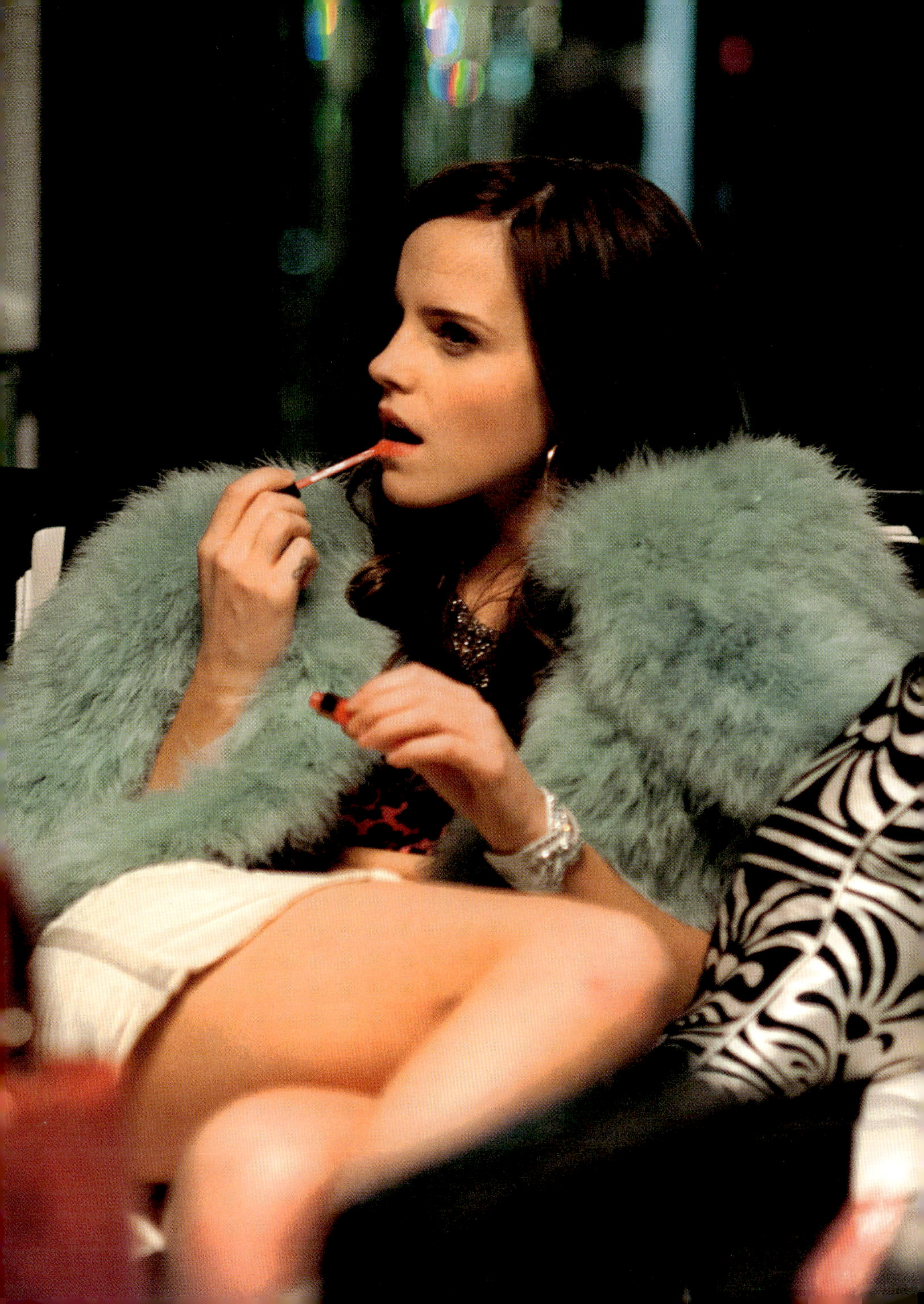

Christian Louboutin shoes named in the *Vanity Fair* piece. Avid magazine readers, the group coveted the noughties aesthetic of fame, and their victims included reality television stars Audrina Patridge (of *The Hills*) as well as an ultimate party-girl icon of the era, Lindsay Lohan. So for the first time in her career, Coppola was able to seek out the real people involved.

Many of Coppola's closest creative collaborators were baffled by her fascination with the story. As an object of showbiz gossip, fine, but as the subject of her next feature film? This woman had fought to gain respect in an industry straining at the bit to call her subject matter frivolous, whose family name often meant she was treated as a beneficiary of nepotism. She had, through skill and intelligence, managed to work around those critiques and be taken seriously as an artist. She had just won the Golden Lion at the world's oldest film festival for her previous project, *Somewhere*. And now she wanted to make a movie about some trashy kids who stole stuff from Paris Hilton's house?

As production designer Anne Ross put it: 'When Sofia told me about the idea I was completely uninterested and couldn't believe that she wanted to spend all this time living in this world...It was so repellent to me and it was repellent to her, too, so I was confused about it.' But Coppola was determined to go markedly against her usual careful prettiness, leaning into what she herself admitted was more obnoxious. The years 2012 and 2013 (the year of *The Bling Ring*) would turn out to be peak years for American films which expressed a certain lurid ugliness and vulgar excess at the heart of the culture: Harmony Korine's *Spring Breakers*, Martin

RIGHT: An appropriately accessory-obsessed poster for *The Bling Ring*.

OVERLEAF: Marc (Israel Broussard), Chloe (Claire Julien) and Rebecca (Katie Chang) congregate outside their high school.

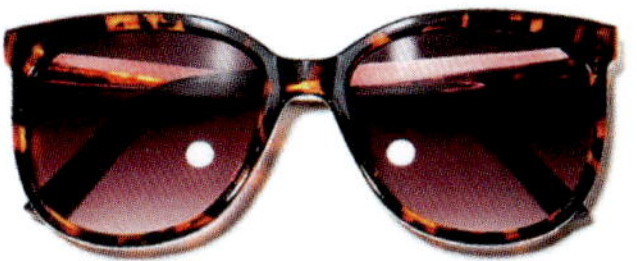
THE MASTERMIND

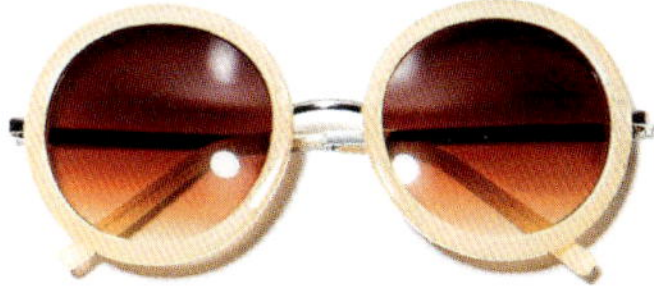
THE LOOKOUT

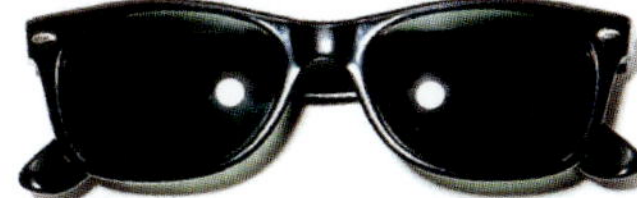
THE RIGHT-HAND MAN

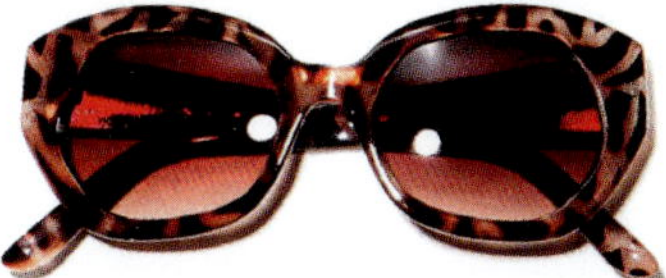
THE WILD CARD

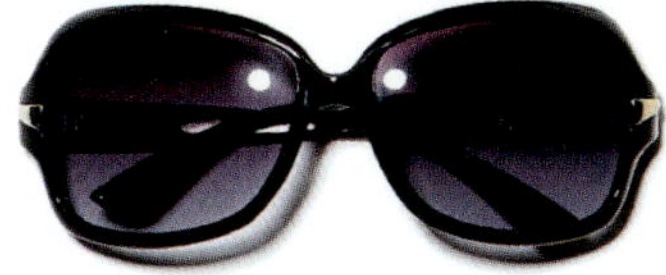
THE STAR

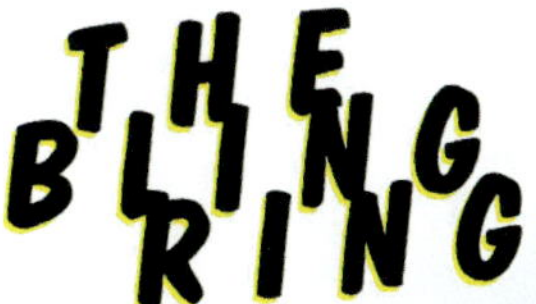
THE BLING RING
Based on Actual Events
Written and Directed by SOFIA COPPOLA
THEBLINGRING.COM
A24
R RESTRICTED
NALA films

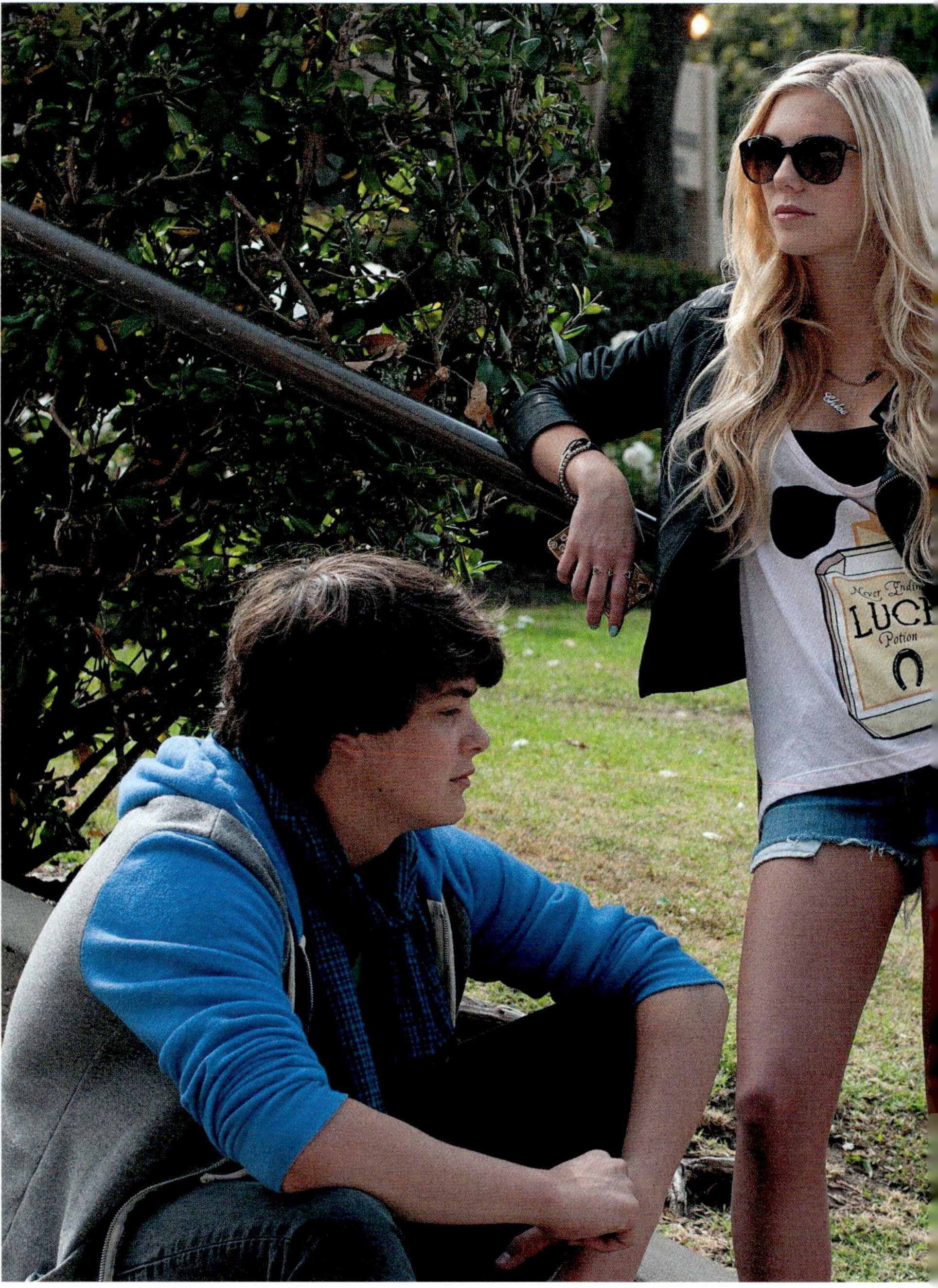

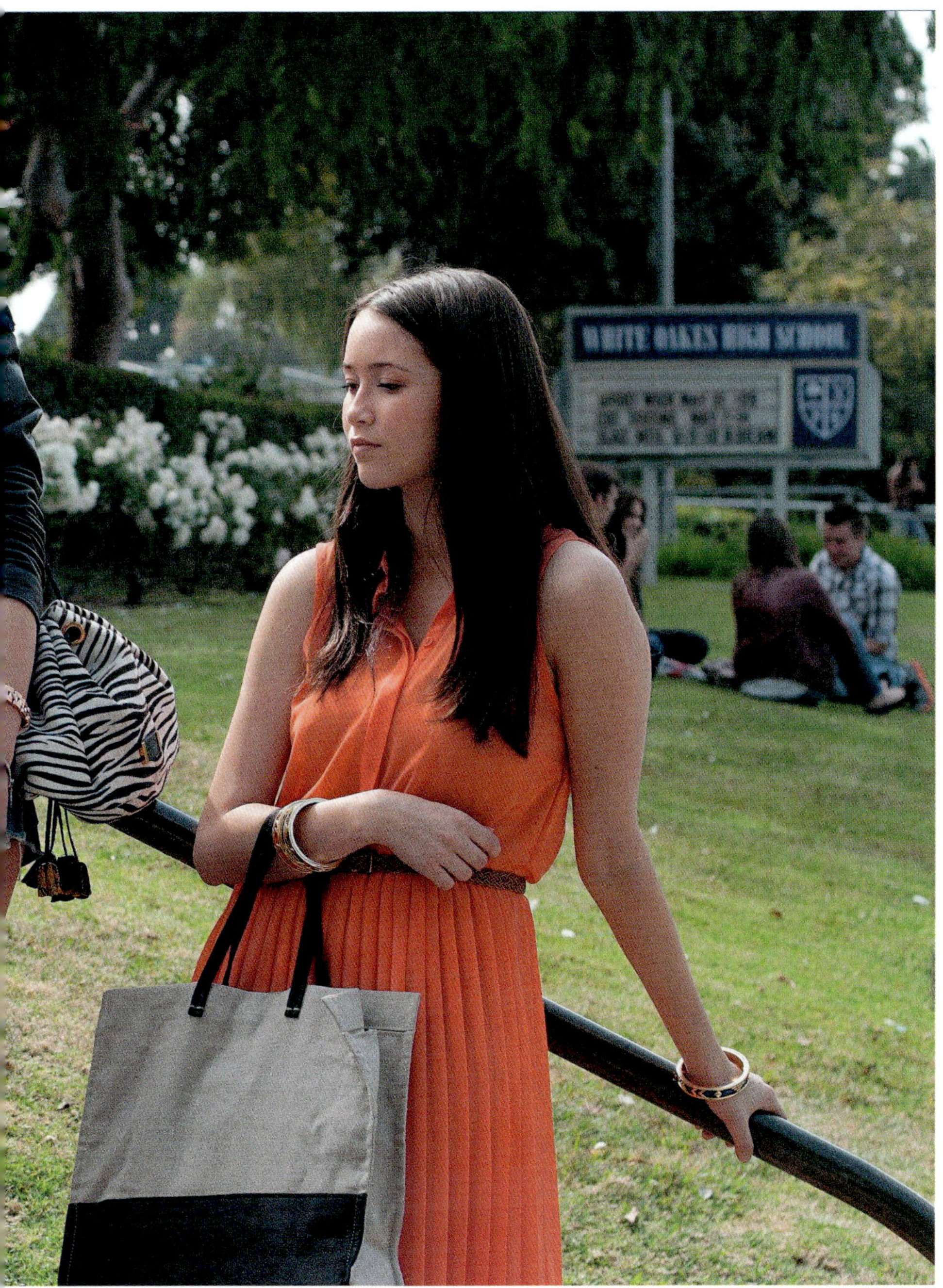
WHITE OAKS HIGH SCHOOL

Scorsese's *The Wolf of Wall Street* and even Michael Bay's *Pain & Gain*.

Coppola understood there was something prescient to be said about this unusual crime, committed mainly by her favourite demographic: teenage girls. She understood the world these kids populated and saw the contrast between the sparkle of Beverly Hills and the relatively beige suburban environs of nearby Calabasas (now, amusingly enough, a neighbourhood heavily associated with the Kardashians, who do not appear in *The Bling Ring* but feel deeply spiritually connected to it).

As Coppola focused on her vision with her production designer Ross and producer Youree Henley, the ideas she had became more clear and aligned. Wanting the film to belong to the subgenre of Cali-girl/teen movies like *Over the Edge* (1979), *Foxes* (1980) and, naturally, *Valley Girl* (1983), it was key to find a delicate balance between entering the mindset of this hyper-specific and much-derided set of adolescents without ever seeming to justify or excuse their actions. But Coppola needed to get to the bottom of the real events first.

Attempting to closely mirror real life, Coppola approached *Vanity Fair* journalist Nancy Jo Sales for her interview transcripts while writing the screenplay. She also eventually spoke to a detective on the case and two of the perpetrators, including Nick Prugo, her protagonist-of-sorts - called Marc in the film and played by Israel Broussard. Marc is new in school, awkward and aching to fit in, when he falls in with the opaque but charismatic Rebecca (Katie Chang), soon to be known as the alleged ringleader of the crimes. For now, they simply enjoy flipping judgmentally through fashion mags, driving around LA blasting out Rick Ross in a cloud of weed smoke, and occasionally checking if parked cars in fancy neighbourhoods forgot to lock up – pilfering whatever's valuable inside. It's a slippery slope; Rebecca and Marc learn about people

Sofia as an online influencer

If ever there was proof that a filmmaker was ahead of her time, it's Gen Z's complete embrace of Sofia Coppola and her aesthetic. While *The Bling Ring* was her only film to ever acknowledge or consider social media, social media remains obsessed by Coppola. There's an entire online cottage industry to memes, TikToks, and inspiration boards driven by a love of her floaty filmic aesthetic. From the depressive, white-dress-clad 1970s ennui of *The Virgin Suicides* to the acid-pink froth of *Marie Antoinette*, there's a lot to love about the way these movies delve headfirst into a look and express it so beautifully, in both costume and production design, lens choices and a host of reference points from literature to photography. For Coppola, born in 1971, it's a rather alien concept; she has expressed confusion at the desire to share so much of your private life online.

they know whose well-off families have left town and start their home invasions, stumbling into far more than expected when they find thousands of dollars in cash stuffed under the bed. One glorious Rodeo Drive spending spree later, and the two kids are hooked; they need to keep riding this high, and they need to find some mansions to rob. That's when they graduate to robbing the stars.

From the get-go, Coppola chooses a glossy, knowingly enticing style, opening the film's credits with a glorious, overwhelming montage of designer goods. She also utilizes flash-back and forward, interspersed with everything from a scrolling Facebook photo album to green-tinged night-vision security camera footage. In the first 15 minutes alone, her camera zips from the pitiful vox pops the teens make to news crews over to real-life tabloid and red-carpet photography of the stars who were

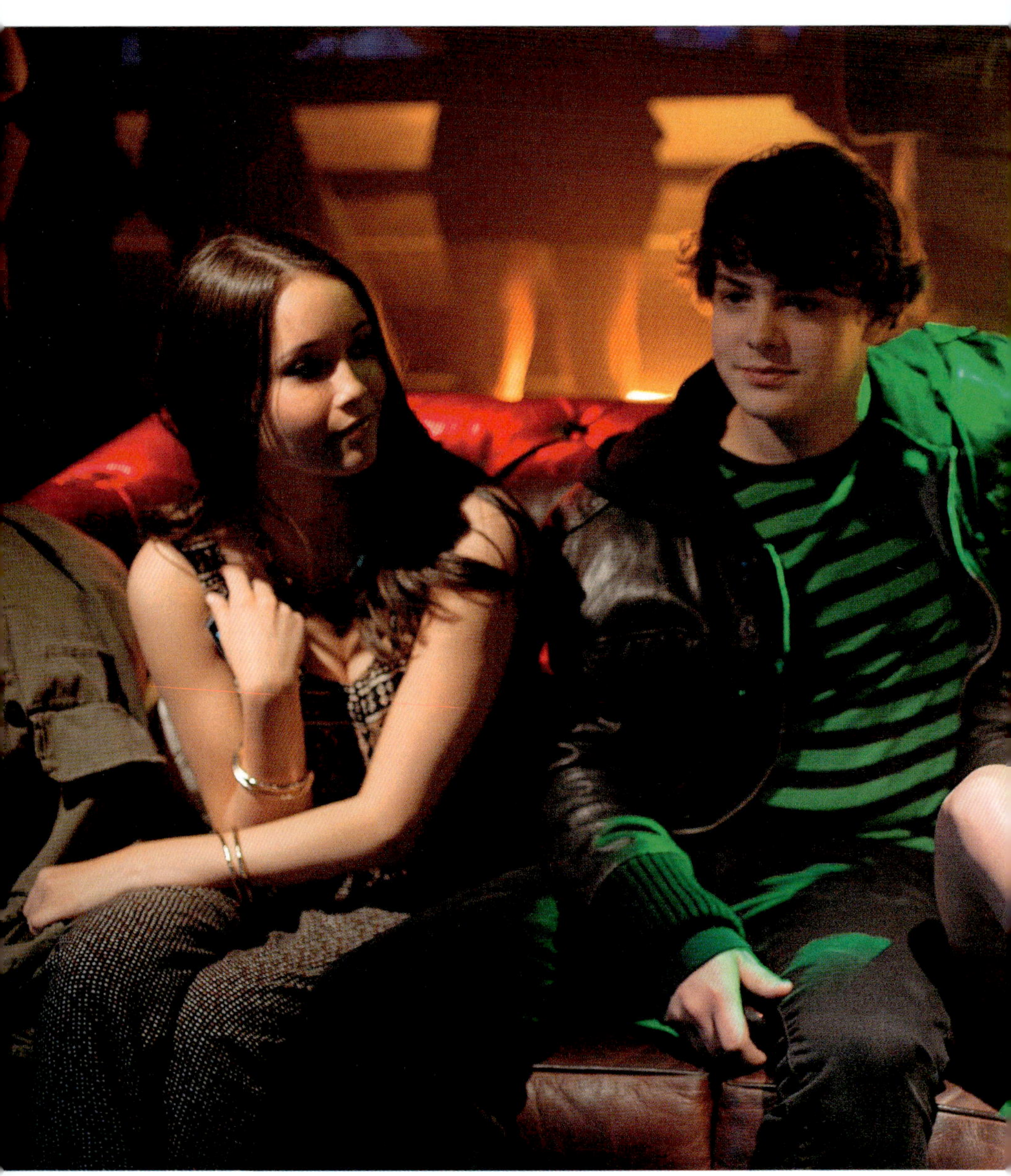

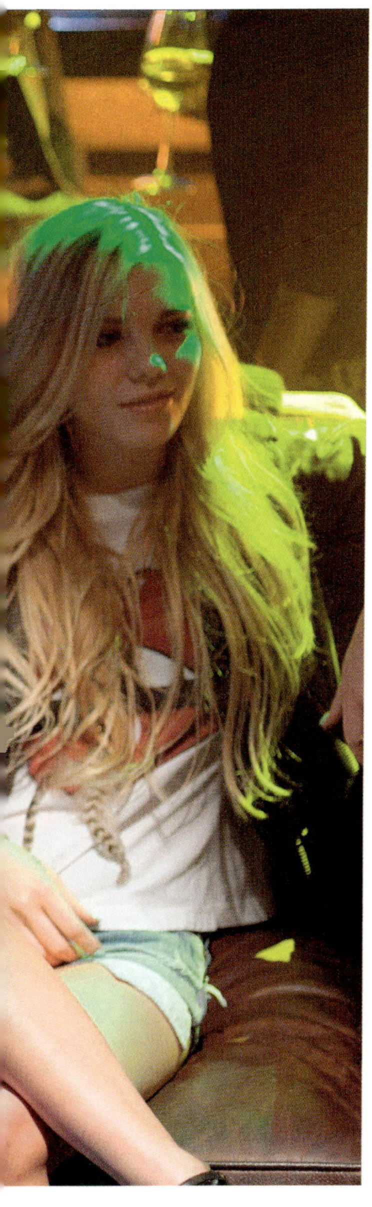

targeted. As such, it's a far more multilayered, 'throw everything at the wall' stylistic approach, using more cinematic sleight of hand than is usually typical of her films. By mixing mediums and giving a garish television news style to proceedings, she is more self-consciously adopting the style of the world she's exploring. It's an assault on the senses, which in no way feels accidental given the rising power of social media and 24/7 tabloid news in this era.

In the main, the perpetrators of these robberies include Rebecca and Marc, as well as a few classmates or friends-of-friends drafted in along the way. That includes bad-girl blonde Chloe (Claire Julien) and Nicki (a wannabe reality TV star played by a deliciously vapid Emma Watson), who brings in her two younger sisters, including Sam (Taissa Farmiga). Chloe's scumbag older boyfriend (a fun turn from Bush frontman Gavin Rossdale) is a nightclub promoter who acts as a fence and provider of substances, among other things. As the crew increasingly dabble in class A drugs, they find more

LEFT: Some of the teens were underage nightclubbers with high-level celebrity connections.

OVERLEAF: Rebecca (Chang) was seen as one of the ringleaders of the crimes; here she poses in the mirror as if she's a celebrity herself.

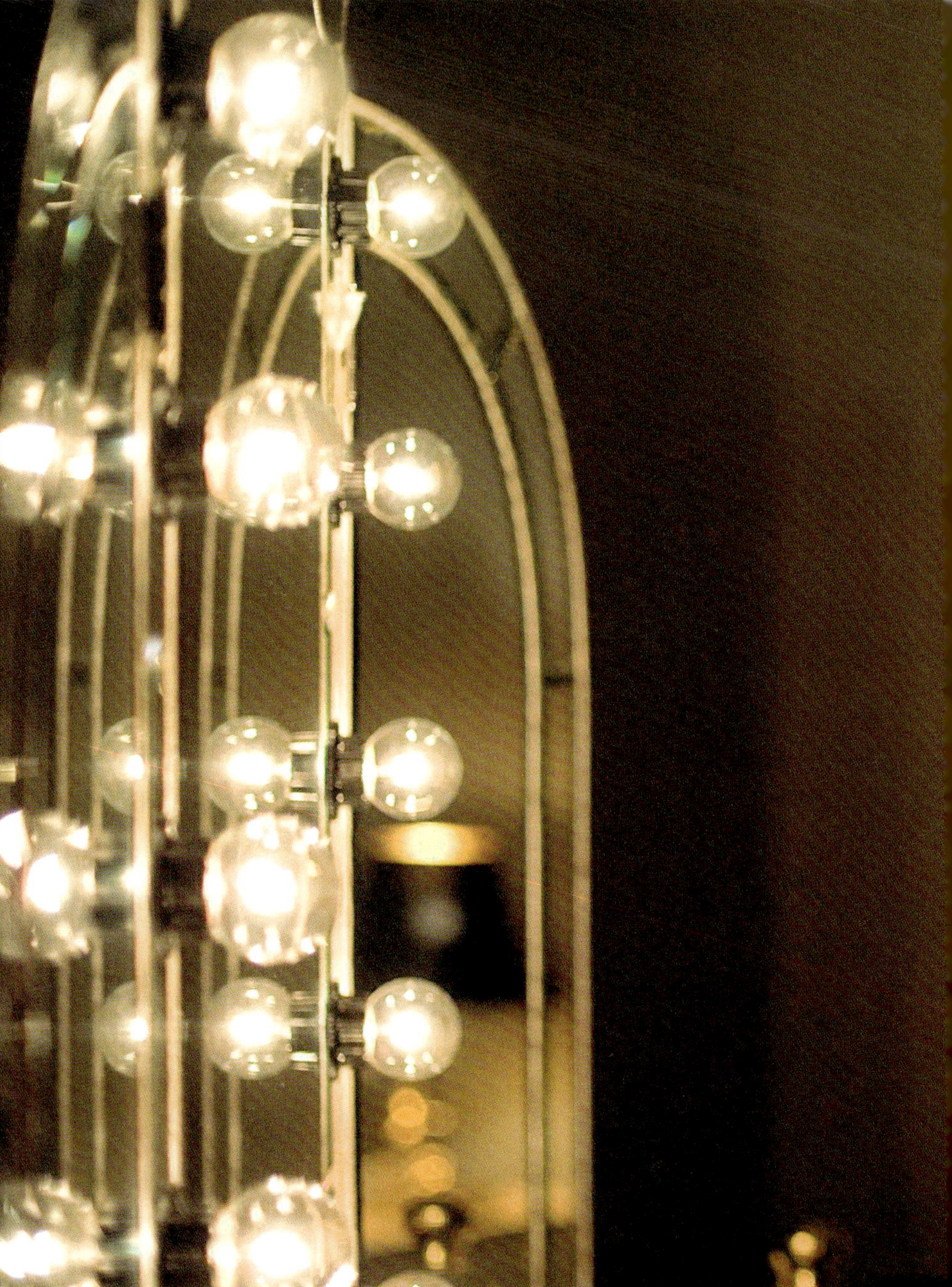

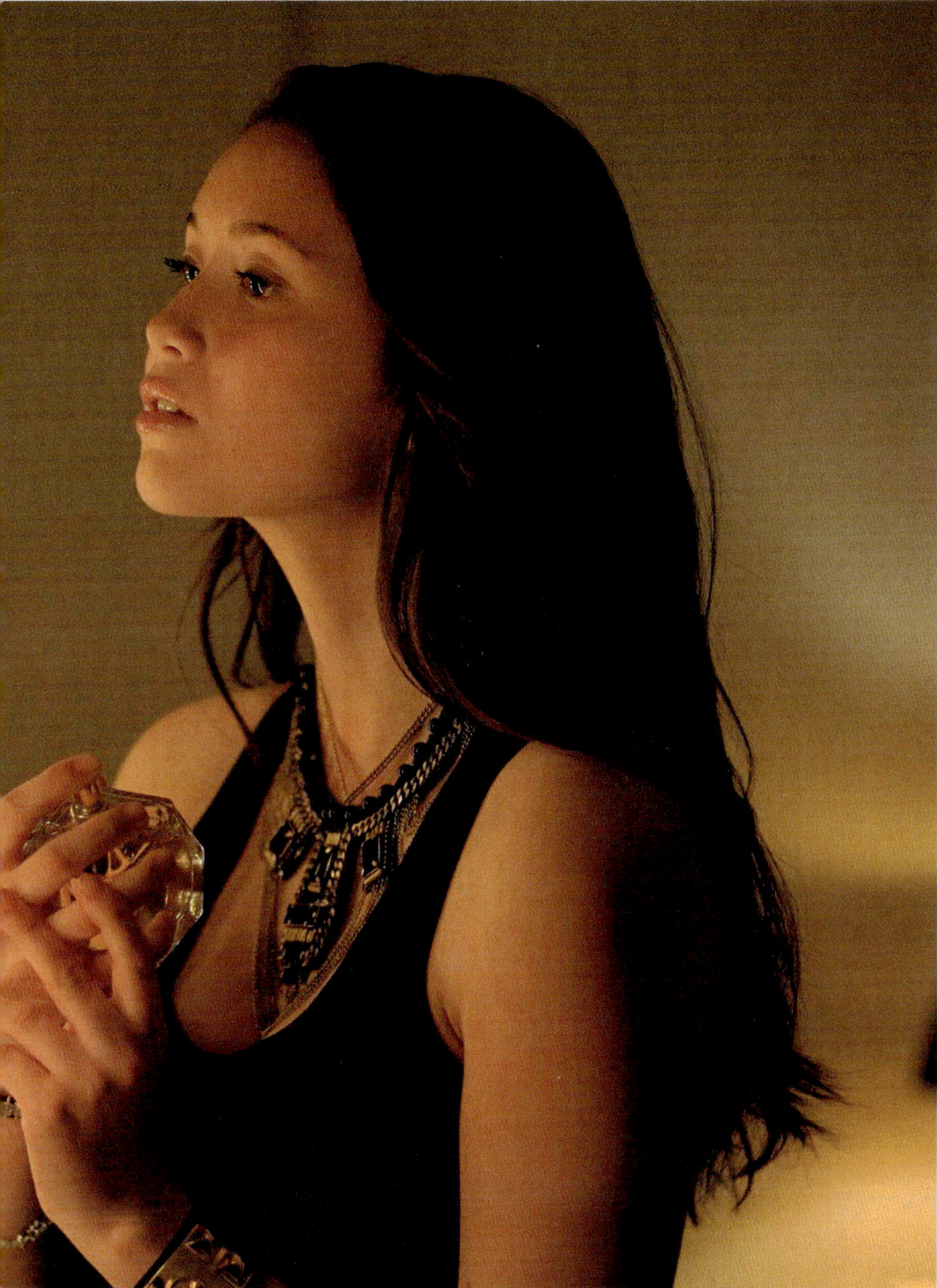

money and stashes to steal, addicted to the thrill of the robbery and the swag they distribute among themselves. The club-hopping teens seem to find being underage no real obstacle to their partying and their local clout, draping themselves in fur boleros and wraparound Cavalli sunglasses to make their entrance. Coppola seductively films the group on dancefloors, snorting drugs and snapping selfies, brandishing it-girl accessories and Swiss timepieces covered in diamonds. They talk about the stars on a first-name basis, voyeuristically opening bedside drawers and examining their medicine cabinets; it's often a queasy experience to watch them, combining the shared illicit thrill of seeing how the other half live with discomfort at the idea of ever being on the receiving end of such an invasion of privacy. Meanwhile, Kanye West blares across the soundtrack, reminding us of the unfettered egomania and materialism rampant across the culture, regardless of where you are in the pecking order.

After *Somewhere*, Coppola had no real intention to make another film set in her native LA, but there was nowhere else on earth that *The Bling Ring* could exist. The wannabes of the film rubbed elbows in nightclubs with the stars they robbed; they knew where in LA's gated communities they might find those homes. To achieve the right contrast between the 'burbs and the stunning mansions of the film, Coppola and her location scouts drove loops around Calabasas, until, as she says, the houses 'all started to look the same'. The peachy-beige blandness of the environment suggests a somnambulant and deeply unoriginal feel. By contrast, the sleek, artful look of one of the celeb's two-storey modernist home is practically a spaceship. In one of the most visually

RIGHT: Marc (Broussard) is perhaps the only truly sympathetic character in the film.

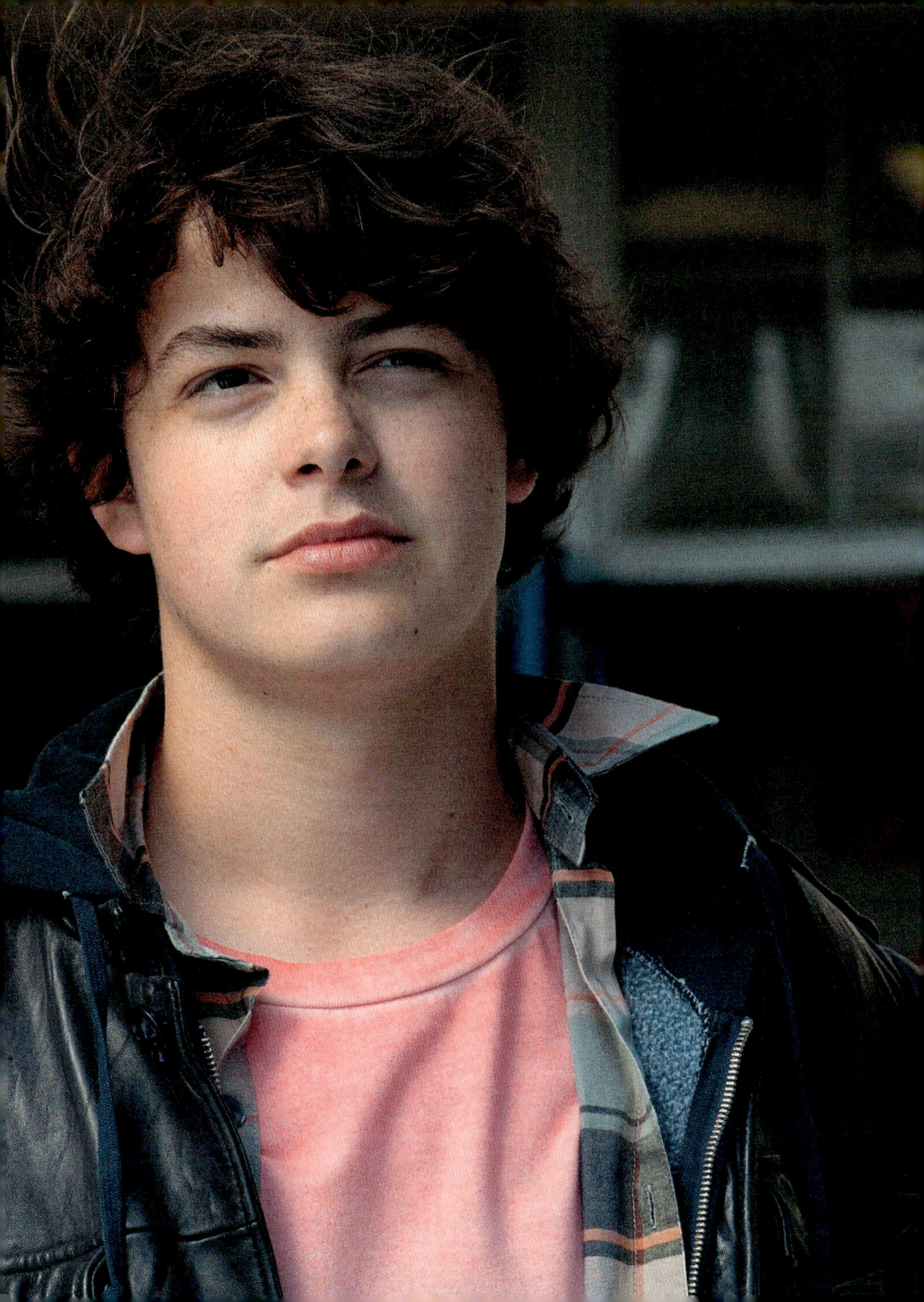

audacious and memorable scenes in the film, Coppola films the kids' break-in with a distant static shot, watching as lights go on and off and they move through the house. Seeing them zip back and forth through the rooms of the beautiful home – all shot by legendary director of photography, Harris Savides – the film contains some bravura work.

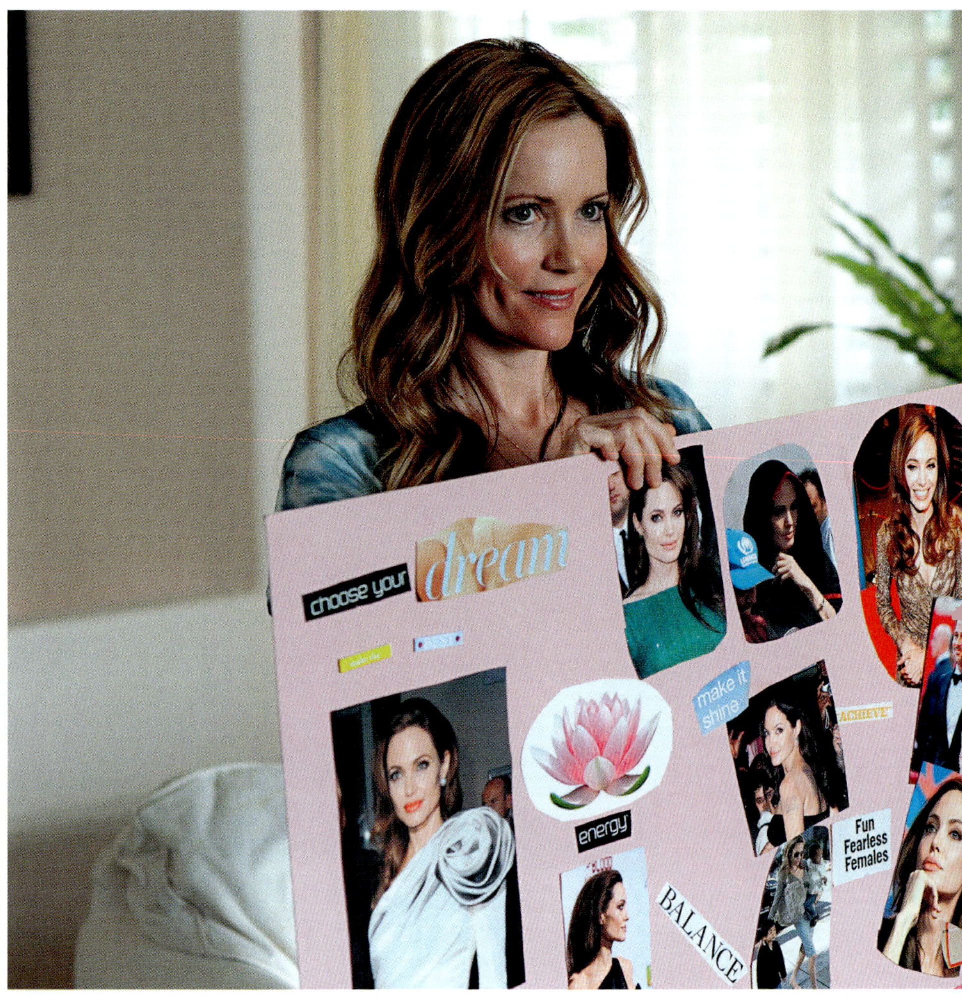

Stylistically, Coppola relishes in all the gaudiness and visual splendour of wealth, borrowing extensive accessories from Dolce & Gabbana, Dior and others to fill the closets the kids rob. Leaning into what we might now call an Instagram aesthetic (although in 2008, when the film is set, Facebook is the place to see and be seen online), she revels in Aladdin's cave-esque images of diamonds and jewels, piles of Louis Vuitton and aesthetically thrilling rows of feathered and bejewelled evening gowns. It also feels fitting that a filmmaker who was determined to get unprecedented access to shoot at Versailles for a previous film would zero in on finding *The Bling Ring* equivalent of that palatial residence: Paris Hilton's house. The heiress and socialite was a fan of Coppola's work, and when approached with the idea to film in her closet and 'nightclub room' where the robberies took place, she said yes. The result is a location unlike any that could truly be recreated artificially, featuring Paris' face plastered across throw cushions and framed magazine covers everywhere. A distressing fact that Hilton herself had not been aware of until Coppola learned about it during her research is featured in the movie: one of the teens seriously considered stealing Hilton's beloved chihuahua, Peter Pan, before being talked

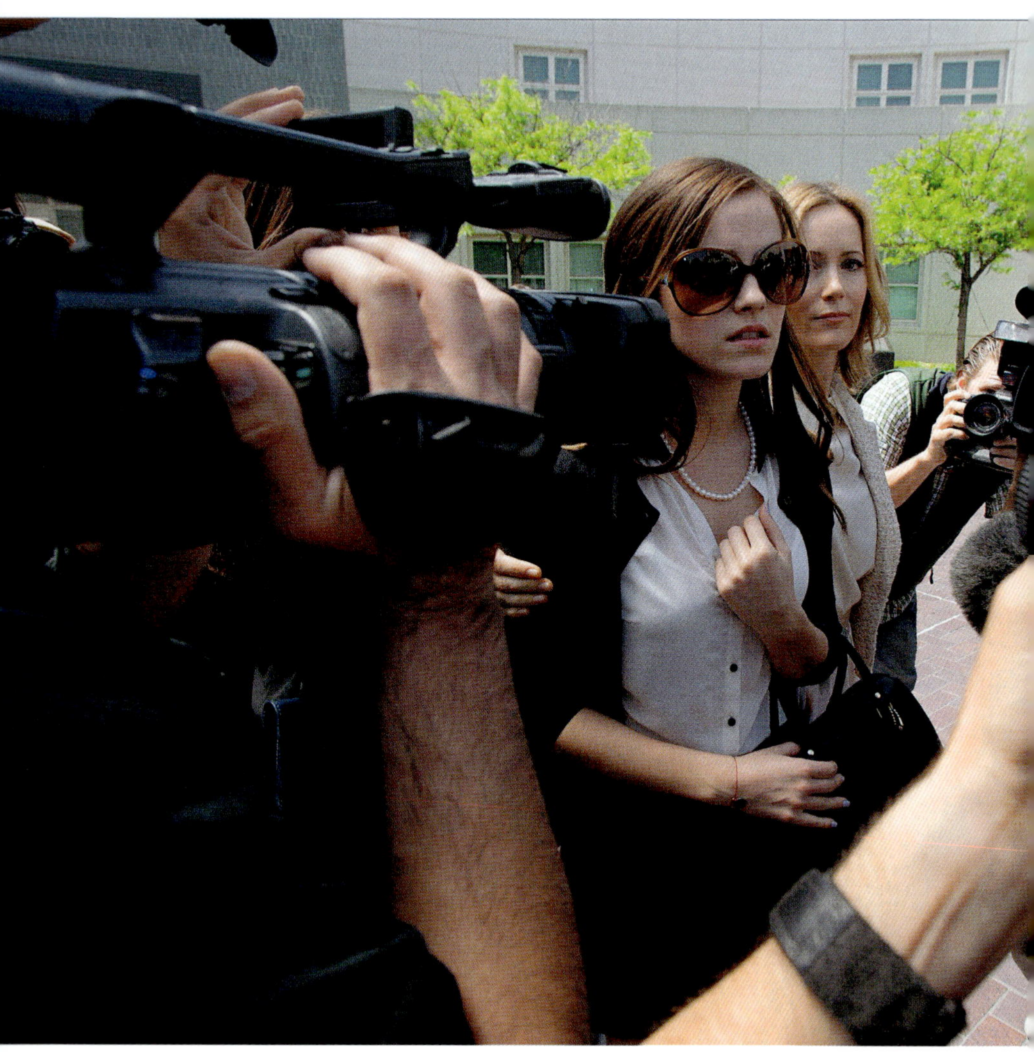

out of it. In the film, it's a throwaway moment, but if you were an audience member inclined to feel unsympathetic to the rich and famous, this tends to bring home the reality of the crime.

The performances had to be carefully calibrated in order to honestly capture the spirit of these try-hard, hedonistic teens

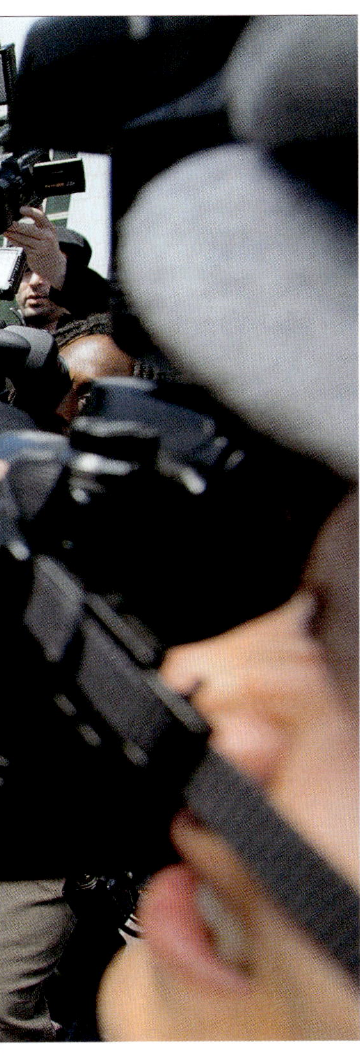

ABOVE: Nicki makes the most out of her 15 minutes of fame once on trial for her crimes.

without turning them into valley-girl caricatures or pure laughingstock. The film manages to toe this thin line, particularly in the form of Emma Watson's Nicki. She combines the much-derided valley-girl vocal fry with a kind of frightening empty malevolence; the naked ambition of Eve Harrington in classic, bitchy showbiz drama *All About Eve* (1950), crossed with the exhibitionism of a Kardashian, trilling on about her potential auditions and her high-minded desire to improve 'like, the peace and health of the planet.' Watson gives a brilliant performance; it takes real skill to depict someone who is so flat in a way which still makes them interesting. A real favourite is one of Watson's line deliveries, said to her sister, who is querying how her butt looks in her outfit. Sitting in bed on her phone, she looks up with sudden, rapt attention, examining the outfit with the seriousness of someone examining a nuclear launch code. 'Your butt looks *awesome*,' she finally says. It's one of the most sincere things she says in the entire film. There is taking vanity seriously, and then there's whatever this is.

When she is finally apprehended and led away by police, though, we do see a chink in Nicki's armour. However unlikeable she may be, when she cries out that the cop is hurting her and asks for her mum, we remember that she is still a child. As Nicki's woo-woo California mother, Leslie Mann gets some portion of the blame. She says, 'Time for your Adderall!' to the girls at breakfast before homeschooling them, encouraging them to make vision boards about Angelina Jolie. Mann is shown attempting, at least, to teach her daughters some values outside of the superficial, but she ultimately proves both useless and spineless in the face of her daughters' searing, selfish ambition to be famous. And outside of Nicki and her sisters' oddball household, we don't get a lot of family time with the teens; both Rebecca and Marc talk about successful parents, but we don't see much of them, and through either neglect or carelessness it seems there's not much to stop these kids from running wild.

At one point, Coppola even had her cast do a rehearsal of a burglary. 'I told them to find a way in and what to take – so they did a practice robbery. I sent someone with a video camera,' she told the BBC. It was good improvisation – to see them fighting over who gets what.'

For the part of Marc, the only male of the group, Coppola went through a host of auditions, finding herself exasperated by tic-heavy or OTT interpretations of the young man. In real life, the inspiration for Marc had been flamboyant and theatrical in personality, obsessed by his own looks and rather campy. But the actor Coppola eventually found went in a different direction. Israel Broussard downplayed the more exaggerated qualities of this young and uncertain gay teen, giving him flashes of wounded insecurity that make you feel rather more fond of him than perhaps of the others in the group. As he lies in his grandmother's thoroughly unglamorous home, secretly wearing a pair of acid-pink stiletto heels stolen from someone famous' closet, you get the sense that Marc's sense of dislocation or lack of self-assurance comes from a much deeper place than that of the girls.

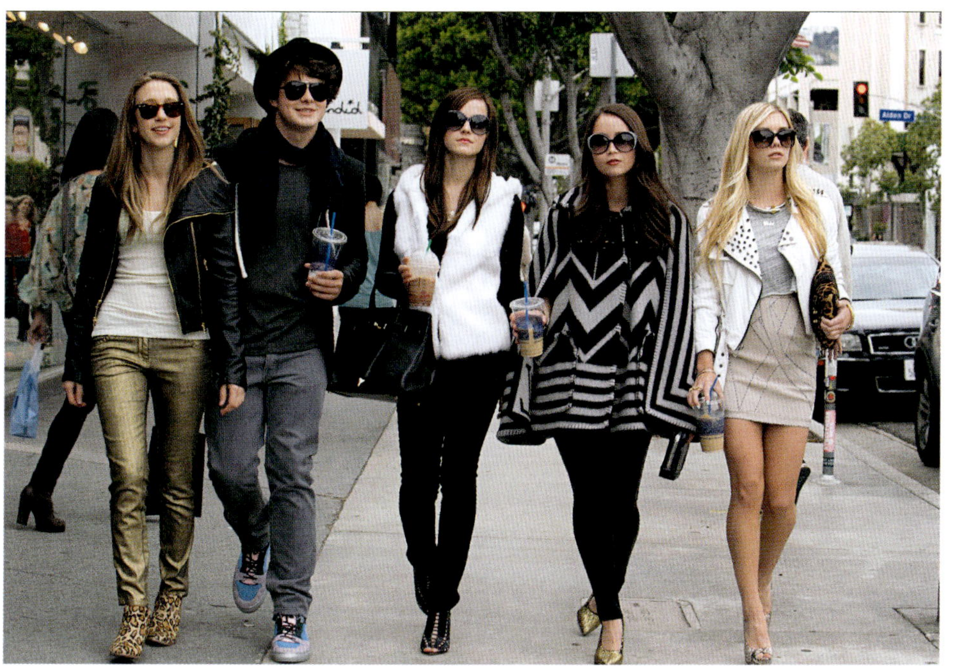

ABOVE: The entire *Bling Ring* crew stroll down Rodeo Drive with their ill-gotten gains.

Coppola has said her favourite moment of the film is seeing the defiant Chloe, ostensibly the 'trashiest' of the crew, moments before the police raid her home. We never see her family prior to this. Coppola and Savides hold a static and beautifully composed shot of her in her parents' grandiose kitchen, as sirens begin to blare worryingly nearer. Her trophy-wife mother makes a smoothie in the background, with the maid hovering nearby. Her dad, in a suit, reads the newspaper. It feels like a revelation: the other kids may be comfortable, but she is *rich*.

Although most of the members of the real-life Bling Ring were more comfortably middle class than wealthy – albeit with a plethora of family and disciplinary issues – the point is well taken. None of them *needed* to do this. Coppola's rendering shows that they aren't especially desperate or disadvantaged, and none can really justify theft on this scale. They might not ever be able to afford a Chanel handbag, but then, that's most of us. The difference is that their need is such that they're willing to risk prison for it; there's real greed in evidence here. But there's also a parallel being drawn with the celebrities themselves, ultimately; the kids and their targets seem to endlessly hoard luxury goods to appear fashionable and cool; turn up at nightspots wanting to be seen; abuse drugs; and seem to need shiny things to shore up their sense of self. Chloe, for instance, is arrested for driving under the influence, which she treats with the same casual indifference as Lindsay Lohan. What becomes clear later on is that if you're ordinary, you don't get away with greed, materialism or bad behaviour in the way that stars do; you're bound to be punished for it.

It's also an interesting gambit when viewed through the lens of the 'crime' film. Traditionally the refuge of the masculine, the fact of the criminals' age and gender are in and of themselves unique and well positioned to provide fresh commentary. Yet Coppola does not side with her teenage girls in this instance; she renders them authentically but is pretty damning of their shallowness on the whole. She offers motivation for their actions up to a point, but none of it is very sympathetic; nor is there any genuine sense of remorse or self-reflection among them in the aftermath of being apprehended by the LAPD. (Nicki maintains her innocence, batting her eyelashes vacantly at a news camera. These kids might be upset about having to face the consequences of their actions, but they're hardly genuinely contrite. In fact, they're even a little bit proud.)

Rebecca, questioned by a detective in custody, rarely reveals her feelings as blatantly as the others, attempting a cool exterior most of the time. But the mask slips when she learns from the cop that the celebrities she's robbed have all been interviewed about her crimes; she's starstruck. 'What did Lindsay say?' she asks.

In the final analysis, this is a story about starry-eyed hangers-on and exhibitionism on social media, about empty aspiration and ugly greed, an obsession with status and materialism but ultimately, more than anything else, simply proximity to fame. The kids of *The Bling Ring* are as interested in touching or wearing the personal items of the stars as they are in showing off or selling them. Hilton later remarked that they even stole some of her bras; clearly this was not simply a matter of monetary gain.

And yet, there's something a bit grotesque about the knowledge that Hilton, for instance, was such a big target because they knew it would take time before she noticed things that were missing. She simply had so much stuff that it didn't matter. It's not an attack on Hilton or her celebrity ilk as such, but it is a darkly compelling point about how heavily weighted the capitalist scales can be in one direction.

If you remade *The Bling Ring* now, you could easily nudge it into the world of the Instagram or TikTok influencer without having to change too much; for a film so deeply rooted in 2008, a few changes in style, designers and celebs du jour would make it feel just as believable in the 2020s. It's certainly just as honest about our unhealthy parasocial love of fame and glamour. Bar the modern tech which would make this kind of crime more difficult, it's just as likely to occur in theory. Take the infamous robbery of Kim Kardashian's jewels in a Parisian hotel in 2016, reportedly planned around her social media posts, and inspired by – so the thieves say – her excessive display of wealth. *Plus ça change*; the rich get richer, and the poor get even.

Yet, from 'cottagecore' and beyond, girls seem to be creating memes and moodboards where their imaginations fill in the gaps so characteristic of Sofia's work. Her filmic ambiguity is a tool which lets them explore what they imagine to be their own corners of that world, adding images of contemporary femme literature, Dior lip oil or other trendy it-girl objects which do not appear in the films themselves but feel spiritually related.

'I was surprised because I'm not very aware of what's happening online,' Coppola told *Polyester* magazine in 2024. 'I don't look at it much, so my kids will tell me that teenage girls talk about me or that I'm mentioned on TikTok,' she says. That fascination with her films is unlikely to end anytime soon, given the current preoccupation with early noughties fashion and culture. Even the intended tackiness of *The Bling Ring* has been, ironically enough, absorbed and reprocessed as inspiration for a bunch of Juicy Couture tracksuit-wearing teenagers. But perhaps with a culture more sensitive to and interested in the difficulties and joys of young women and girls, Coppola's ongoing relevance online is all the greater a sign of her artistic staying power.

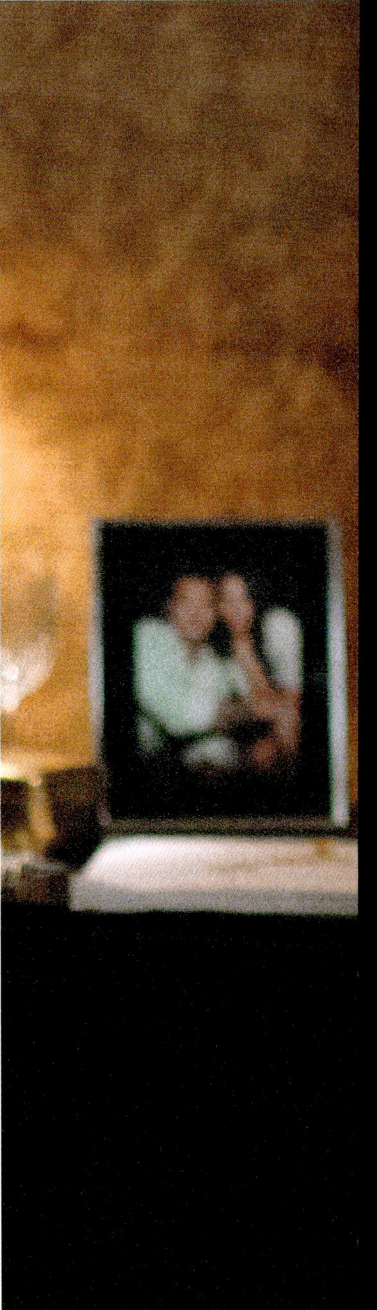

RIGHT: Nicki (Watson) enjoying a bit of power when she gets hold of a gun.

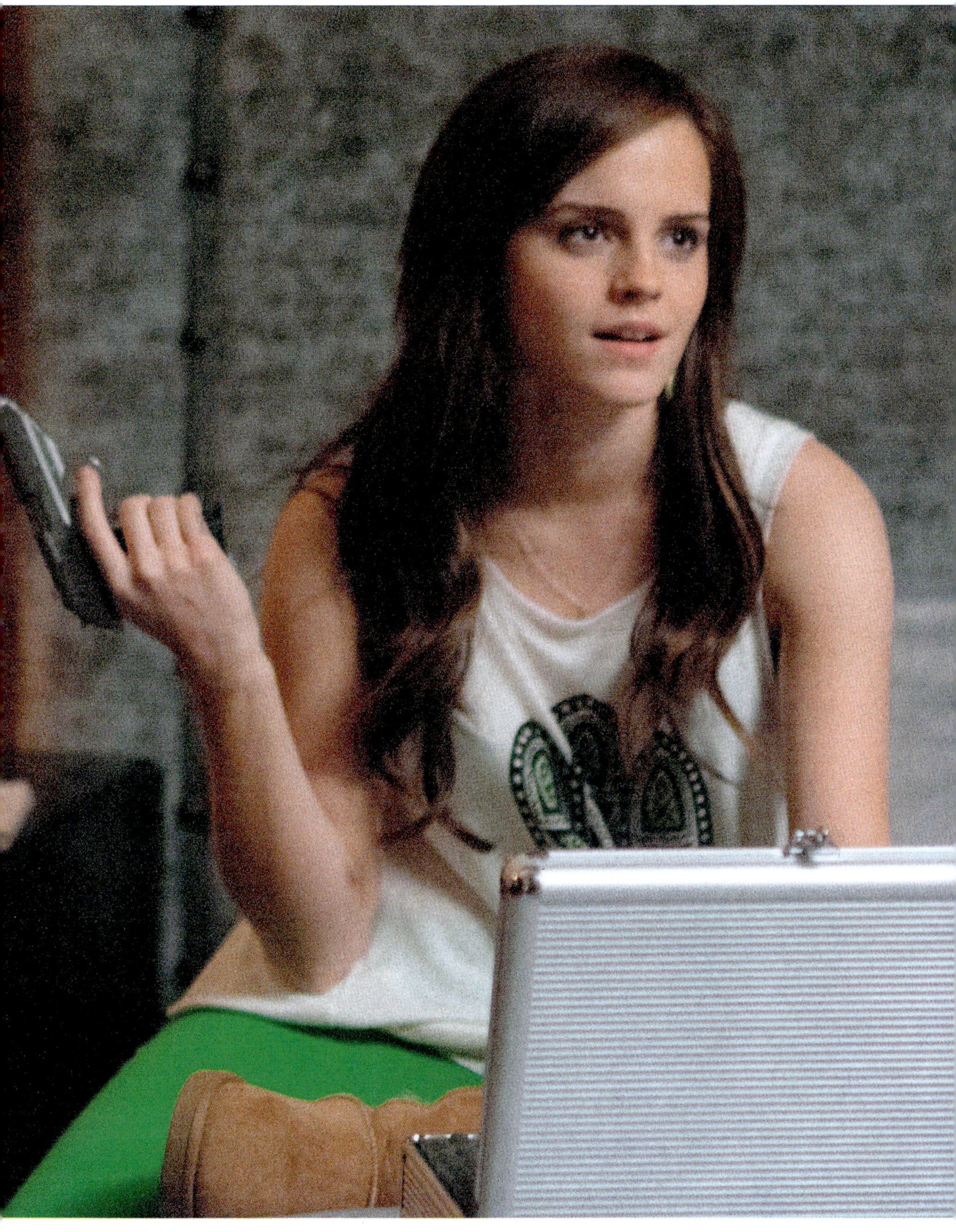

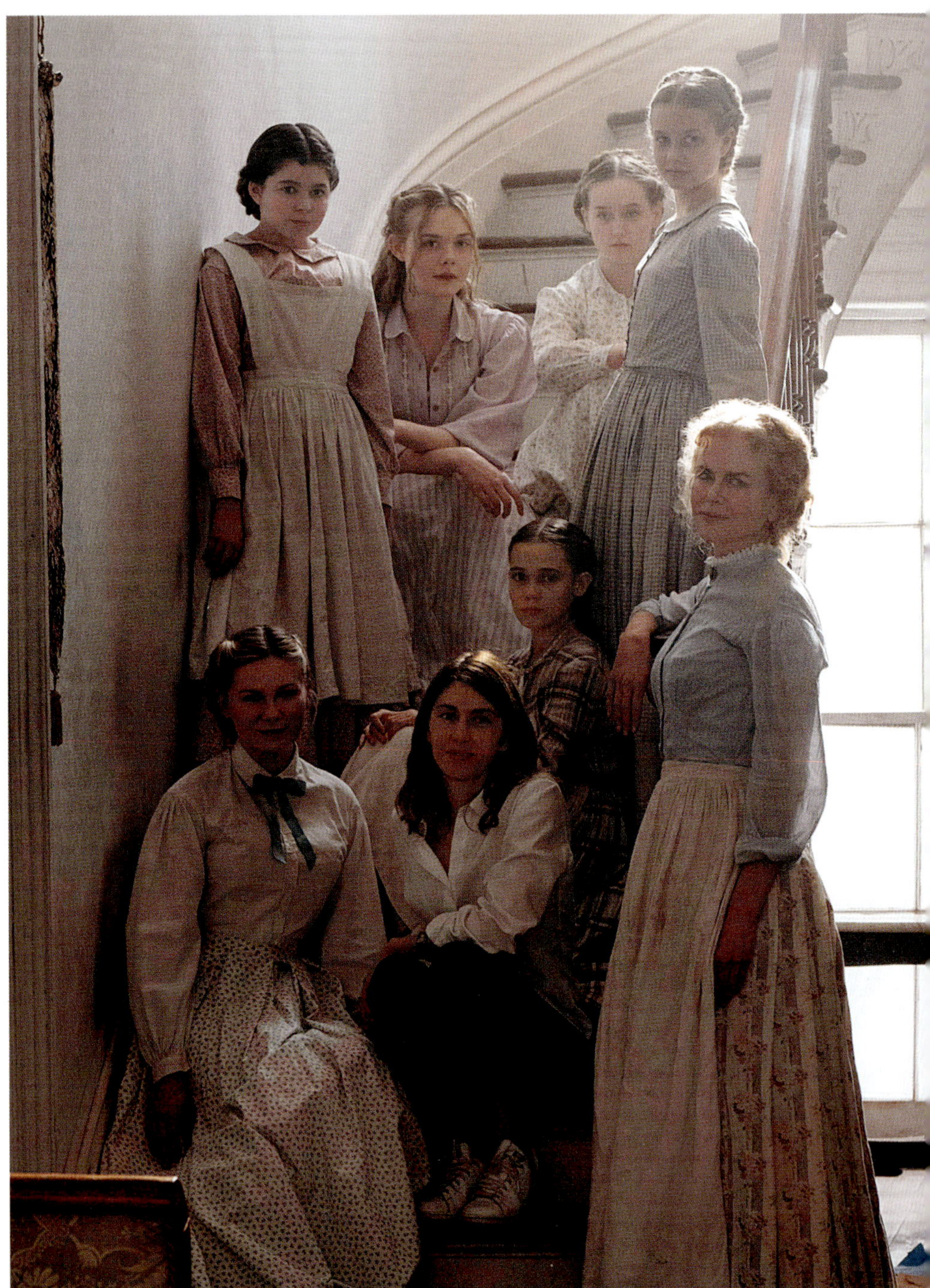

'All bravery is, is doing what's needed at the time.'

THE BEGUILED
2017

After exploring the gaudy ugliness of contemporary American life with *The Bling Ring*, Sofia Coppola could be forgiven for wanting her next project to be focused on making something beautiful. What's surprising is that *The Beguiled,* her 2017 Civil War-era drama about imperilled Southern belles, is both one of her most gorgeous aesthetic achievements and, simultaneously, her most violent and perverse film to date. If Coppola has long been accused of a preoccupation with the pretty, there's a real poisoned-apple quality to the dark fairy-tale she tells here. She called the movie a combination of 'psychological drama and gothic horror' and saw it as her most genre-oriented work so far. But it also fits perfectly alongside her other films in its fascination with an ornamental and cloistered world of young women and girls, and more pointedly, one where that ornament hides a vicious, black-hearted core.

Coppola first came across the material when longtime production designer Anne Ross encouraged her to watch Don Siegel's Southern gothic drama *The Beguiled* (1971), a film which takes place three years into the Civil War in the Confederate territory of Virginia. It stars Clint Eastwood as Colonel John McBurney, a Union Army deserter who, injured and desperate, prevails upon an isolated school full of Confederate women for help. They take in the enemy soldier and nurse him in spite of their

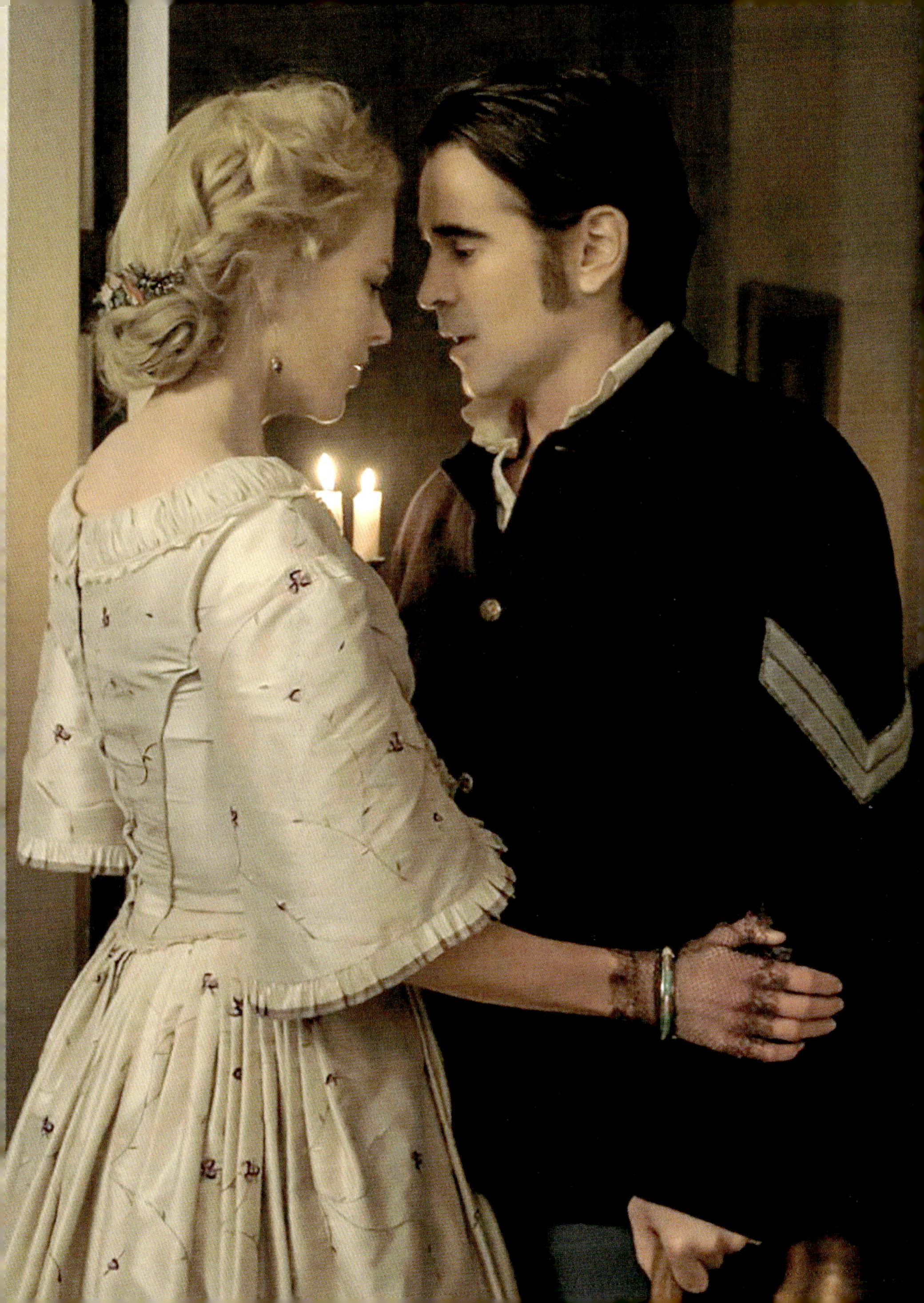

reservations, citing their duty as Christians. But as McBurney attempts to manipulate and seduce the supposedly chaste women of the school, including prim headmistress Miss Martha Farnsworth (Geraldine Page), the hothouse atmosphere of desire and jealousy comes to an unexpected and explosive peak. Part melodrama, part thriller, the film was what Hollywood might call an 'interesting failure'. It was not as popular as Siegel's other macho projects with Eastwood (together, they'd already made *Dirty Harry* in 1971), and its seeming interest in the feminine mind only appeared to confuse viewers expecting more action.

It's a fascinating but flawed project exploring lust and gendered power dynamics in an enclosed space, but it's also one which centres on and sympathizes with its lusty male protagonist. Most of the women in the film are slapped with cheap Freudian ideas about their cruelty deriving from sexual repression, and the film doubles down on this by using bosom-heaving fantasy sequences wherein they reveal their urges or their lurid histories. As Siegel himself said, he felt the story was about 'the basic desire of women to castrate men'.

The original screenplay was based on a 1966 novel by author Thomas P Cullinan, which got Coppola thinking: how had this story about women, desire and power been told exclusively from a male perspective? And so she decided to reimagine it for the screen herself, this time from the point of view of the wilting, hungry Southern women in the seminary itself. As an opportunity to capture the picturesque spookiness – and underlying brutality – of an era long relegated to the old, bad past, Coppola set herself a challenge in terms of presenting a difficult socio-historical era, but she also saw it as an allegory ripe for reinterpretation. Her version of *The Beguiled* is both authentic to the spirit and letter of its time, and much more interested in this self-contained 'fox in the henhouse' tale as an exploration of men and women.

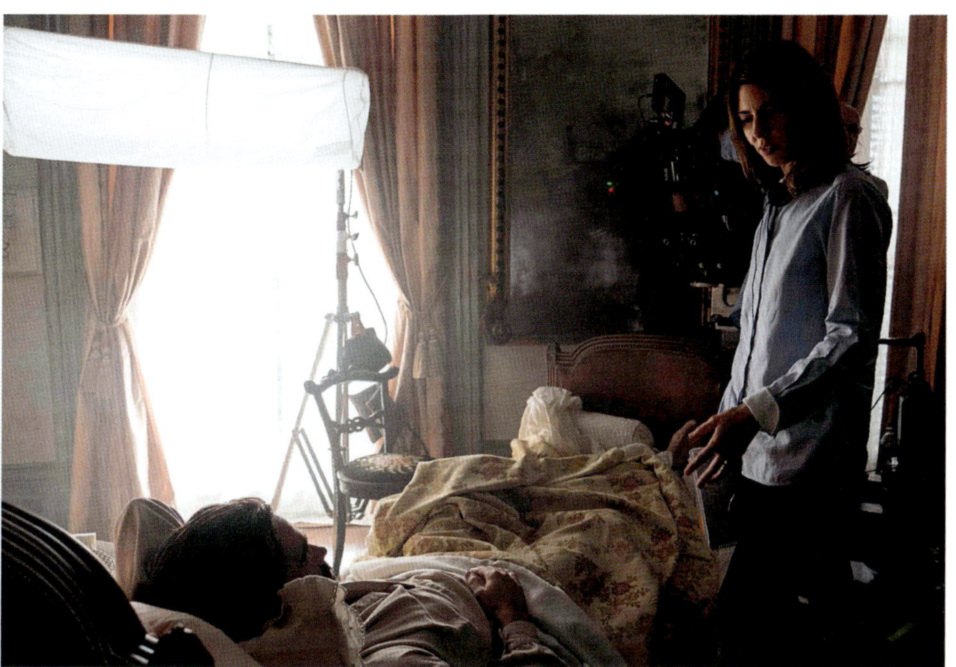

ABOVE: Coppola directs Farrell from his character's
sickbed, where he lies in wait for much of the film.

As in the original film, *The Beguiled* starts three years into a war
which the Confederate Army is losing badly. Deep in rural Virginia,
Miss Farnsworth's school for girls – the kind where they might
have otherwise learned to become proper antebellum ladies –
holds a handful of strays who for one reason or another do not
have safe passage back home. The war wages on just beyond
them in distant rumbles of cannon fire, while ragged processions
of men drop by for a meal or steal their chickens, depending on
which side they might be on. The slaves who would have worked
their gardens and served their tea have long run away; they're
mentioned once at the start and not heard about again.

Things seem increasingly dire, but the two adults in the grand
old plantation house run it as much as they can as though nothing

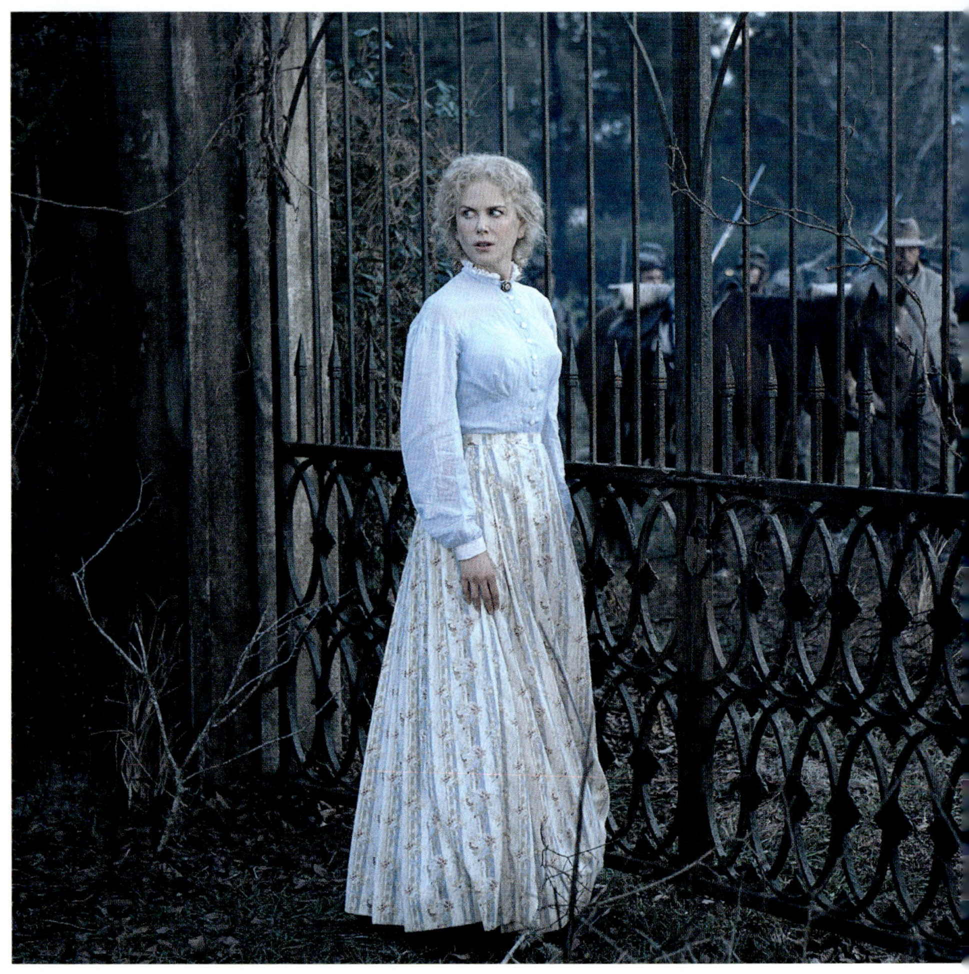

has changed. The five remaining students run from just under 10 years of age to their late teens. The oldest two are Miss Alicia (Elle Fanning, all grown up since last we saw her in *Somewhere*, and beautifully mutinous) and Miss Jane (Angourie Rice, whose good Southern girl is horrified at the thought of sheltering a 'Yankee'). They're all presided over by Miss Martha (Nicole Kidman, imperious and excellent) and teacher Miss Edwina (Kirsten Dunst,

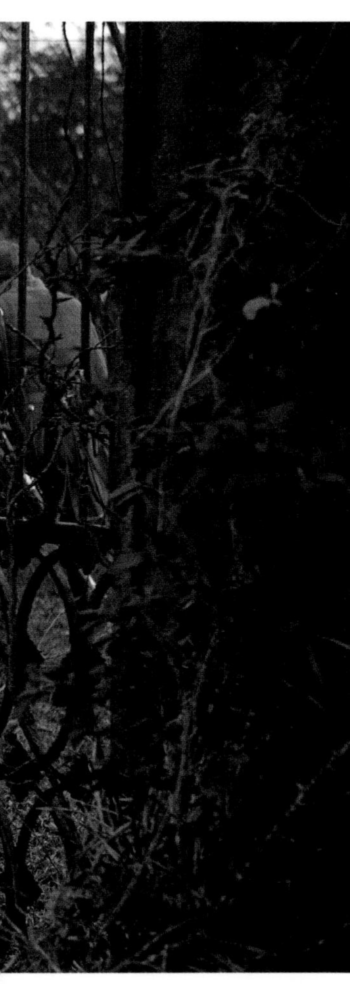

downhearted but with a delightful twinkle of insubordination behind the eyes). Miss Martha clearly runs a tight ship, with daily and nightly prayer sessions, a hawk-eye on straight stitches and French lessons even as the girls wilt in the Deep South humidity. With wisps of hair sticking to their cheeks and pristine cotton blouses damp from perspiration, the ladies work their small farm and vegetable patch to sustain themselves, risking callouses and dirt now that there are no slaves around to do their bidding.

Coppola, who shot the film with director of photography Philippe Le Sourd in part on a real 19th-century plantation in Louisiana, depicts the environment as simultaneously rich and verdant with life – sun-dappled gardens under Spanish moss, deafeningly loud summer crickets and birds – and the plantation itself as rather dilapidated, overgrown and ill-cared for in the years since the war began. It's a beautiful visual symbol of a lifestyle and a world which is becoming antiquated in real time, fading slowly into darkness like an old tintype photograph.

It is this monotonous, isolated existence that Col John McBurney (Colin Farrell) interrupts, when young Miss Amy (Oona Laurence) discovers him while foraging for mushrooms. He is faint and

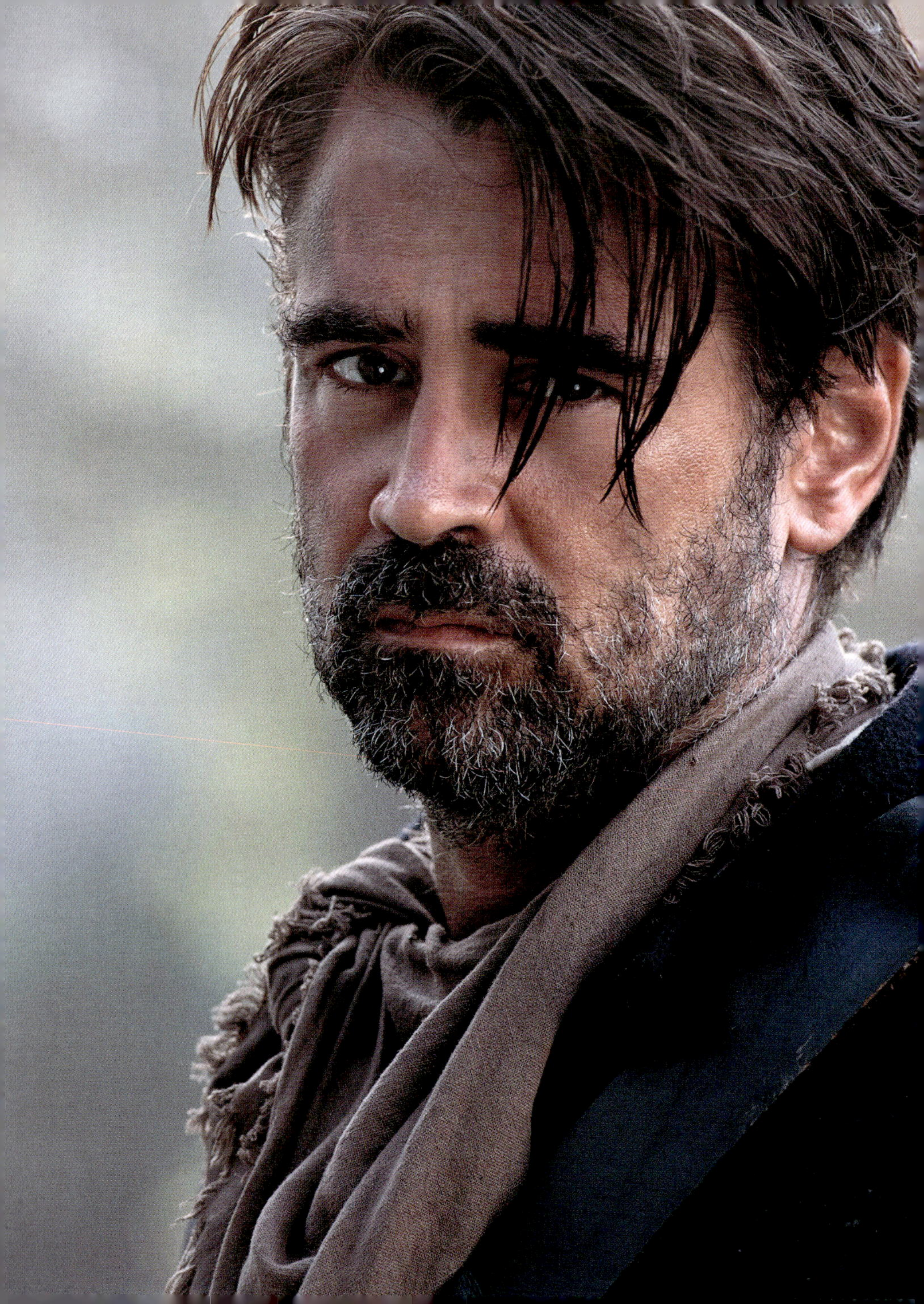

bleeding from a shrapnel wound in his leg, and the Christian thing to do is to take him in. Deciding they will try to save his life and then pass him on to the next patrol of Confederate troops who come by the gates, it soon becomes clear that McBurney is a deserter and has very little desire to return to his post. A recent Irish immigrant out of New York, his past is fuzzy. Finding through sheer luck that he has been offered safe refuge from the danger outside – and surrounded by fluttering women in pretty gowns who feed and nurse him – it's not difficult to see why he might find any excuse to try and turn his good luck into an opportunity, be it sexual or otherwise. Charming and respectful at first glance, McBurney soon reveals a talent for sweet-talking, and little specificity for the target. Be it favouring Miss Martha with admiration of her 'courage' in hard times or Edwina and her 'delicate beauty', he wheedles and manipulates in the hopes that he can bide time.

Coppola films Farrell, cast in the Eastwood role with plenty of the masculine swagger and good looks the role needs, as what she later called 'a sex object'. From the moment of his arrival to the school, as Miss Martha is perhaps a bit too attentive in the task of giving the unconscious man a sponge bath, the camera luxuriates over his bare torso and arms, following droplets of water as they tangle in his chest hair and splash gently over his hipbones. This might be a medical necessity, but Coppola's lingering camera makes it clear that the man has piqued her interest in more ways than one.

LEFT: The handsome but cunning McBurney is the proverbial fox in the henhouse.

OVERLEAF: Miss Martha has a number of tricks up her sleeve to keep McBurney from taking advantage of their Southern hospitality.

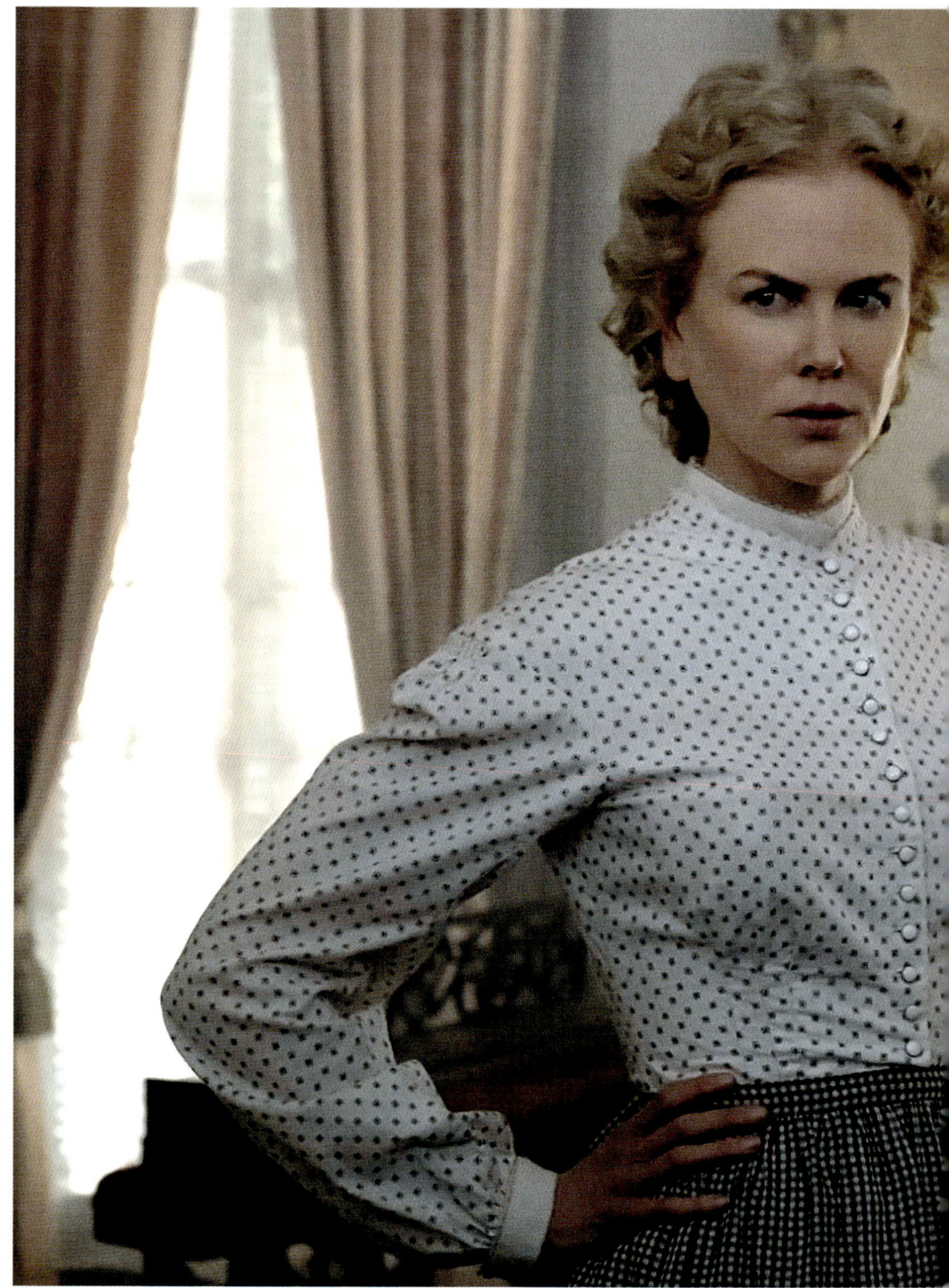

Across age groups from childhood to middle age, it's fascinating to see the group dynamic and each character's relationship to desire blossom uncomfortably. The older women haven't touched or been up close to a man for three years as the war has raged on, while the youths' interest is naturally piqued with new, hormonal curiosity at something so alien to them. They titter and giggle among themselves, making obvious doe eyes at McBurney as he begins to recover and finds his way into working in the garden.

Ultimately, though, McBurney grows smug on the doting attention of the girls, seizing on the rarity of his situation, particularly in a time when unaccompanied women were unusual and the dogma of sexual purity was ironclad. This liminal, chaotic period of wartime is ripe for usually rigid social norms to collapse, and so the boldness of the young women increases in relation to the fact that no one seems to be watching. The little ones sneak into his room to give him books, wearing pilfered pearl earrings; the older ones simper and flirt.

To get these dynamics right, each casting choice had to be perfect. Farrell, whose familiar status as a heartthrob and dark intensity lend a great deal to the part, is asked to move from silver-tongued seducer to raging madman throughout the film. He described the film as 'a really great, contained tale about the more animalistic aspects of human behaviour that are provoked by times of war.' Nicole Kidman, who Coppola had also never worked with before but had long admired, was who the director had in mind when writing the screenplay. As Elle Fanning put it, 'Everyone stands up straighter when Nicole is around.' Her own professionalism and authority only boosted the hierarchical dynamic of a boarding school.

As the pair go head-to-head, in some respects, their scenes together have urgency and frisson – particularly as Miss Martha

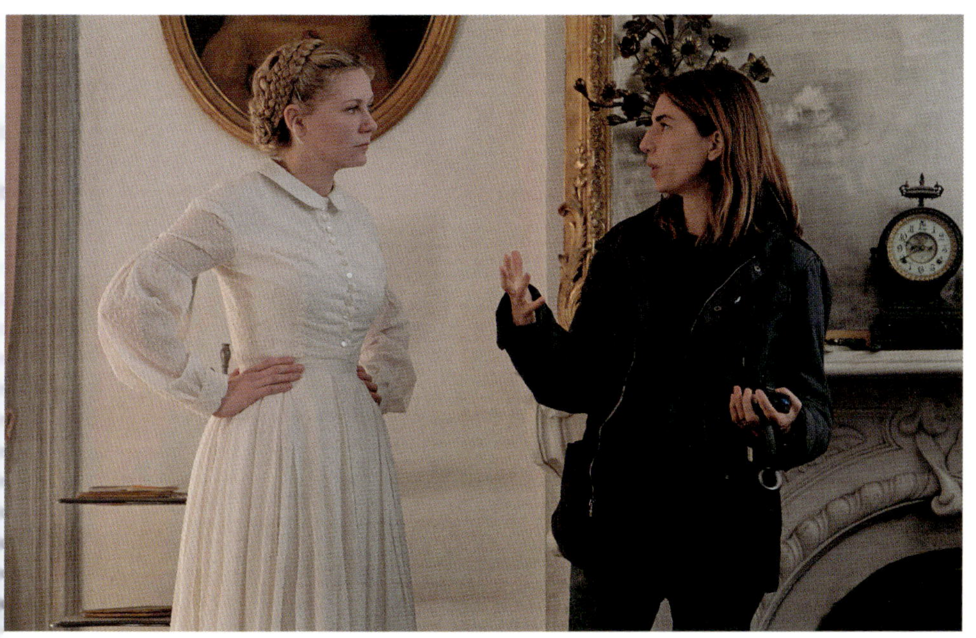

ABOVE: Coppola directs friend and star Kirsten Dunst, as the desirous and unhappy Miss Edwina.

works so hard to avoid her attraction to McBurney. But it is Edwina who proves to be the apple of McBurney's eye; she is of marriageable age and his motivation for confessing his love to her soon becomes evident. As a deserter from the army, he would face execution if he was caught by his superiors; if he ran into the enemy, he'd become a prisoner of war. But if he had the chance of securing a Southerner's help, he might have a chance to escape. And yet, it seems that McBurney believes he can have his cake and eat it too, taking advantage of all the attention being lavished on him. In a pivotal moment, he is caught having a nighttime tryst with the flirtatious young Miss Alicia, shattering all of his schemes. It becomes clear to Edwina he is a deceiver.

The colours and particularly the lighting in *The Beguiled* are among the director's finest work; her painterly images here are

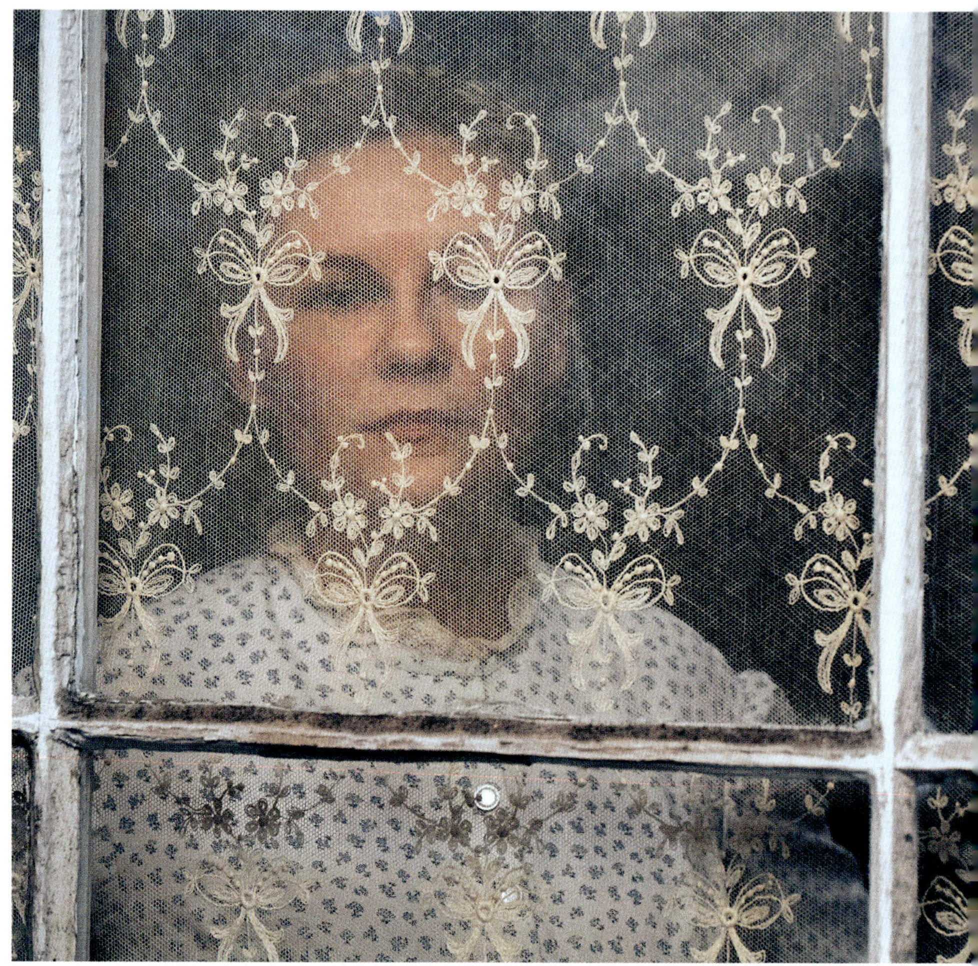

often breathtaking. Her continued interplay between darkness and light gives the film much of its sinuous power as a story of innocence – or so-called innocence – spoiled. There's a marked contrast between the pale pastels and virginal whites the women wear at the sunny start of the film and the dark navy of Farrell's army uniform, tucked in a crepuscular music room in his sickbed. The women are all characterized by a certain blondness and

lightness, while McBurney is darker of mien and often shrouded in shadow, face partly obscured to imply his own shifting and ambiguous intentions. As the film progresses, it grows intentionally claustrophobic and darker, with the women often ensconced by the evening darkness, and the inky blackness of night proving a cover for various misdeeds.

Director of photography Le Sourd and Coppola only shot their exteriors at specific times of the day, using dusk and sunset to 'amplify the sense of immediate danger'. The look was inspired by everything from Peter Weir's film *Picnic at Hanging Rock* (1975) and the pictorialist photography of Edward Steichen to the sfumato of Renaissance painting, a technique which allowed colours to melt into one another, softening the transition between objects or tones and giving a hazy effect to them.

The approach to sound design was rather less traditionally characteristic of Coppola's work, although it still was created by Phoenix. The band created a moody, understated synth score for the film which Coppola only deploys sparingly. More pared down than her usual soundtrack work, Coppola uses diegetic sounds of nature and the often-unnerving rural quiet around the school to ratchet up the unease. The most notable intrusion on that quiet is Phoenix's reinterpretation of Monteverdi's classical 'Magnificat', which they slowed down to the point of distortion.

The colours of the period costumes, with all their petticoats and hoop skirts, were carefully calibrated for both realism; the everyday wear and frequent washing has begun to bleach out any brightness, giving them a lived-in look in spite of their prettiness. You can imagine that they were once pristine, but like everything about the school, they now seem rather forlorn. Costume designer Stacey Battat chose to make most of them rather than rent them, using fabrics and buttonholes that would have existed at the time. And while verisimilitude was important, there's one symbolic moment early in the film that reveals much about Coppola and costume. After first finding the injured McBurney, the gathered girls drag the prone man onto their porch. Looking down at him, breathless with the strain of moving him, they remain elegantly buttoned up to their throats and wrists, brooches and ribbons in place. All except for Miss Alicia, whose top button has come undone, revealing just the slightest patch of her collarbone. Of course, it's she who will eventually go to bed with McBurney first. It's a tiny thing, but precisely the sort of foreshadowing, via costume, that a visual storyteller like Coppola is brilliant at doing.

In another, more pointed scene where clothing takes on great importance, the women sit down to a fine dinner with Col McBurney. Each is preposterously overdressed for the occasion, wearing her finest silks and bows; clearly no one has had any excuse for finery for a long time. Coppola lingers on the girls dressing for the meal, only to show Miss Alicia mutinously remarking on the fact that Miss Edwina, her teacher, is allowed to reveal her shoulders in her duck-egg blue silk gown. Instead of reprimanding the student, an equally jealous Miss Martha politely advises her second-in-command to cover herself with a shawl.

You can practically see Dunst's cheeks burning with embarrassment in the candlelight.

In reality, the spirit of the production was far from the bitchiness shown onscreen. The three youngest girls quickly befriended one another, and Coppola asked them to journal from the point of view of their characters in order to explore their backstories. Meanwhile Fanning and Dunst, long acquainted, enjoyed a sisterly relationship.

In one of several tense dinner scenes in *The Beguiled*, there's even what feels like an echo of *The Virgin Suicides*, where Kirsten

BELOW: Miss Martha leads the girls of the school in Christian prayer.

OVERLEAF: McBurney and Edwina share a tender, charged moment.

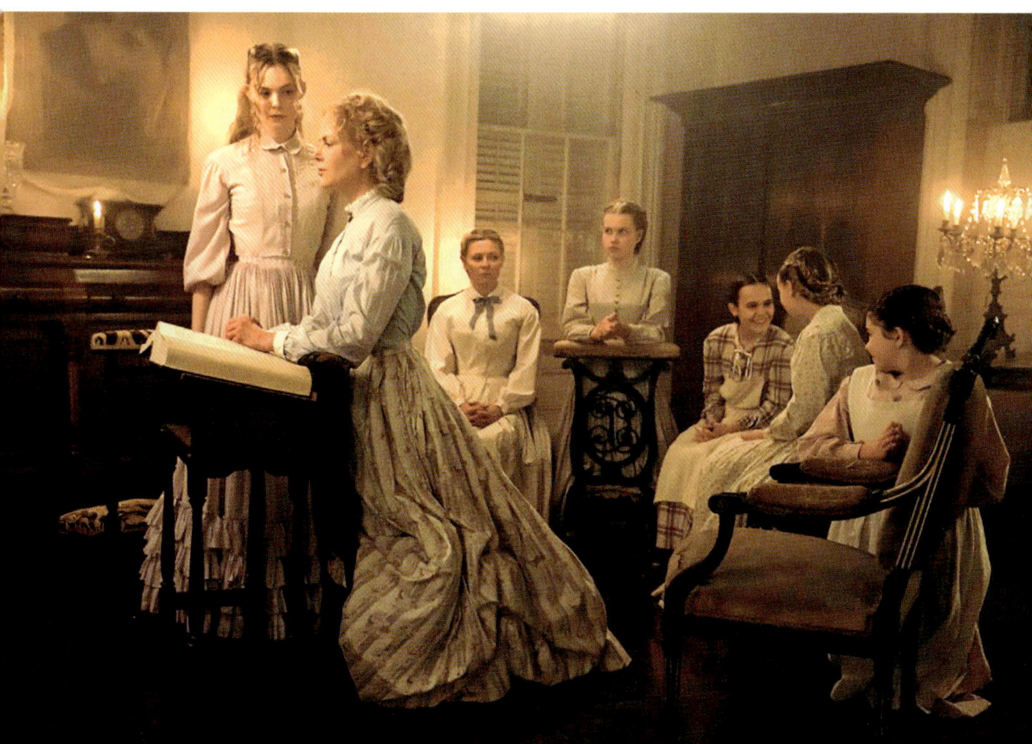

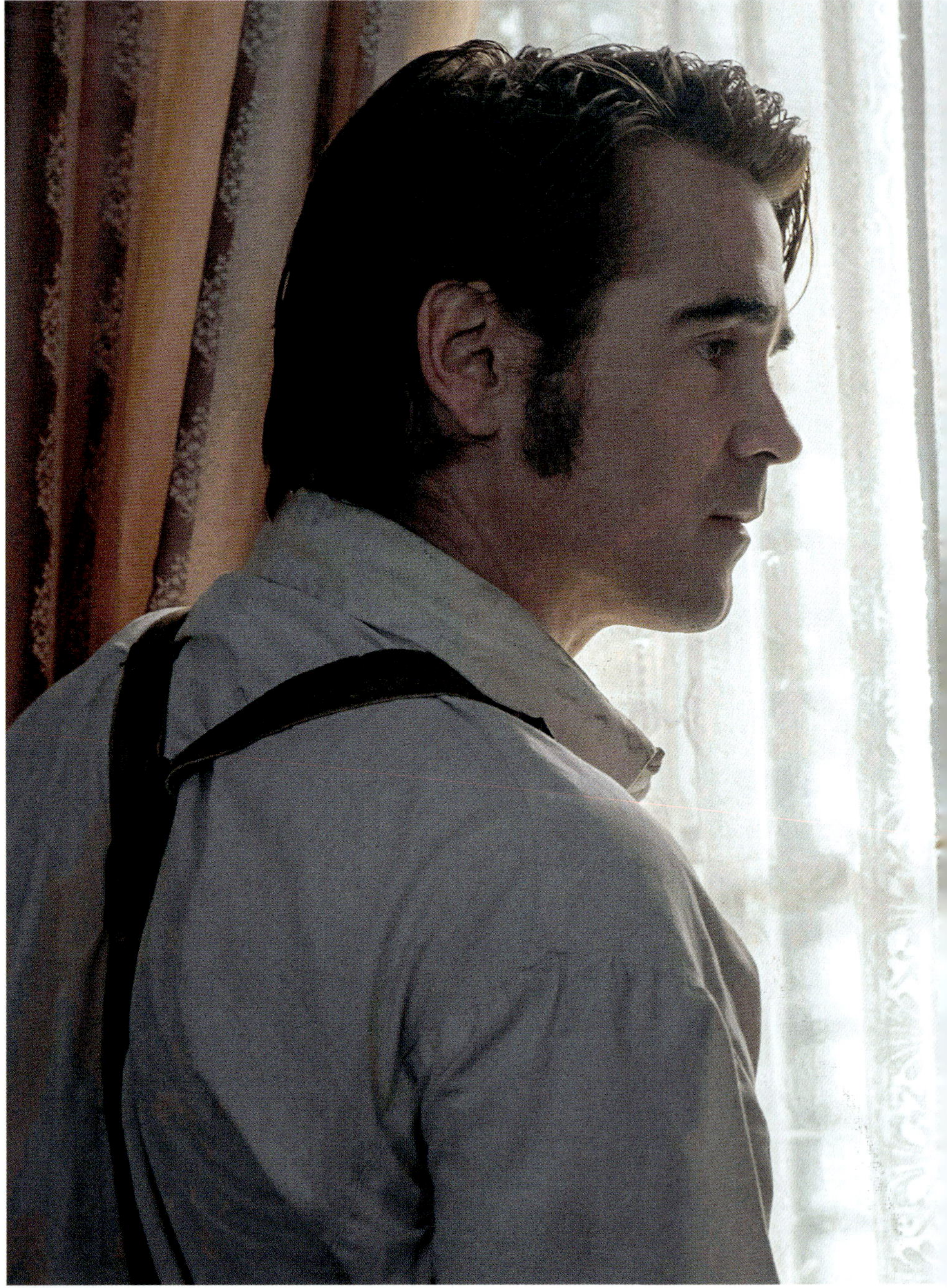

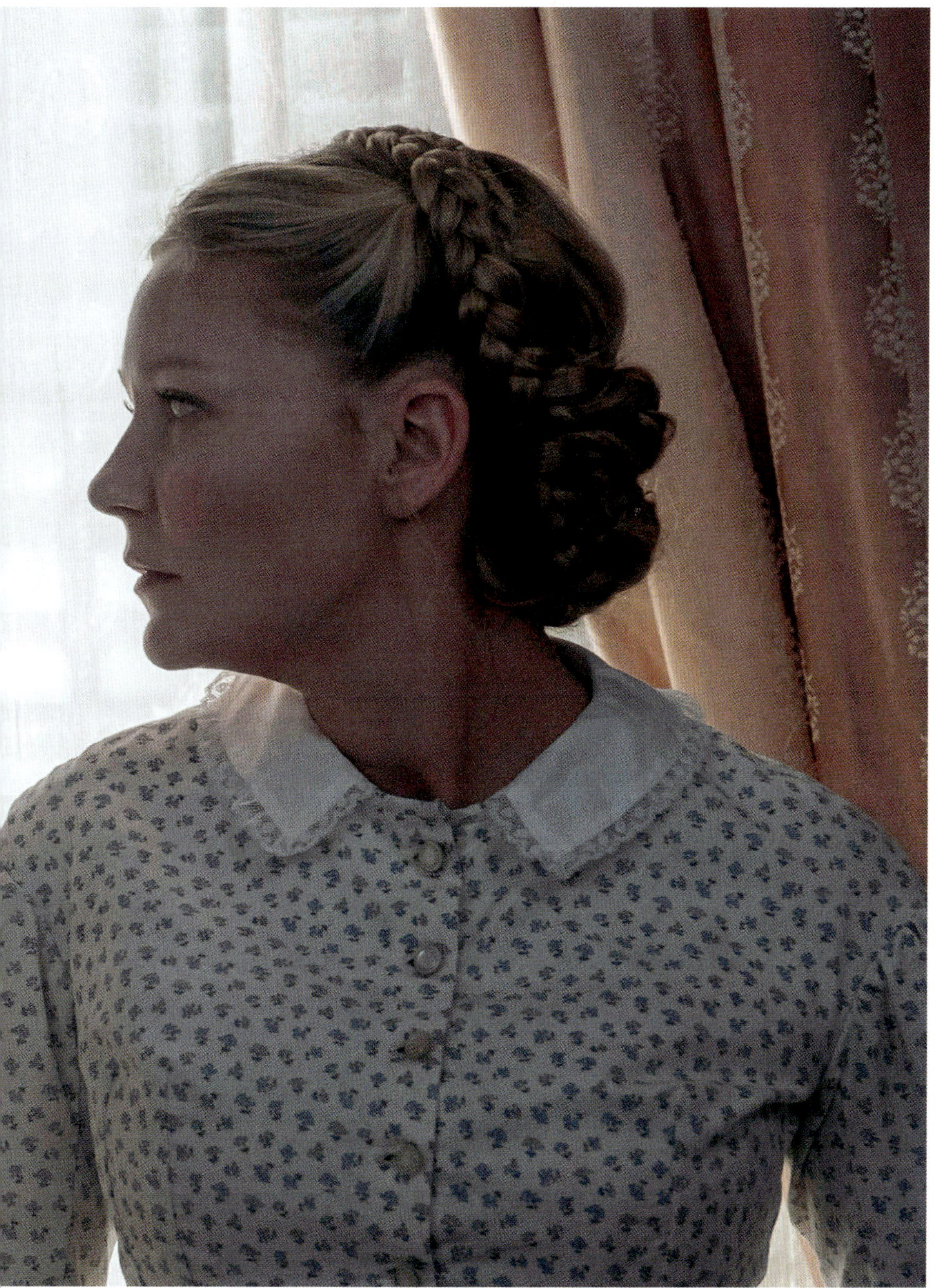

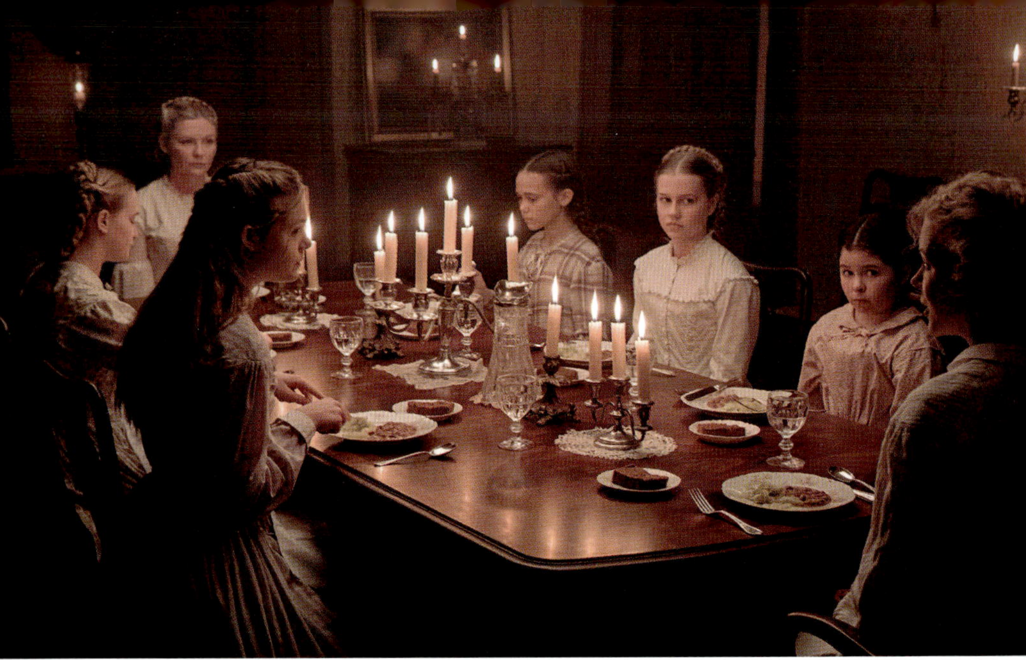

Dunst also sat at a table full of repressed authority figures and flirted covertly with a dinner guest. The camera here pans in a notable circular motion around the guests at the table, tracing the jealousies, suspicions and ulterior motives of each of their expressions.

Finally, when Edwina, hysterical at the sight of McBurney with Miss Alicia, shoves him down the stairs, his already-injured leg is damaged past the point of fixing. The women are forced to amputate. It seems that the 'threat' has been removed; with his difficulty getting around, he can no longer pose a serious danger to any of them, either literally or sexually. It's not hard to read between the lines and see this as a clear castration metaphor.

It's worth saying that *The Beguiled* is not a straightforwardly 'feminist' film in the sense of simply having female heroines and a male villain. For all their grit and eventual solidarity, these women

Sofia and female desire

The insistent, steady hum of female desire is buried deep throughout Sofia Coppola's work as a filmmaker. It's often under-discussed given the focus on her aesthetics, soundtracks or other more obvious signifiers of her work, but her interest in sex and sexuality has been present from the very start, in her debut film. As a disassociated and repressed Lux Lisbon takes a series of random boys onto her suburban roof to make love to them, desperate for any sensation of rebellion and fun, Coppola's film does not judge or condemn her. Instead, it shows the voyeurism and superficial concern of the boys next door who watch her, and the obsessive policing of the Lisbon parents over their daughters' bodies. In *Marie Antoinette*, *The Beguiled* and *Priscilla* – all period pieces set in times which were far more constrained about women's sex lives – a lack of sex or the enforcement of purity is the bane of these women's lives, oppressive and pushing them to increasingly frustrated and outlandish behaviour.

While Coppola has never been particularly overt in her depiction of sex – she foregoes sex scenes in the main, hinting at them with Marie Antoinette's coquettish fan and stockings scene or the rolling-around-the-bedroom antics of Elvis and Priscilla – she does feature one sex scene prominently. That's late in the running time of *The Beguiled*, in a visceral scene that proves both disturbing and satisfying. When the meek Edwina abandons propriety, physically shoving her headmistress away to chase after the raving, gun-brandishing McBurney, the pair end up on the floor, with McBurney pawing at the woman's layers of petticoats and both of them heaving with sweat and need. The man might be terrible, but in the final analysis, he's also disposable: a girl's gotta do what a girl's gotta do.

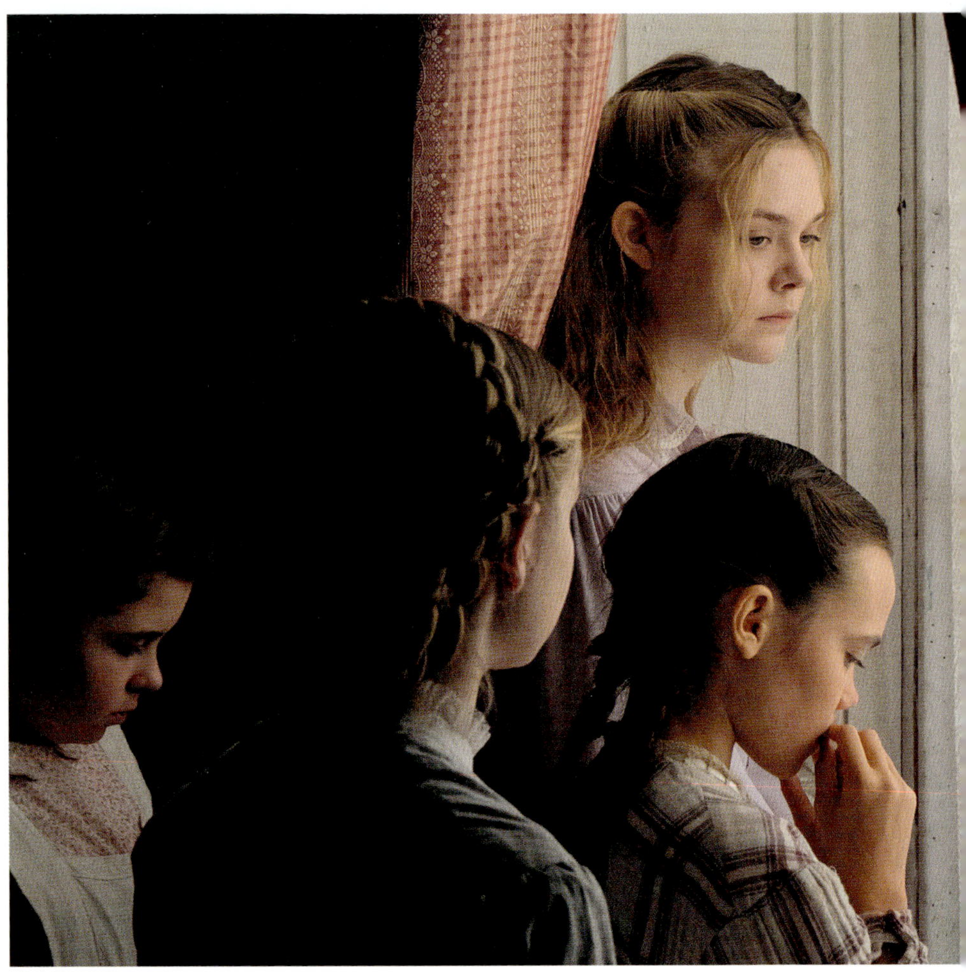

are also shown as catty, scheming and capable of murder in the name of self-protection. Their final decision to poison the Colonel could be read as righteous self-preservation, but ultimately, it also seems like a reaffirmation of their insularity and their fragile sense of Southern purity and womanhood. It's about much more than any physical threat, but about a challenge to their way of life, perhaps even to their acceptance of reality that times are

changing and the war will be lost. These young women are being trained to exist in a society which will no longer be there in a year's time.

And with the exception of Edwina, no one in the film emerges as particularly decent. The sly, arrogant McBurney is shocked by the women recognizing his deceit, while the hypocritical Miss Martha punishes those around her for their unseemly desires, preaching Christian virtue while barely repressing her own urges. It's tacitly understood that Miss Alicia's claims of attempted rape are suspicious, and that everyone knows it may well have been consensual; but no one says so, mainly because it's too impolite and unpleasant to admit that a young woman of her breeding would willingly submit to premarital sex – one of the gravest sins of her era.

There's something else that's unspoken but simmering beneath the surface in this heady mixture of sex, violence and repression: the absence of slaves or Blackness in the film. Coppola's vacuum-sealed depiction of white women's sexual jealousies and cruelties is interesting when considering an incredibly common practice among the ladies of antebellum households. It was their lot to ignore the frequent sexual abuses and assignations of their slave-owning husbands with the Black women they regarded as property – so much so that a law was written which absolved white slave-owning men from parental responsibility for any children born of slaves.

It's no wonder the women of *The Beguiled* are so good at turning their heads the other way in response to sexual transgression and impropriety. As a society, these Southern belles would have been tacitly complicit in their menfolk's appalling behaviour for decades. Although this reality is never made explicit in the film – and arguably might have been better served if it had – it seems to inform the atmosphere of moral rot and puritanical hypocrisy that these characters trade in. ('Keep your stitches straight,' Miss Martha tells the girls as they sew up Col McBurney's body bag.) These are far from being any kind of figures of feminist empowerment. As *Vulture* film critic Angelica Jade Bastien wrote, '*The Beguiled* is a curious reckoning of the myths of white womanhood – how they use fragility as a shield for deviousness and insulate themselves from the horrors of a world that they too are responsible for.'

The film went on to win Coppola the Best Director prize at the 2017 Cannes Film Festival, marking only the second time up until that point a woman had won the award. But others met *The Beguiled* with a chillier reception, particularly around the excision of a Black character – a slave woman named Mattie – who is in the novel and depicted by Mae Mercer in the 1971 film. Some critics felt Coppola was guilty of whitewashing, choosing to zero in on these white Southern belles at the expense of the cruel historical reality. Coppola responded in writing to the backlash, saying: 'I did not want to perpetuate an objectionable stereotype where facts and history supported my choice of setting the story of these white women in complete isolation, after the slaves had escaped. Moreover, I felt that to treat slavery as a side-plot would be insulting.' It is understandably difficult to parse the differences between a film about white myopia and the possible myopia of its creator, but it seems evident that *The Beguiled* takes a damning view of nearly every white character depicted.

The final shot is a powerful one. Seen in outline through the wrought-iron gates of the school, shut tightly against outsiders, the women stand in unnerving stillness, grouped together as though for a daguerreotype photograph. They are frozen in aspic there, entrenched in their own lost Scarlett O'Hara delusions, fading into history. That, ultimately, is where they belong.

BELOW: Coppola and Dunst greet each other enthusiastically at an event for *The Beguiled*.

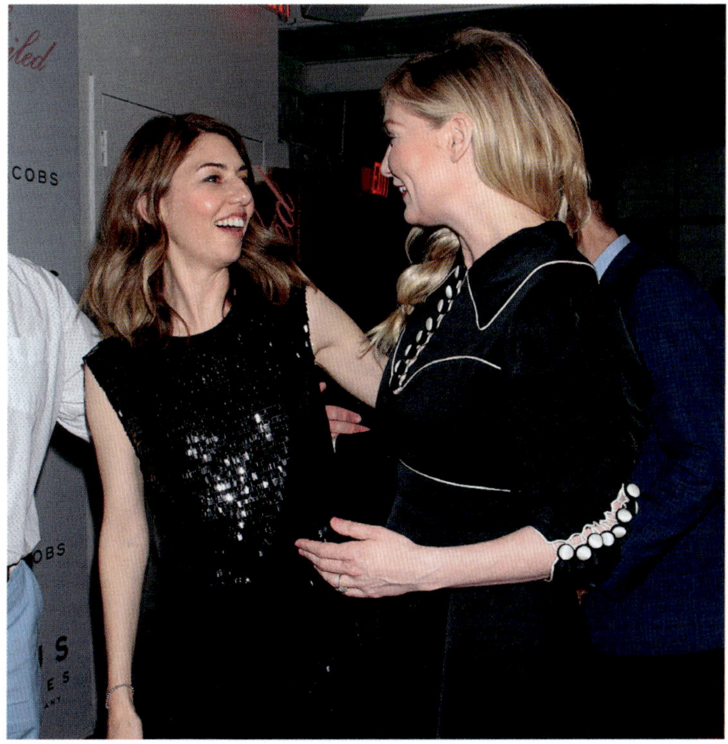

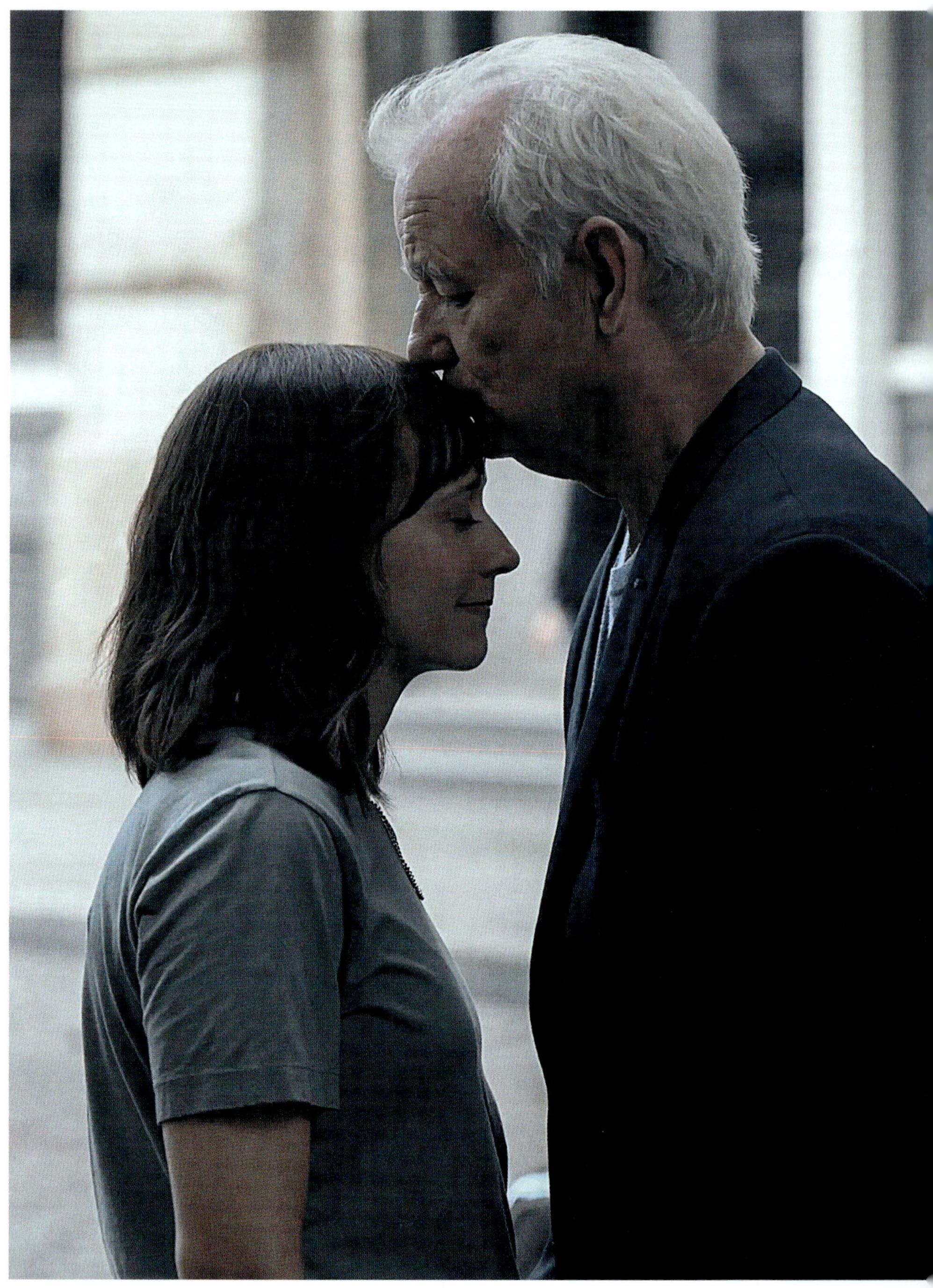

'And remember, don't give your heart to any boys. You're mine.'

ON THE ROCKS

2020

The underrated and gently poignant screwball comedy-drama *On the Rocks* was a significant change of pace for Coppola. It's a film that came three years after her last and feels rather unlike her others in some respects – sprightly, less consciously muted, talkative and more overtly humorous. It tells the story of Laura (Rashida Jones), a married New York City mother of two young girls, a novelist meant to be working on her newest book, and the wife of Dean (Marlon Wayans), a burgeoning businessman who works long hours away from home. At the start of the film, there's a cut from a fleeting glimpse at the pair's wedding day to their current domestic life. Coppola shoots Laura's bare feet and hands as she picks up her toddler's detritus from all over her floor; the statement is succinct in its cut from romance to domestic chaos (as the old joke goes: it begins while you sink in his arms and ends with your arms in his sink).

Laura's daily life is dictated by school runs and bedtimes, in the fashion of all parents of children this age; she withstands the over-therapized stream of babble from her fellow school mum (played comically by Jenny Slate) and oversees the family schedule in an effort to rise above the general din of chaos. The rest of the time, she spins her wheels at her keyboard, suffering from writer's block and feeling creatively suffocated. Her husband Dean, meanwhile, seems enthusiastic and enlivened by his own growing business,

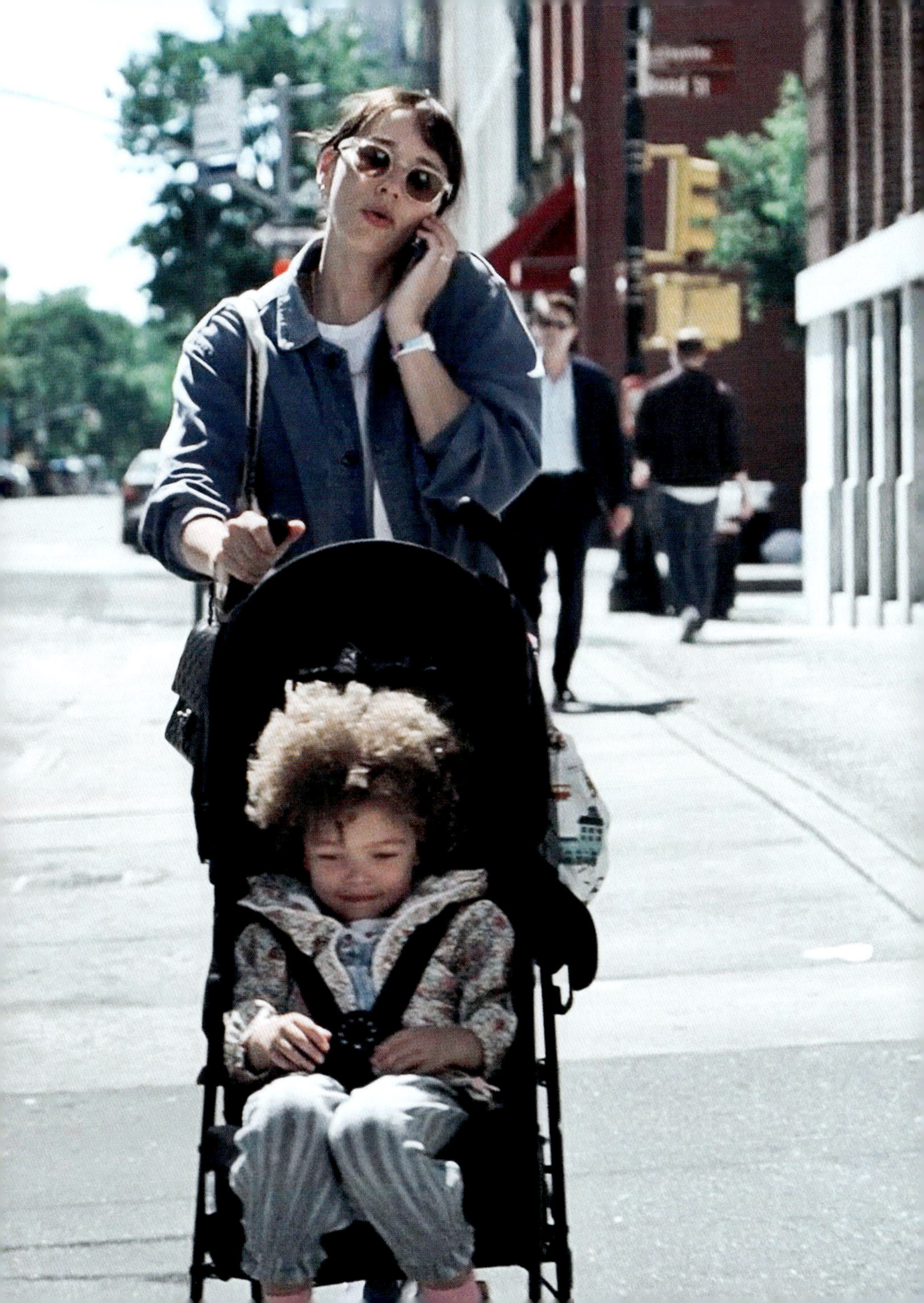

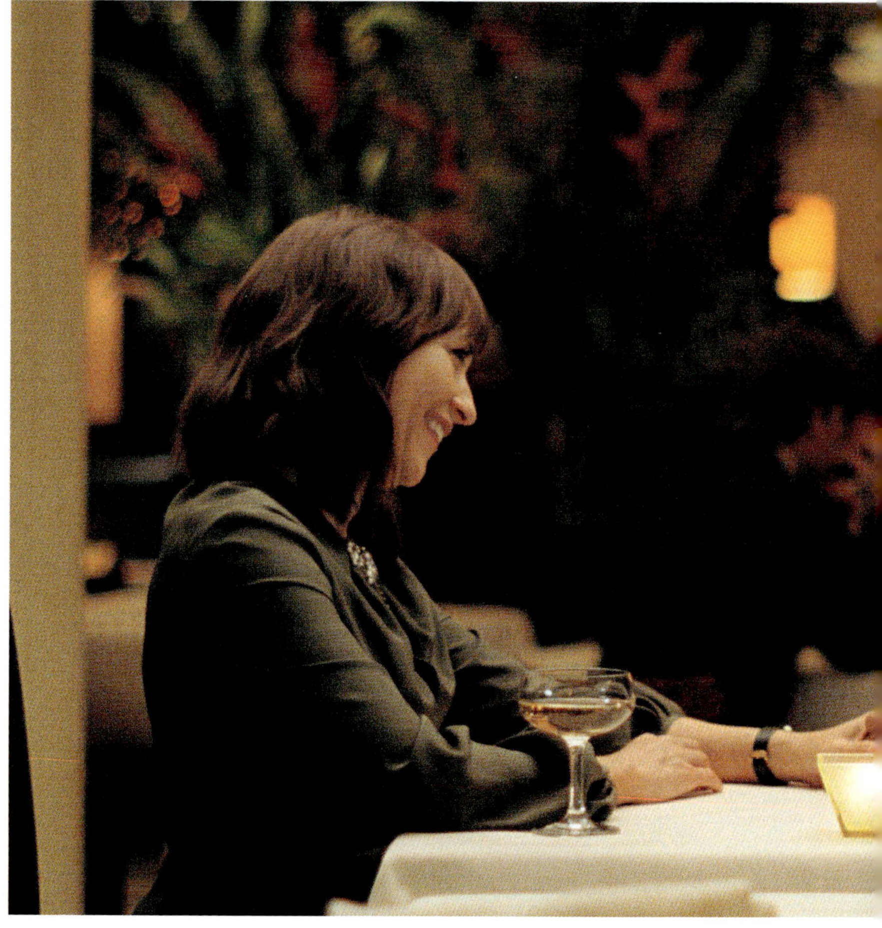

and his bursts of chattiness about it seem only to reinforce Laura's own sullen uncertainty about her own career post-motherhood. Without drawing any overt attention to the contrast, it's clear that parenting has impacted one's career much more than the other, and it has little to do with any wilful neglect or poor behaviour from husband Dean. It's simply the way the burden tends to fall.

As if that weren't enough, Dean's attractive new assistant Fiona (Jessica Henwick) seems to always be a half-step behind

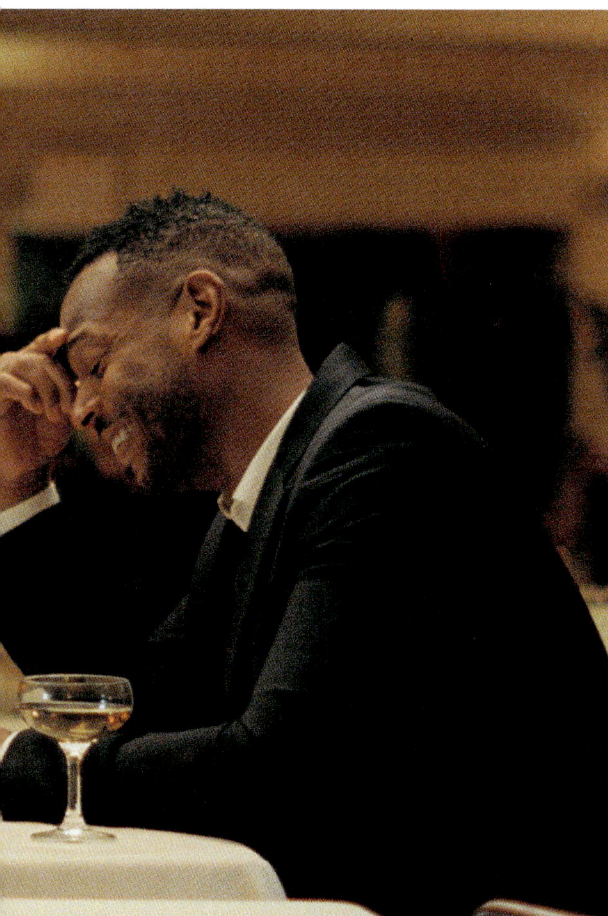

him, accompanying him and his team on work trips while Laura handles the home front. And so it begins: feeling out of sorts, like a 'buzzkill' and uninspired at work, Laura is already feeling off-kilter when she finds Fiona's toiletry bag in Dean's suitcase. Suspicion only grows from there.

Enter Laura's dad, Felix (Bill Murray), a charismatic and mercurial art dealer of some renown, legendary for his womanizing. He turns up, lavishes affection on his granddaughters and is a real man of the world, prone to monologuing philosophically about life, women, Monet and especially about 'how men think'. He is both enormously intelligent and thoroughly a product of his male-dominated generation, as Laura exasperatedly points out when she sighs: 'Can you ever just act normal around *any* woman?' Or, in fact, when he has a barrel of fun with Laura's two girls but leaves them with the passing thought that they should 'wear our hair long and pretty, the way boys like it.' Coppola later remarked that as she was writing the screenplay for *On the Rocks*, she suddenly recalled that an older friend of her father's told her precisely this when she was young.

It's no surprise, then, that when she asks for his opinion on Dean's fishy behaviour of late, Felix jumps immediately to an affair ('He's a man. It's nature,' he says). It's what *he* would be doing, after all. And it's what he did to Laura's mother, who remains unseen throughout the film. And so, although Laura is reluctant initially, the father and daughter end up on a madcap journey to follow Dean and uncover his possible infidelity. Her dissatisfaction and insecurity drive her need to know. At one point, Felix turns up in a zippy vintage red Alfa Romeo sports car, with a pile of caviar and crackers for a snack, in a ridiculous attempt to shadow his son-in-law. It's clear that this is as much about Laura and Felix's own individual, inherent feelings of loneliness than it is any real desire to unmask Dean as a cheater; ultimately, it's Laura's relationships to both of the major male figures in her life that are illuminated in surprising ways.

Coppola, living in New York at the time with her own two young children, Romy and Cosima, admits she wrote *On the Rocks* when she herself was feeling off kilter about motherhood, and presumably how it affects identity and marriage. Although she has always been a fairly private person, Coppola told *Indiewire*, 'There's a bit of an identity crisis – how do I connect with who I was

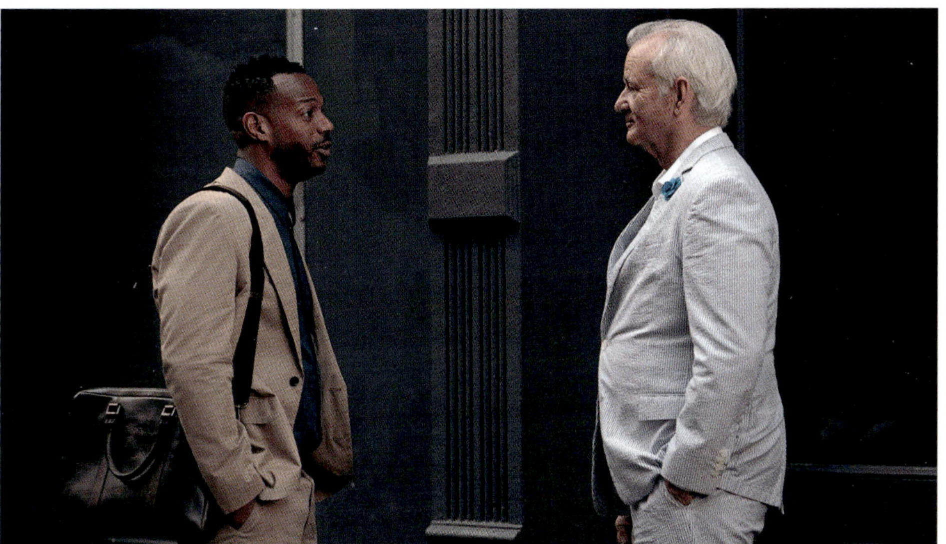

before all that and still work?' A friend of hers told her a story that she really had taken her dad and gone and spied on her husband while hiding in the bushes, a story too amusing not to steal for the screen. But Coppola also considered her relationship with her own father, thinking about how those things change once you have children of your own.

The rather privileged existence of both father and daughter as they drink cocktails in swish locations like Soho House and the Carlyle does not go unnoticed. This is not a domestic scenario where money seems to be one of the primary concerns. Rashida Jones, likeable and witty in the role, is a longtime friend of Coppola's (and who, interestingly, has a slight resemblance to Coppola, if you squint). She also knows what it is to be the daughter of a very famous and important father (music producer Quincy Jones, in

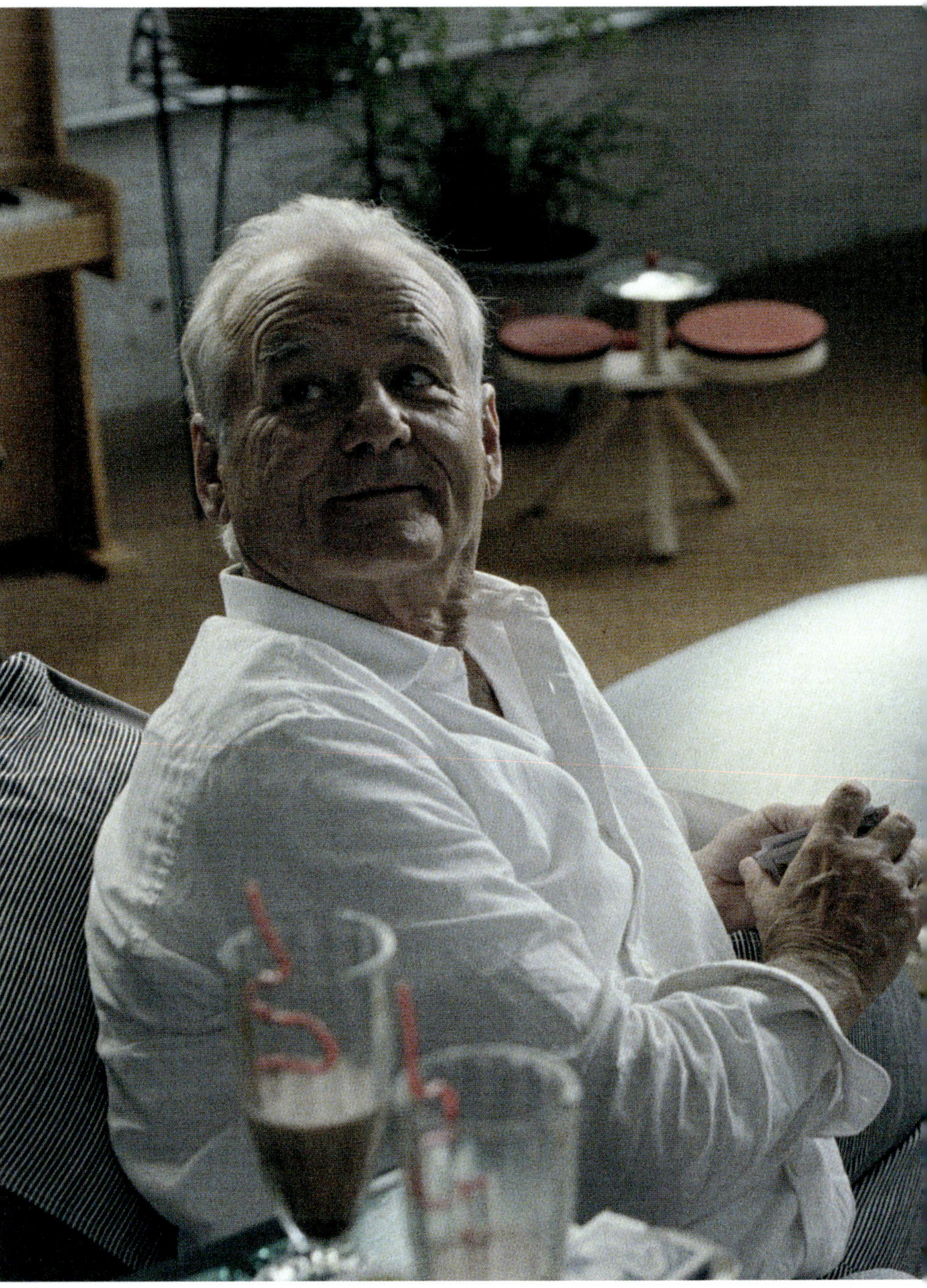

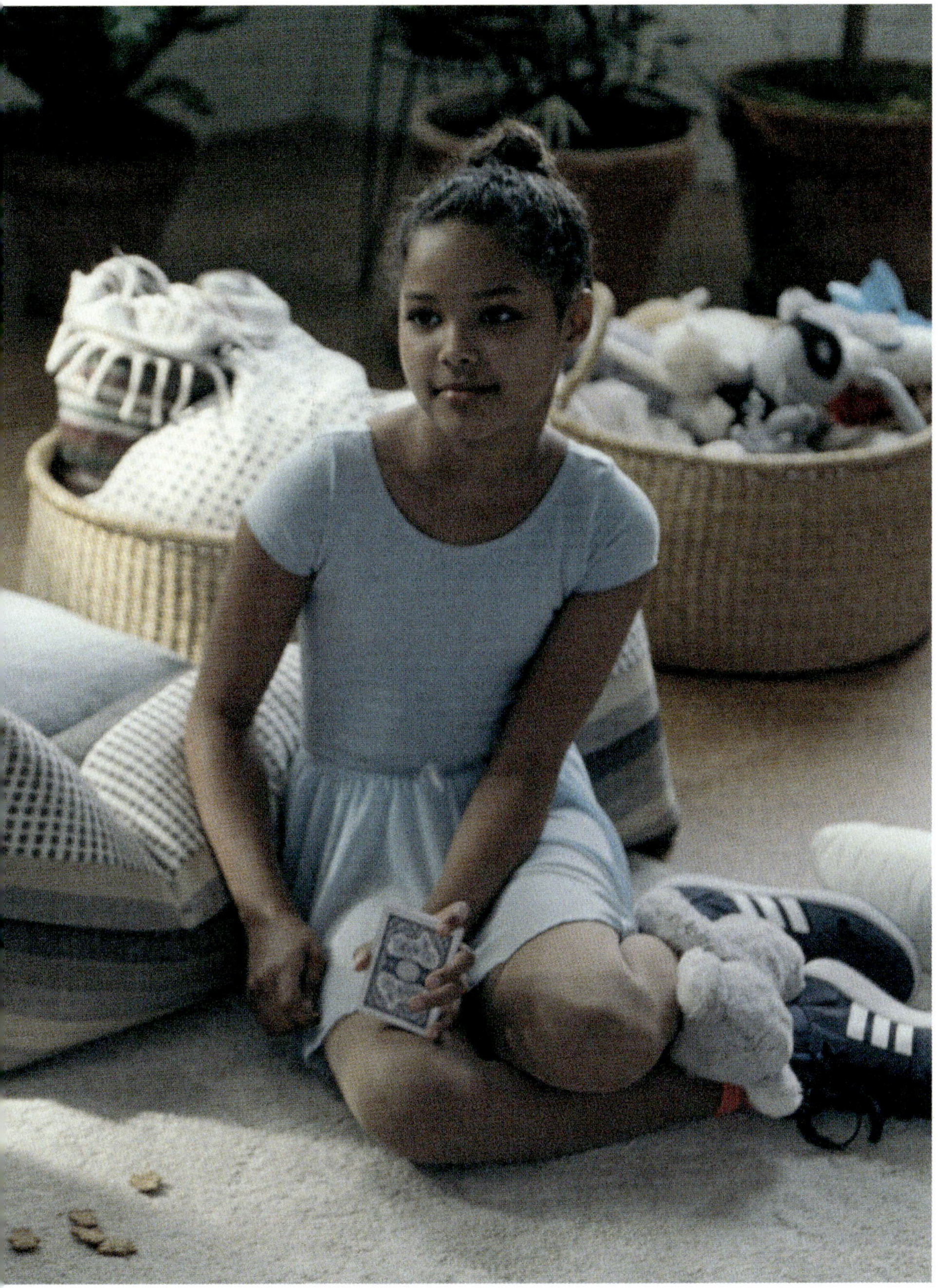

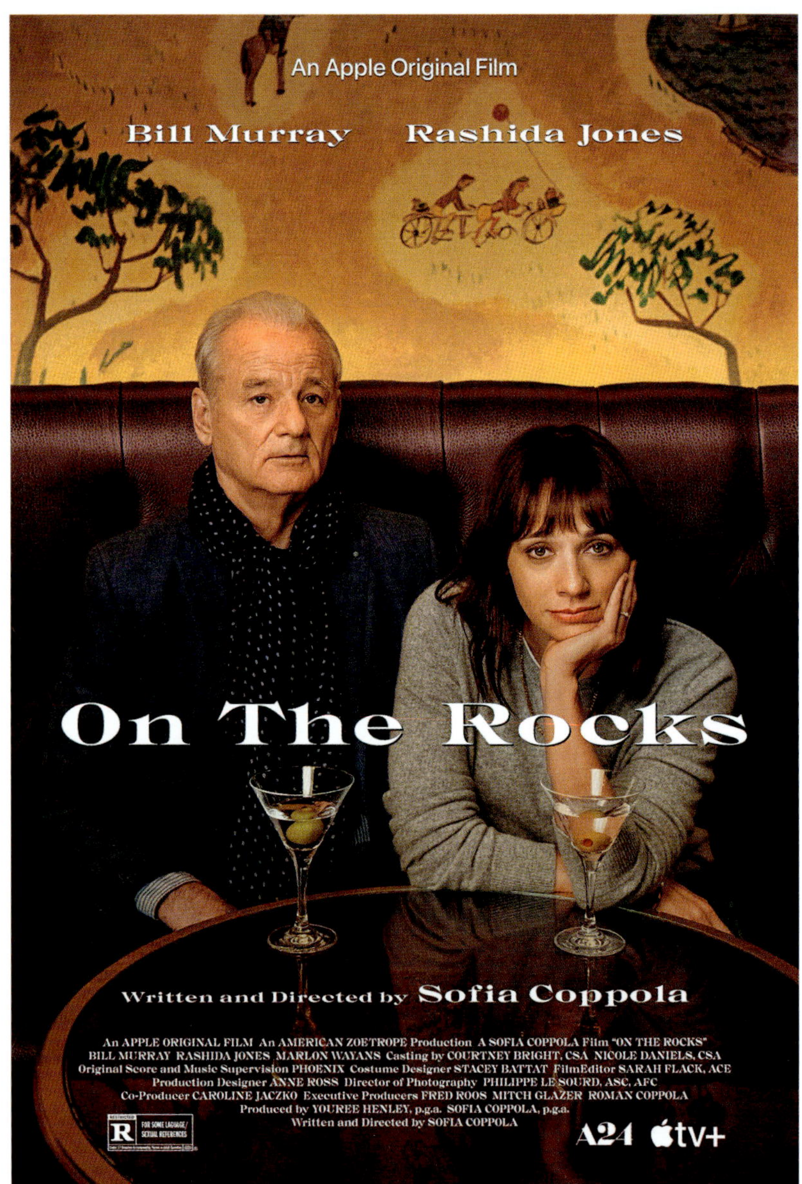

An Apple Original Film
BILL MURRAY   RASHIDA JONES
ON The Rocks
Written and Directed by Sofia Coppola
An APPLE ORIGINAL FILM An AMERICAN ZOETROPE Production A SOFIA COPPOLA Film "ON THE ROCKS"
BILL MURRAY RASHIDA JONES MARLON WAYANS Casting by COURTNEY BRIGHT, CSA NICOLE DANIELS, CSA
Original Score and Music Supervision PHOENIX Costume Designer STACEY BATTAT FilmEditor SARAH FLACK, ACE
Production Designer ANNE ROSS Director of Photography PHILIPPE LE SOURD, ASC, AFC
Co-Producer CAROLINE JACZKO Executive Producers FRED ROOS MITCH GLAZER ROMAN COPPOLA
Produced by YOUREE HENLEY, p.g.a. SOFIA COPPOLA, p.g.a.
Written and Directed by SOFIA COPPOLA
RESTRICTED R FOR SOME LAGUAGE/ SEXUAL REFERENCES
A24
tv+

this case). This is a relevant piece of shared history given the subject matter of the film. Watching a scene in *On the Rocks* as dad takes daughter for a swanky birthday drink in a posh hotel and they share martinis, you can't help but ponder the possible parallels in both of these creative women's lives. There's real warmth and affection between Jones and Murray as her father, but equally a sardonic sense of humour as he tells his daughter that his new assistant 'doesn't talk, she just listens', and she immediately replies: 'That sounds perfect for you.'

For the part of Felix, Coppola says she initially hesitated at the thought of working with Bill Murray again, even though they'd remained close and she had long seen him as a 'big brother' figure. Since the success of *Lost in Translation* 17 years before, she felt that expectations would be too high – and too fixated on his character in that movie – to try something new. But Murray was perfect for the part and it felt distinct enough from their previous film together for it to work, and he is predictably brilliant as this swaggering but loving father, dispensing high-minded advice even while trying not to pinch a waitress's backside. From the first moment of the movie, it's Murray's voice we hear insisting that his daughter not give her heart to any boy, and the familiarity of it feels immediately paternal. Coppola gave Murray wide remit to explore without forcing him to stick strictly to her written script, knowing his essential charm and sly humour would sparkle best if his personality came through. Rashida Jones and Bill Murray had one brief scene together in Coppola's one-off comedy special *A Very Murray Christmas* (2015), which got the wheels spinning about the pair's rapport.

LEFT: *On the Rocks* poster, Apple TV, 2020.

Coppola, a professed lover of *The Thin Man* movies, also used cues from classic screwball, a mode of romantic comedy popular in 1930s and 1940s Hollywood which produced the likes of *The Philadelphia Story* (1940), *Bringing Up Baby* (1938) and *His Girl Friday* (1940). These films utilized manically fast-talking characters who were often faced with the apparent breakup or reunion of a marriage – and who go on ridiculous and slapstick adventures in the process of falling in or out of love. 'I was really trying to push myself out of my comfort zone to be a little bit more silly. I was in the mood to make a romantic comedy,' Coppola told British *Vogue*.

Known as 'battle of the sexes' comedies for their worldly and amusing take on the differences between genders, it's not hard to see that classic film DNA in *On the Rocks*: the clueless husband, the eccentric supporting ensemble, the wild goose chase by car through New York streets, the abrupt decision to trail Dean all the way to Mexico only to have to hide in the bushes at a luxury resort. All it's missing is a leopard on the loose, à la *Bringing Up Baby*. All of this, though, may have been a factor in *On the Rocks*' somewhat muted critical reception. Some felt the film didn't feel sufficiently 'like' a Sofia Coppola project, and her script deviated from the norm with her far more garrulous pages of dialogue. Still, Coppola kept her screenplay open to interpretation and was always keen to have her actors' input. As Rashida Jones said, there was an understanding and identifiability for her from a personal perspective, as someone trying to find her place in her own life and to distinguish it from behind the shadow of her prominent father.

It's strange to think that Coppola's artistic reunion with the great Bill Murray did not garner more fanfare. Of her eight feature films, *On the Rocks* may arguably be the one which has been the least discussed and celebrated, and unjustly so. One of the factors

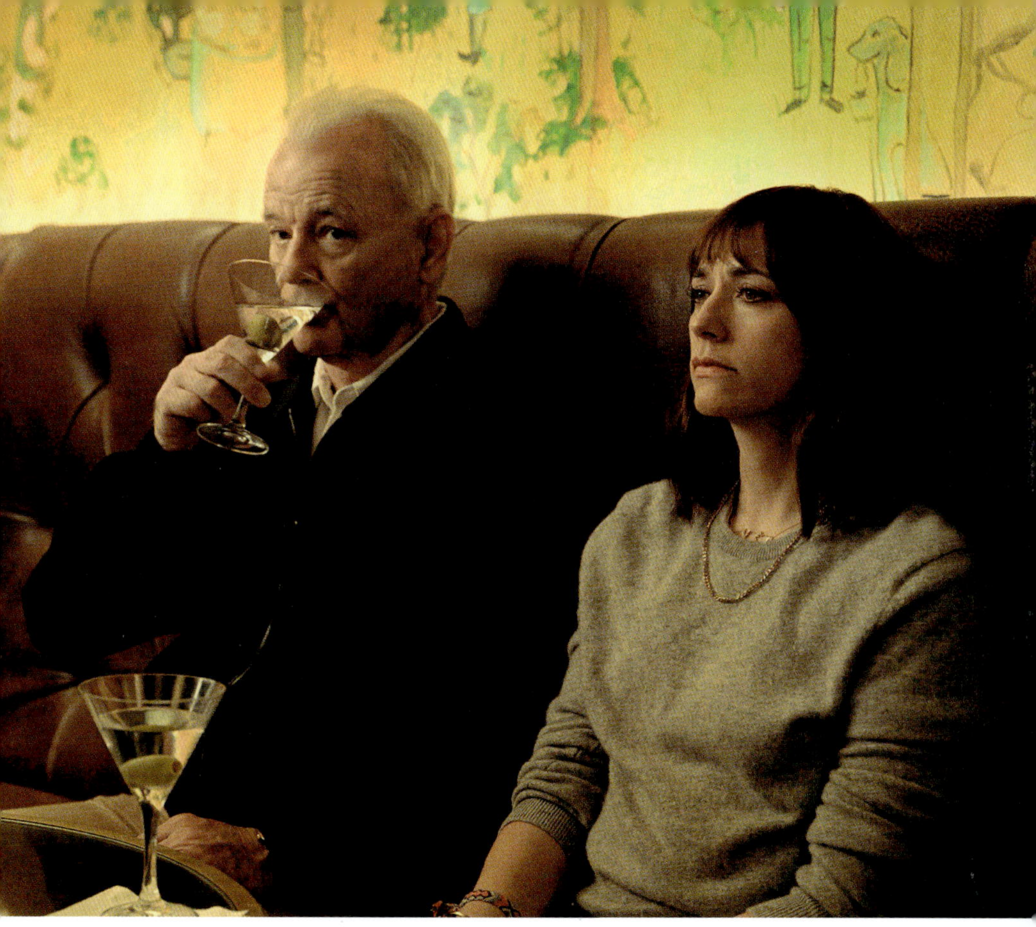

ABOVE: Father and daughter drink martinis in a luxury Manhattan hotel while contemplating infidelity.

might be that the film is so understated after all the prettified frippery and festival buzz around *The Beguiled*; Coppola has a tendency to sometimes move away from the 'type' of project she did immediately previous. (From the knowing tackiness of *The Bling Ring*, she took on the period trappings of *The Beguiled*; after the contemporary *On the Rocks*, she moved back to a confectionary period piece, *Priscilla*.)

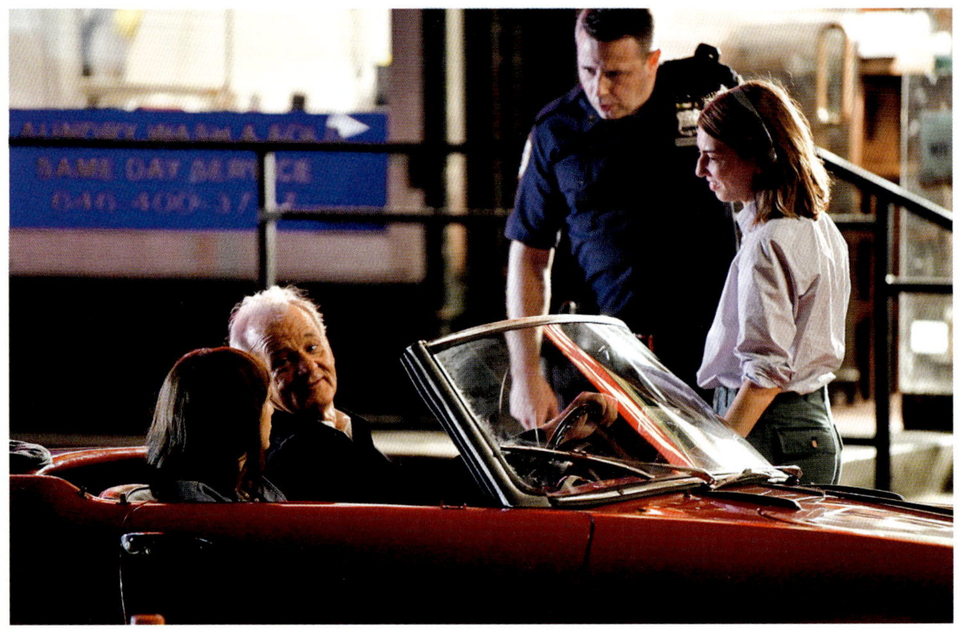

ABOVE: Coppola directs Murray and Jones in a vintage Alfa Romeo on the streets of New York.

But the biggest factor was most likely an obvious one: the Covid-19 pandemic. Filmed in the summer of 2019 with her father's company, American Zoetrope, and hip indie A24, the movie was intended for a cinema release as with all of Coppola's previous films. And then, mass lockdowns changed matters. Although it was generally well reviewed by critics, being left to a streaming-only release on Apple TV didn't especially help its rep. Premiering it at a drive-in theatre in New York City and then left to a streaming release on Apple TV, it seems the film disappeared into the ether of many non-theatrical releases of this liminal pandemic period.

For her cinematography, Coppola worked again with Philippe Le Sourd, but this time on a very distinct project from their previous film. For her first time shooting in New York, it was pivotal to her that the city not appear simply by the visual and cinematic shorthand that's always stereotypically used for a film set there. Instead, she worked with Le Sourd to achieve a slightly burnished vintage look, shooting on 35mm as is her preference. 'When walking through New York, you have this enormous range of lighting conditions, ranging from the brightness of Time Square to the deep darkness when looking down a long alley,' Le Sourd described; it was key to him to capture this gradience in light and shadow for a film containing so many nocturnal scenes.

It's interesting that so many of the integral moments of *On the Rocks* do come at night. There's one comic vignette where Felix and Laura race through the city in Felix's old Alfa Romeo, running stop lights in an effort to chase down Laura's husband in a taxi. It vaguely recalls some of the heady 1960s Italian movies like Federico Fellini's romp *La Dolce Vita* (1960); Fellini was always inclined to explore the spiritual decay of debonair playboy types. There's a free-spiritedness, particularly to the Felix character, that borrows from the spirit of those late-night adventures. But there's also a certain philosophical bent to the film. It's once again under the safe cover of darkness that father and daughter have a tender discussion about his infidelity in his marriage to her mother, revealing both the genuine loneliness and regret of his choice – but also of the complexity of his affair and the feeling of grief in learning of the death of his former mistress. Fellini had an outsize influence on Francis Ford Coppola, and here, as one critic put it, his daughter has 'whipped a meringue from 50 or 60 pages from a cinema history textbook'.

Still, the backbone of the film is ultimately the marriage between Laura and Marlon Wayans' Dean. (It's interesting that Coppola cast Wayans, an actor with a comic reputation, best known for his work on *The Scary Movie* franchise. She felt she'd never seen him in this type of role before, and her instinct that he

The Sofia gang

It's something of a well-received fact that the Coppolas have an extensive showbiz family tree, and they tend to love working together. Along with father Francis' American Zoetrope as production company, Sofia's brother Roman is a presence on all of her films, as producer and unofficial adviser. Add cousin Jason Schwartzman to the occasional cast, late mother Eleanor as a former behind the scenes filmmaker, and husband Thomas Mars as musical collaborator, and you can see how creatively and practically involved Sofia's family is in the making of her films. The Coppolas long saw filmmaking as a family business – Francis Ford always enlisted the help of his family and friends too.

But there have also been a host of longtime regular collaborators outside of the family who, as Coppola says, she has a shorthand with, and who intuitively understand what it is she might need from a scene. That includes her longtime editor, Stacey Flack, who has been able to approach everything from the sedate pace of *Somewhere*, fluid and impressionistic, to the jabbing, frenetic rhythm of coke-fuelled *The Bling Ring*.

Production designer Anne Ross is so close that she even first introduced Coppola to the idea of making *The Beguiled*; Kirsten Dunst, when not starring in Sofia's films, has successfully identified the right actors for Coppola to work with (Cailee Spaeny for *Priscilla*, for instance). Regular directors of photography Lance Acord and Philippe Le Sourd both work very closely with Coppola (who she is never physically far from on set, always carefully surveying the camera work), and always on 35mm film, as is her preference. Her cinematographers are some of her closest allies and confidantes in the making of her movies, such is the pivotal nature of how she composes her elegant shots. And finally, producers Youree Henry and Fred Roos have known Coppola for decades; they understand she has a uniquely feminine command of her projects, but she relies on a known and trusted group of technicians, artists and businesspeople to get things done.

could achieve it was accurate. There's no trace of that former ridiculousness to Wayans, and he carries himself like a consummate if ambiguous family man.) His Dean comes across as a relatively caring partner, happily playing with his children when home and FaceTiming his wife on her birthday when he can't be there, surprising her with (albeit misguided) gifts. As such, the film hardly leans heavily into the brokenness of an irreparable marriage or follow expected dramatic cliches around marital strife: this is not Ingmar Bergman's *Scenes from a Marriage* (1973) or Derek Cianfrance's indie tearjerker *Blue Valentine* (2010).

Rather than zero in on the kind of deep-seated stagnancy, toxic dynamics or other long-term issues which eventually may prove enough to capsize a marriage altogether, *On the Rocks* looks at a strong marriage which nonetheless strains under the pressure of responsibility, career and parenthood. Coppola never over-emphasizes the problems between Laura and Dean but hints at the corrosiveness of emotional distance and doubt between two people. 'I like to be deceivingly simple, hopefully that's easy to take in but that you think about later,' Coppola says. 'It isn't all wrapped up for you. I like things that are impressionistic.' *On the Rocks* is about the rough patches and awkward transitional phases a long-term relationship must go through, and in many ways, is all the more touching because of its lack of fatalism.

Still, the underlying questions that Coppola explores are major ones, and largely unanswerable: What does it take to keep a contemporary marriage together in busy modern life, and why is it always the wife who seems to grow frantic and insecure? Why do men so often seem – frankly – clueless? How much do our parents inform our idea of romance and relationships, and do fathers

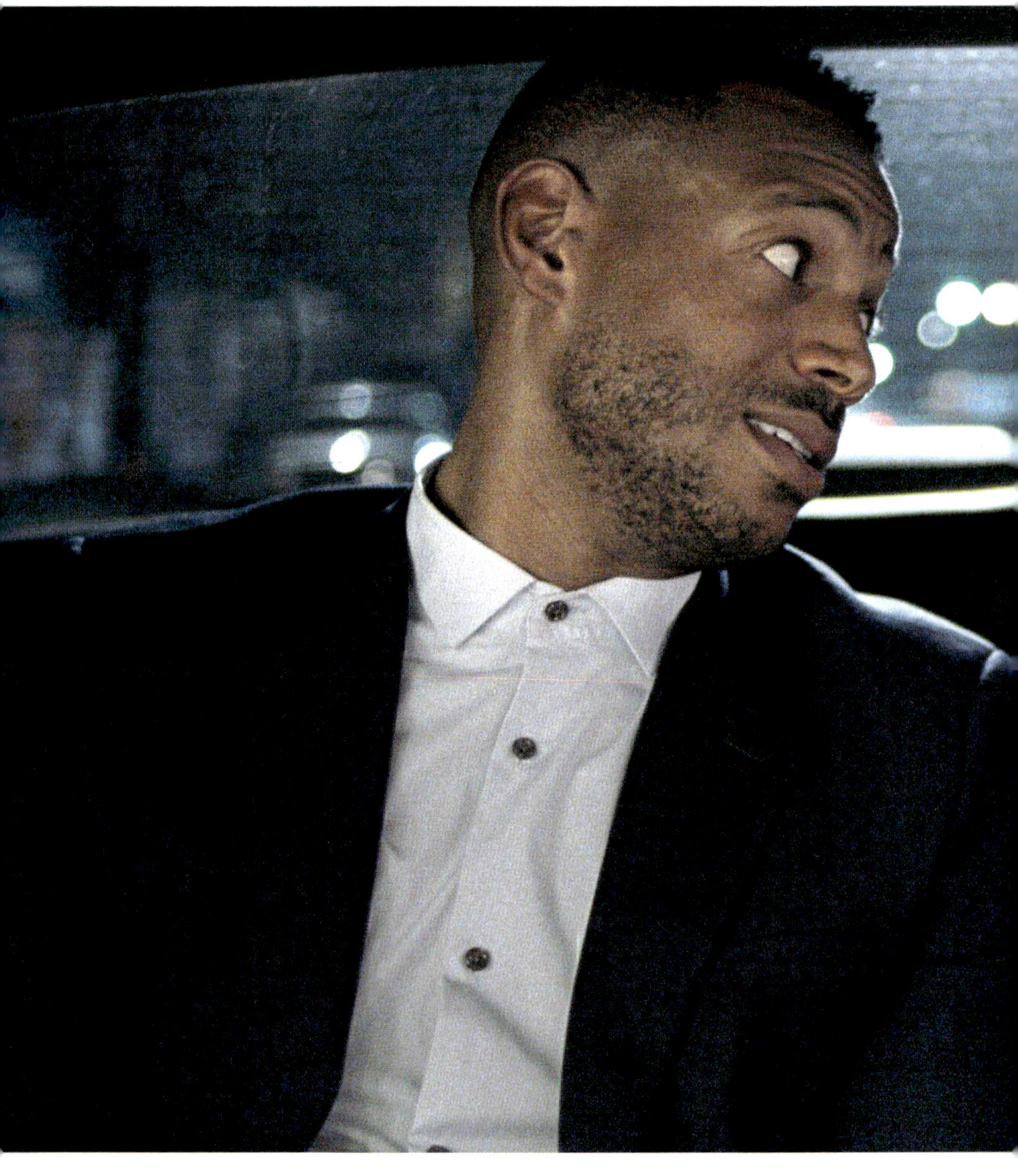

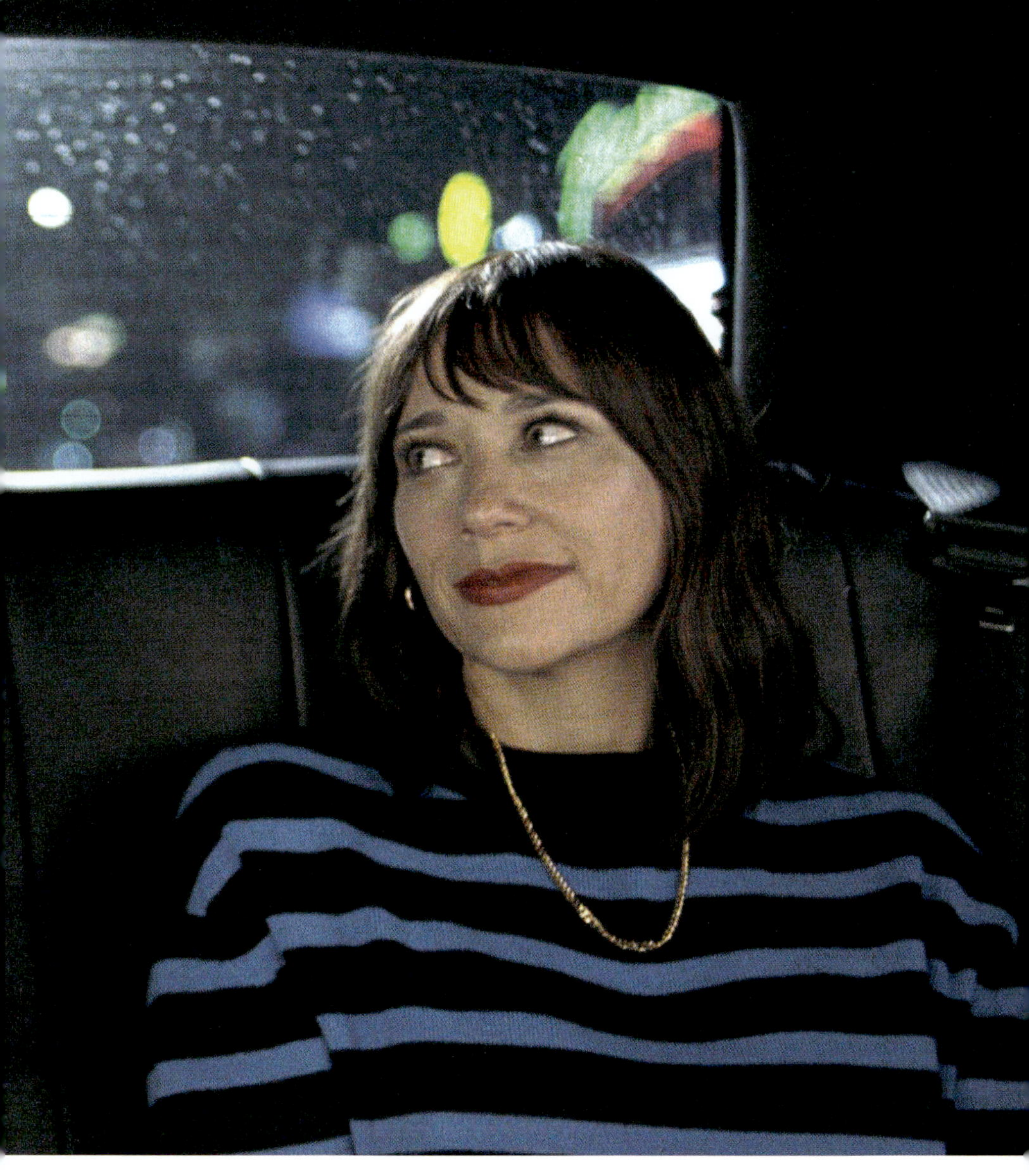

imprint on their daughters about the way men behave? Can evolved men and feminist women find equilibrium in their lives, balancing between domesticity, work, money and eroticism? The answer to that last, endlessly complex question feels like a 'no' in the eyes of Coppola's movie, but that's no reason to despair: we soldier on together, aware there is no way to juggle everything at once and doing our best to course-correct those imbalances as we encounter them.

One of the acknowledged influences on *On the Rocks* came from a somewhat unexpected place in this regard – not any highbrow photographer or arthouse film but relationship psychotherapist and popular podcaster Esther Perel. Perel's 2007 book *Mating in Captivity*, about maintaining intimacy in committed relationships, has been translated into 24 languages. Coppola considered using some audio of Perel's podcast at some point within the film, perhaps even having Laura listening to it or choosing it over the final credits, but ultimately couldn't quite find the right place to put it. Instead, as part of a bonus feature on Apple TV, Coppola and star Rashida Jones did a lockdown Zoom video chat with Perel to discuss the themes of the film generally, which turned out to be a rather illuminating one.

In it, Coppola expresses her concern with the balance between fulfilling responsibilities as a parent and maintaining enough mystery and curiosity in a romantic relationship to keep the flame alive. While she is never specific in terms of her own marriage or circumstances, it's a completely identifiable set of questions to

RIGHT TOP: Coppola directs Murray and Jones.

RIGHT BOTTOM: Murray and Coppola share ideas on set.

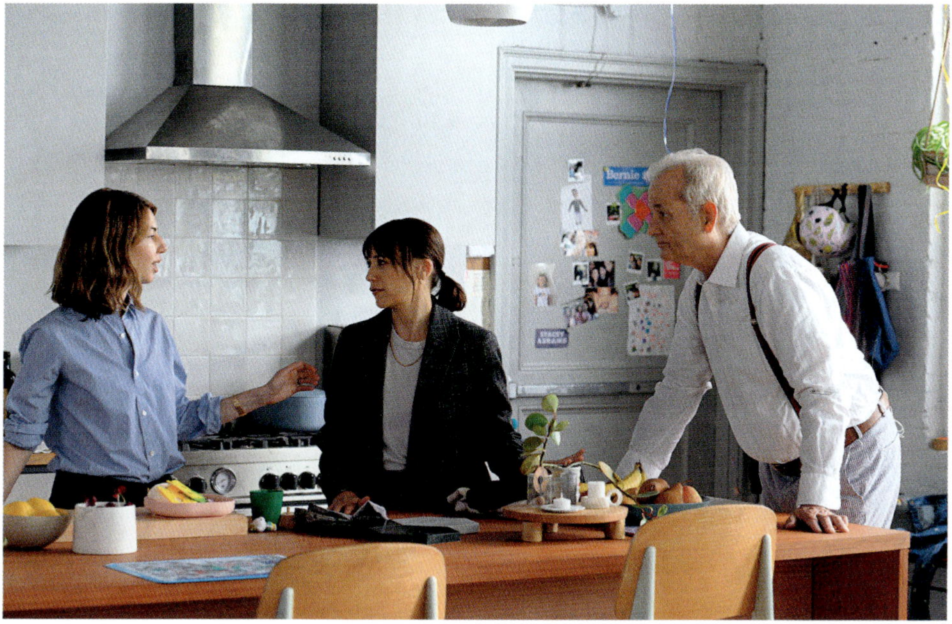

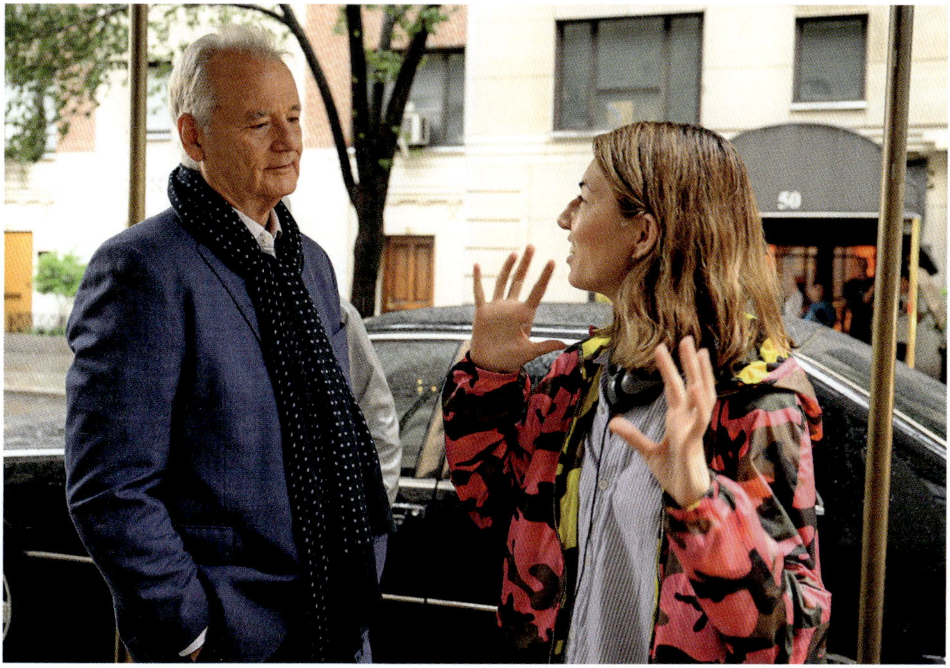

most modern women seeking to strike a balance in the never-ending battle to 'have it all'. Even in this casual chat, it seems clear that Coppola's interest in girlhood and, as her career and life has progressed, womanhood, is one which colours much of her filmmaking.

Although her films often frame femininity as something of a prison, or certainly womanhood as rather isolating in terms of finding connection and understanding, Coppola also finds humour and optimism throughout. Think of the upbeat whoosh of the Jesus and Mary Chain's 'Just Like Honey' kicking in at the close of *Lost in Translation*, even as the would-be lovers separate possibly for good. Or here, in *On the Rocks*, with its madcap, almost slapstick sense of fun.

Although *On the Rocks* is fundamentally about a marriage, in many ways the most fun and fascinating scenes are between Laura and Felix. He sweeps in like a fairy godmother character, providing a break for Laura from her domestic monotony, but ultimately there's a price to be paid for that kind of thrill and charm. Certainly, the scene which culminates in Mexico, where the pair chase Dean around only to finally realize that he is innocent, feels very much like the key confrontation of the film. Once Laura realizes she's been led on a wild goose chase and her husband is not, in fact, cheating, she explodes in frustration at her dad, pointing out his own lifelong selfishness. But the pair soon reconcile back in New York, where Felix will undoubtedly innocently try and show his young grandchildren *Breaking Bad* again. At the close of the film, he tries to tempt Laura on another adventure away from home. But she is entrenched in her domestic life and kindly turns him down.

It seems to be a sign that Laura's restlessness has calmed, and with it, she sees that father's own mistakes could also be hers in an entirely different way. She resists his urge to escape family and

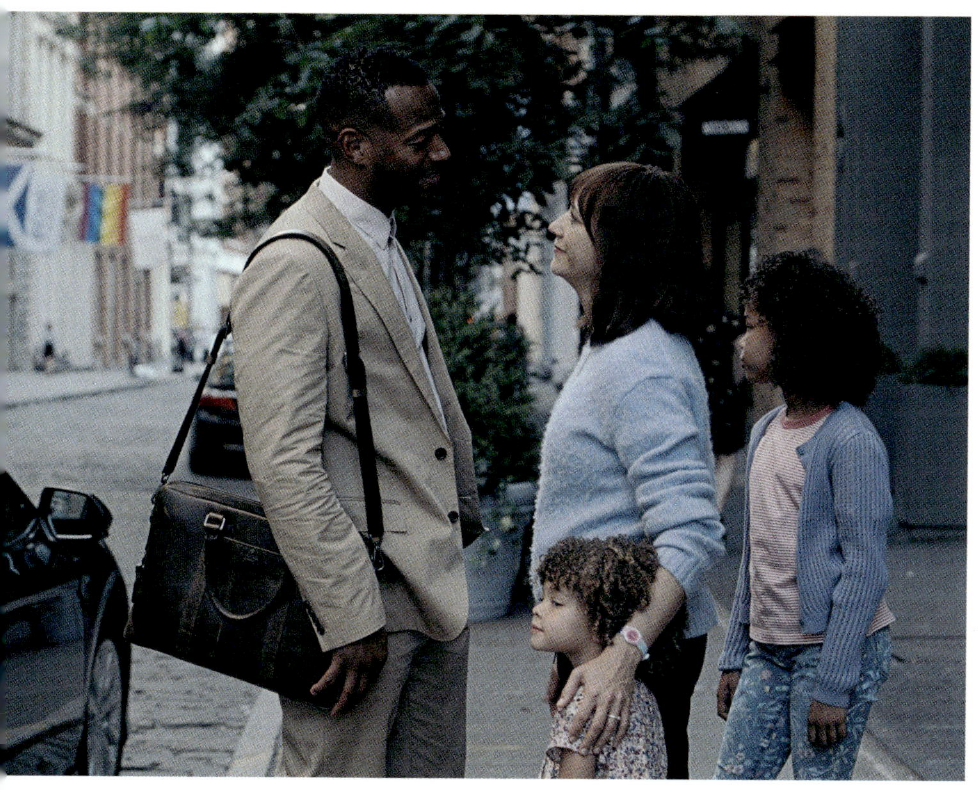

ABOVE: The family, reunited.

obligation, ultimately, knowing that putting the work into her relationships is what will make them worthwhile. Running off to sip martinis and talking about the ancient Romans might be fun – and it might be a way to salve the wound of alienation that runs between the father and daughter. But it can never be a permanent fix, as their cross-generational misunderstandings throughout prove. Laura understands this, accepts her father for who he is, and in a quietly sad scene late in the film, replaces his hand-me-down watch on her wrist with a birthday gift from her loving husband.

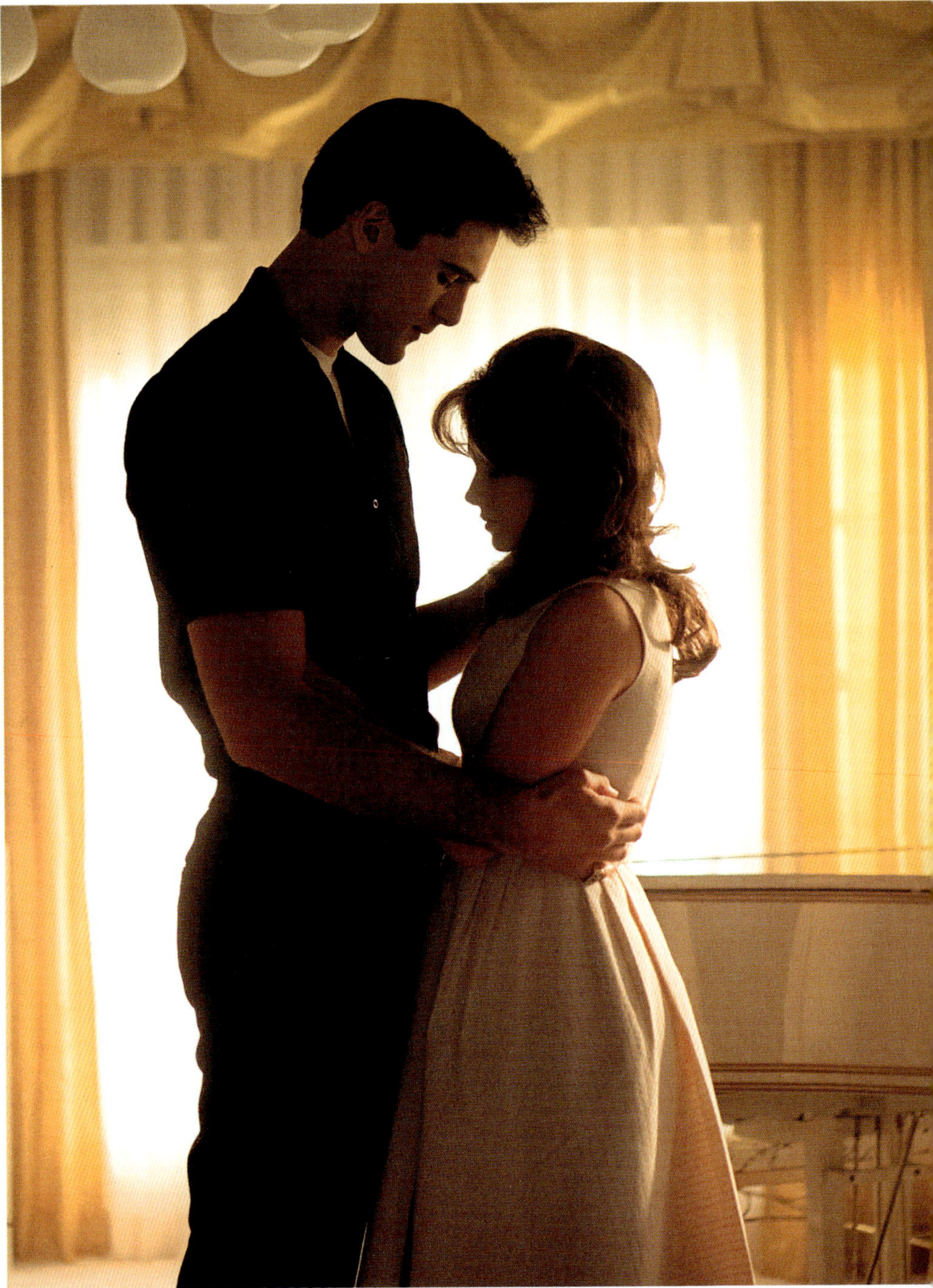

'You're losing me to a life of my own.'

PRISCILLA
2023

On first hearing that Sofia Coppola was making her next film about the life of Elvis Presley's glamorous wife Priscilla, it was natural to think: oh, that's *perfect*. Given the director's long fascination with music, the fact of her finally making a feature film directly set in the iconography of rock 'n' roll felt like a natural conclusion. But her adaptation of Priscilla's 1985 memoir *Elvis and Me*, about the tumultuousness of her married life with the King, is as much about being a young girl on the periphery than it has anything to do with the mid-century music business. The film arrived after a handful of stalled projects for Coppola; one as producer-director, for an adaptation of Edith Wharton's 1913 novel *Custom of the Country* for television. Another was a stymied *Little Mermaid* remake with Disney which ended in creative differences. So when Coppola picked up Presley's memoir for a beach read on vacation, she saw an opportunity to go back to plain and simple directing, and decided to do what she does best.

The film tells the story of obscure and beautiful teenager Priscilla Beaulieu, a 14-year-old army brat uncomfortably relocated to her father's military base in West Germany. She meets Elvis at a party while he, a decade older at 24, was stationed there, and it was swoon at first sight. The real Priscilla recalled that up until that point, she had only watched the musician on *The Ed Sullivan Show* through a crack in the living room door, because her parents had

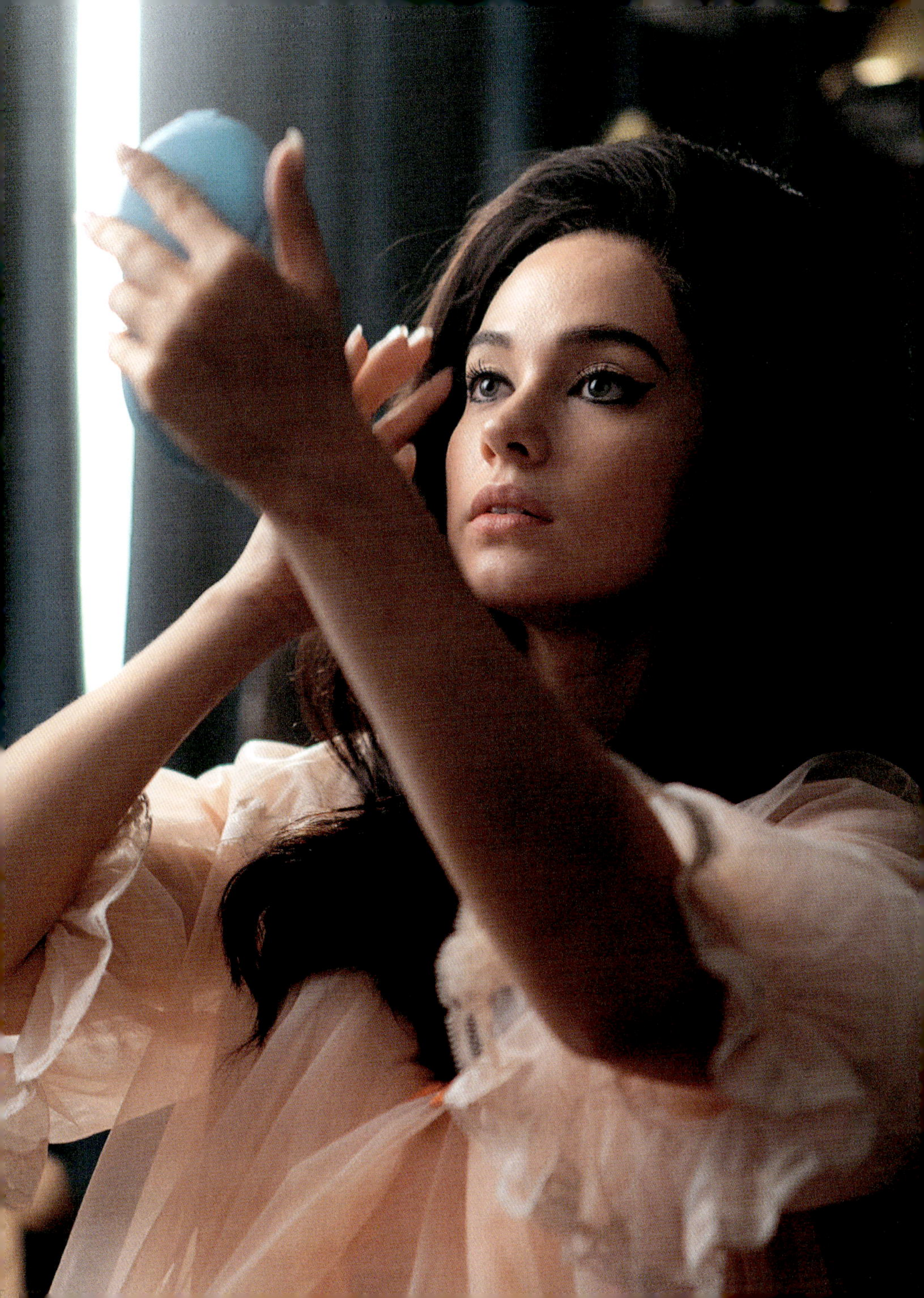

deemed him scandalous. Little did any of them imagine that Priscilla would become the King's only spouse before separating in 1973 and his untimely death in 1977. Seeing the courtship, marriage and eventual breakup through the starry-eyed and inexperienced eyes of the teen, Coppola depicts the dizzying highs and isolated lows of a girl who relocates to a high school in Memphis to be close to her much-older beau, with the begrudging acceptance of her highly concerned parents. ('My parents were really beside themselves,' the real Priscilla told *The Hollywood Reporter*. 'I basically threatened them and told them, "If you don't let me go, I'll find my way."')

Coming hot on the heels of the 2022 big-budget Oscar-nominated Elvis biopic from Baz Luhrmann, wherein the Memphis rock star played by Austin Butler is shown to be every bit the hip-shaking genius and sympathetic hero audiences might hope for, Coppola had her work cut out. In the wake of such a well-liked performance and film about the King, her position on him was wildly different. And while *Priscilla* was never intended as a 'hit piece' or designed to foster dislike for Elvis, it does take a different tack, focusing on his emotional immaturity, infidelity and a difficult domestic life. Some people were bound to be unhappy about it. Ultimately, Coppola was refused permission to use any Elvis Presley songs by his protective estate. For a story about Priscilla's years at Elvis' iconic Memphis home Graceland, that could be a pretty big problem; but Coppola did not hesitate.

Featuring Priscilla Presley herself as an executive producer, *Priscilla* is less a traditional biopic and more the portrait of a strange, seductive and ultimately poisonous marriage from beginning to end. Actress Cailee Spaeny – recommended to Coppola by Kirsten Dunst, who had worked with the then 25-year-old on Alex Garland's film *Civil War* (2024) – was tasked with the challenge of portraying her character from the ages of 14 to 30.

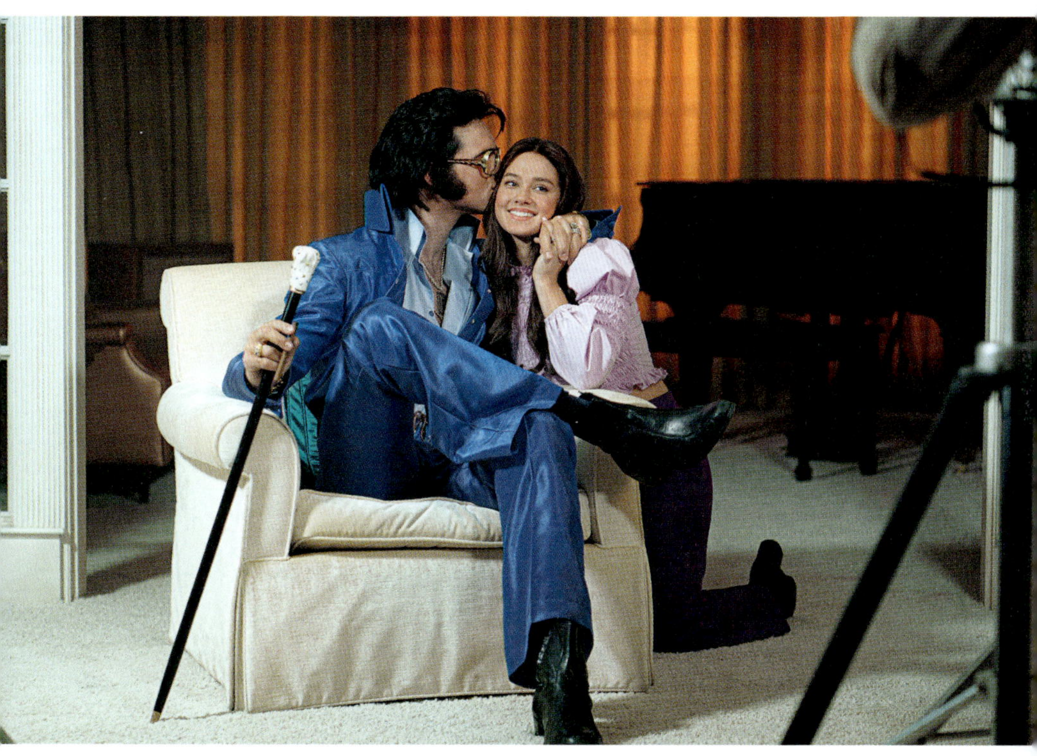

ABOVE: Priscilla (Spaeny) and Elvis (Jacob Elordi) have iconic photographs taken.

Spaeny does a remarkable job at radiating a softness and innocence that is not to be mistaken for stupidity or lack of backbone. From a saddle-shoe-wearing army brat sipping milkshakes in a West German diner to a self-assured mother who takes it upon herself to end a marriage with one of the most desired men in the world, Spaeny takes us every step of the way.

Rather than weave a story merely of suffering or manipulation, Coppola looks at this world through a teenage Priscilla's eyes. It's all about the swooning ache of first love and the rhinestone-encrusted glamour of Vegas during Pax Americana. Coppola's characters often plunge into the darkest of human experiences, be they suicide or abuse, but they retain an innocence and a levity that never makes her work miserable to watch.

This is a film that touches on topics which did not have socially-understood terminology in their era, but today might be called grooming and coercion. As written in the *Elvis and Me* memoir and depicted throughout the film, Elvis didn't like for his woman to have a job or to wear certain clothes; he could grow petulant and bullying at times, even blackening Priscilla's eye in a pillow fight at one point. Yet the feminine passivity that the American mid-century idealized is not the only thing on display here, and *Priscilla* avoids portraying the young woman as a mere victim. Equally, Coppola deploys her typical psychological acuity and nuance in Elvis' direction. Rather than a treatise on his evil, Elordi portrays the man as a rather vulnerable manchild, often a victim of his own fame in his inability to mature beyond a certain point. (A scene where he casually decides to demolish a building on his property with a bulldozer, with a crowd of his yes-men cheering him on, goes some way in revealing this.)

To find someone to play Elvis, Coppola knew she had a difficult task at hand: she needed someone who could make him as much a swaggering, spoilt man-child as a

ABOVE: Just a teenager at the time of their romance, Priscilla does her homework at Graceland.

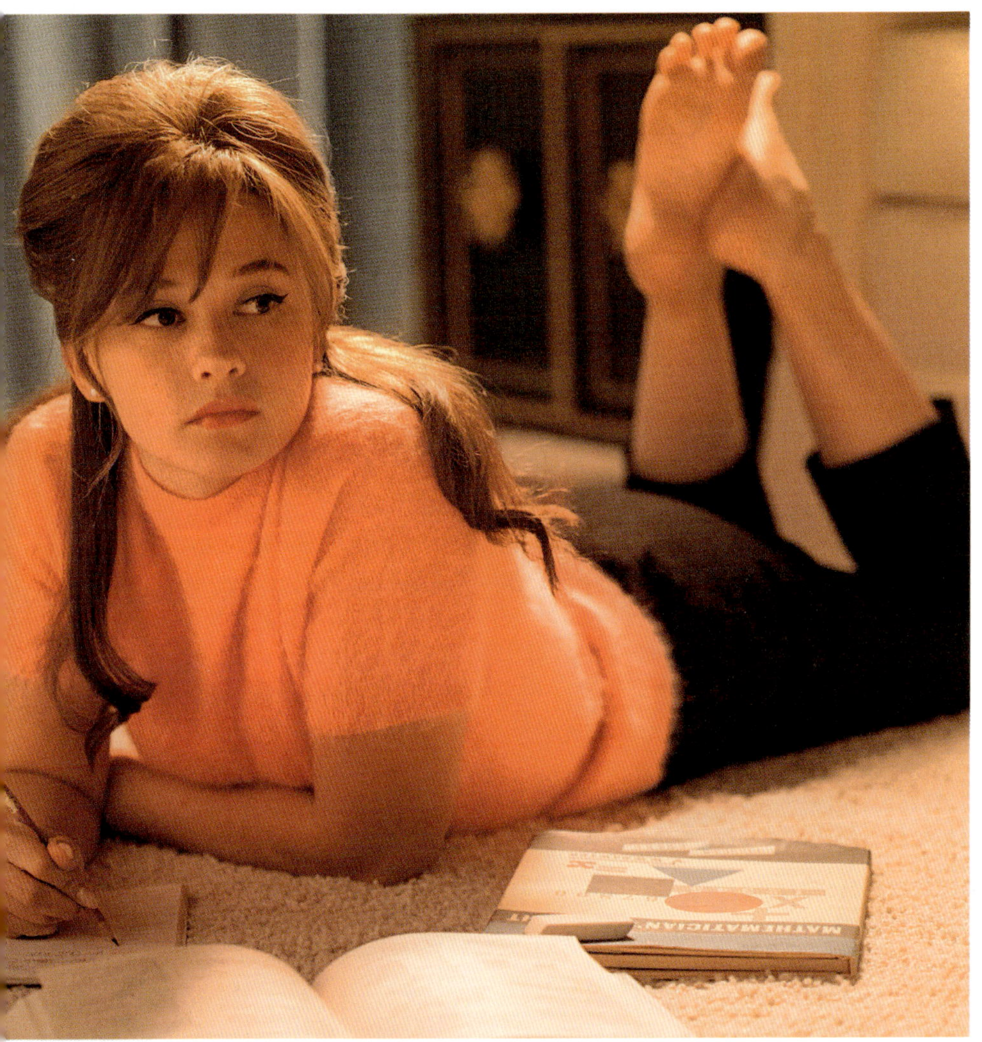

heroic artist, and crucially, of course, he needed to be able to do *that* voice. Jacob Elordi, the Australian-born actor who broke out in *Euphoria*, met Coppola at a New York coffee shop and she immediately felt the part click into place. 'All the girls in the room just turned to him, they gravitated,' Coppola says. 'I just felt like,

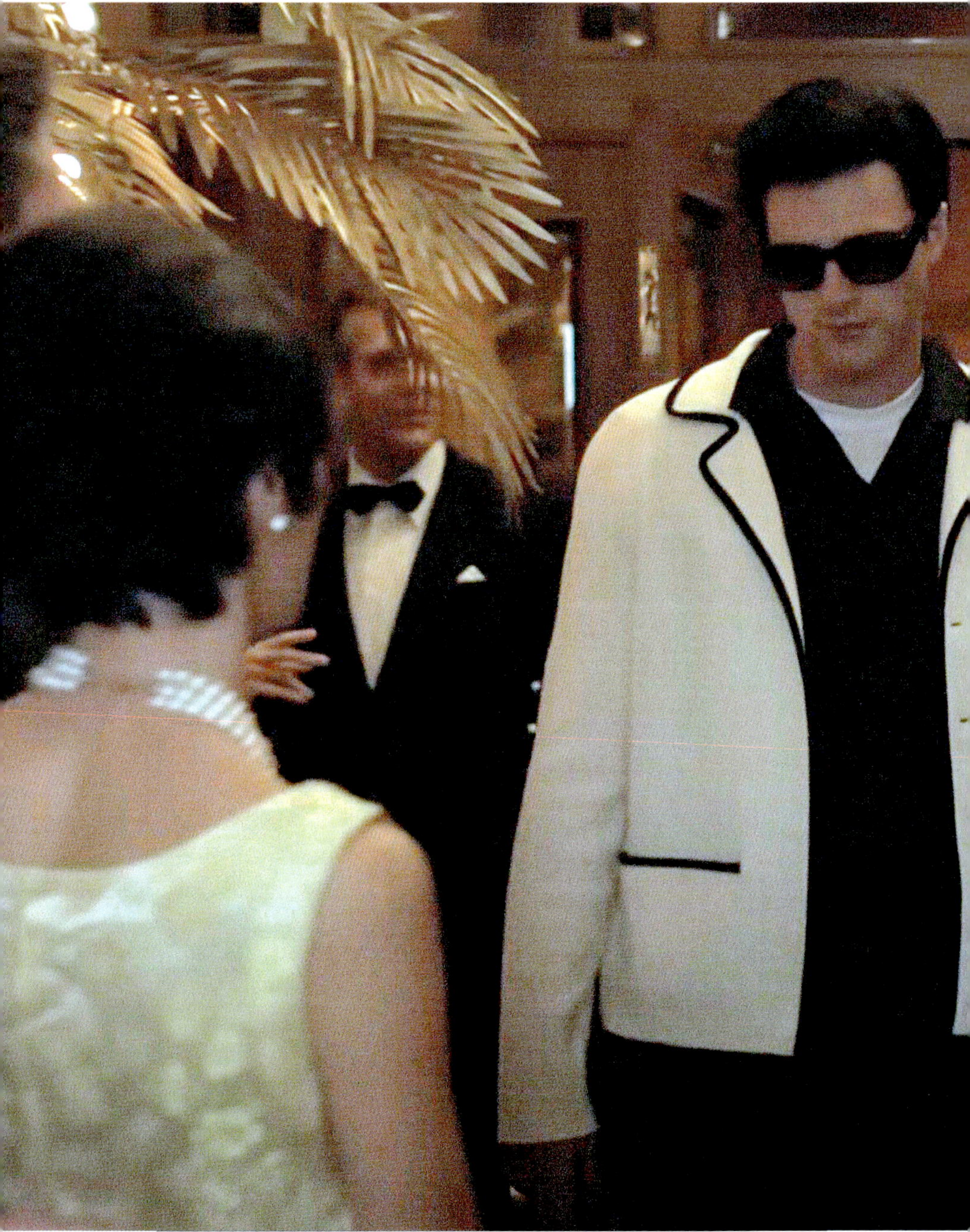

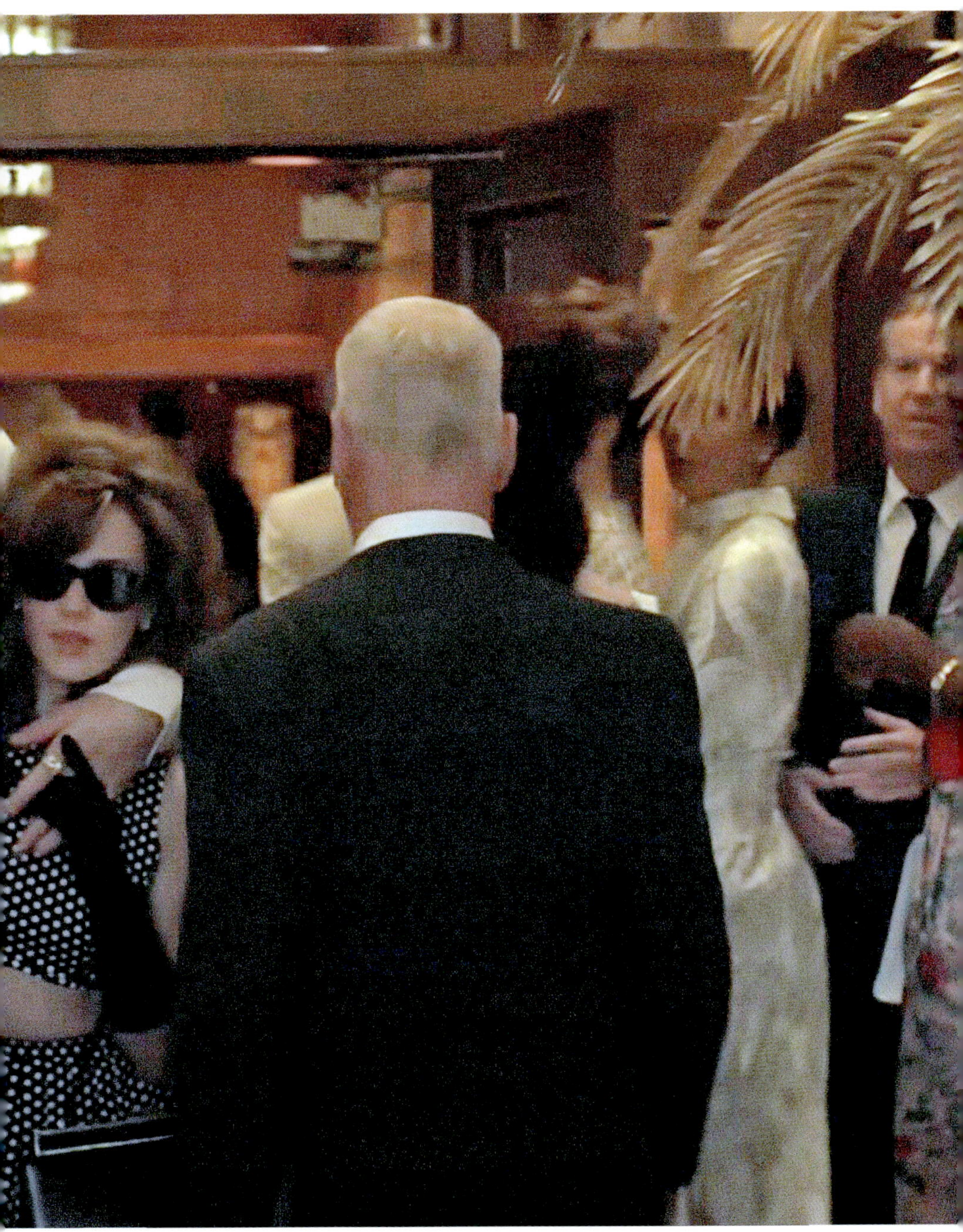

'Yeah, he has that kind of charisma that I imagine Elvis had.'

Elvis' square-jawed magnetism is indeed well portrayed by Elordi, whose considerable height (6ft 5in/196cm to Cailee Spaeny's petite 5ft 2in/157cm) also offers a handy visual metaphor of his towering presence both as a public figure and in Priscilla's life. She looks up to the older man and adores him; it's easy and seductive to be drawn into his arms and his protective, if suffocating, world. In fact, Coppola and director of photography Philippe Le Sourd attempt to reflect the psychological impact of Elvis' presence by changing the parameters of Graceland according to whether he's home or not. The rhythm of the editing and sense of excitement ratchets up when he's there; when Priscilla is left home alone, time drags slowly, boredom and claustrophobia setting in. Elvis prefers if she doesn't leave the house too often, chased and hounded as she is by his fans and gossip-hungry press; and so she and her little dog are cloistered in Graceland's expansive walls. She seems to be a guest in her own home.

PREVIOUS: Jacob Elordi as Elvis Presley and Cailee Spaeny as Priscilla Beaulieu Presley.

RIGHT: Elvis' whirlwind courtship of the teen girl was glamourous and exciting.

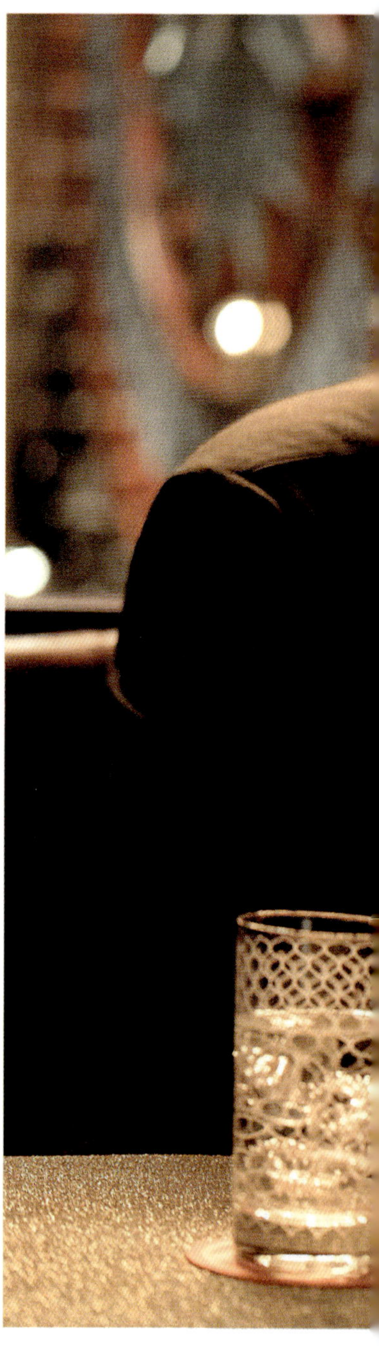

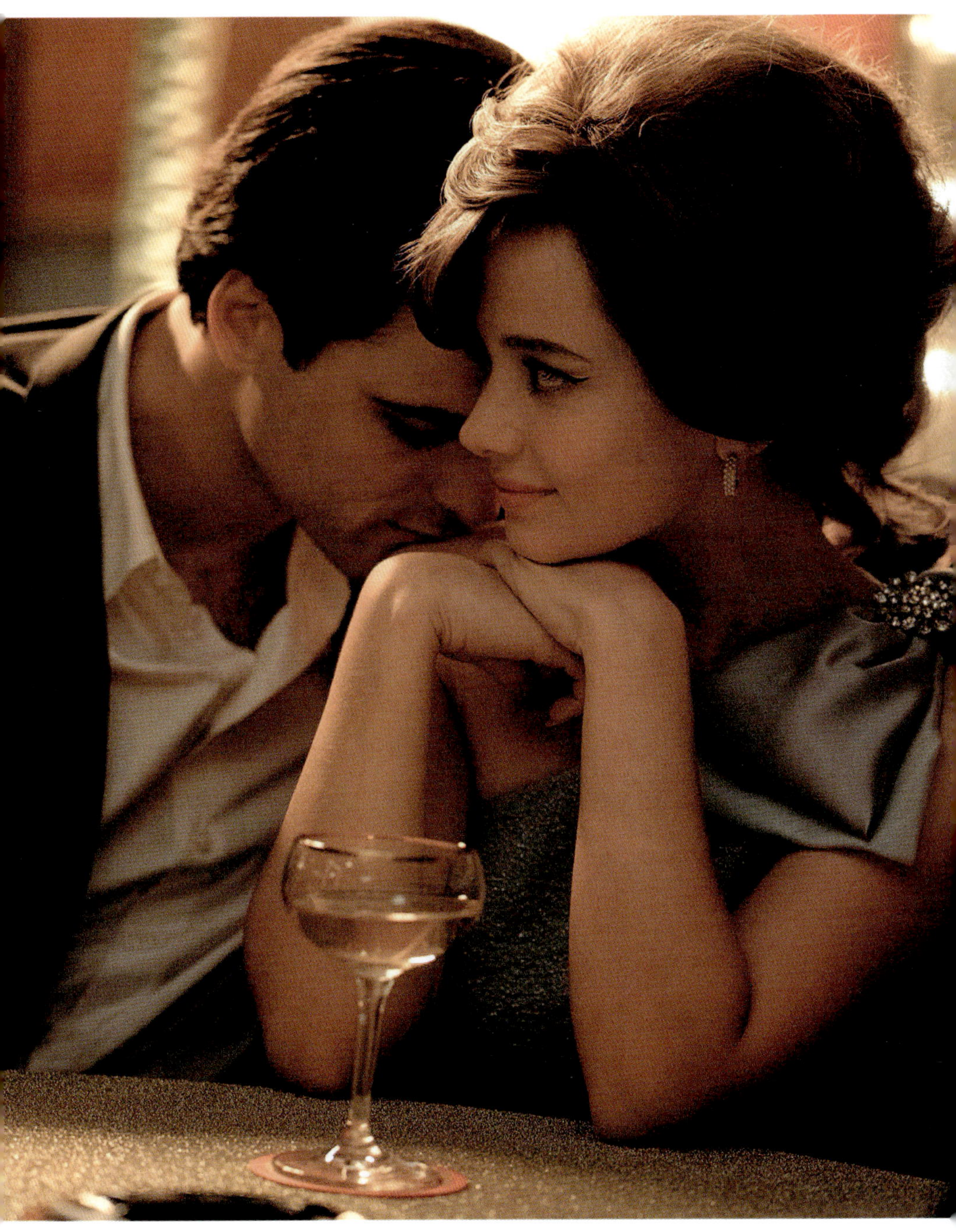

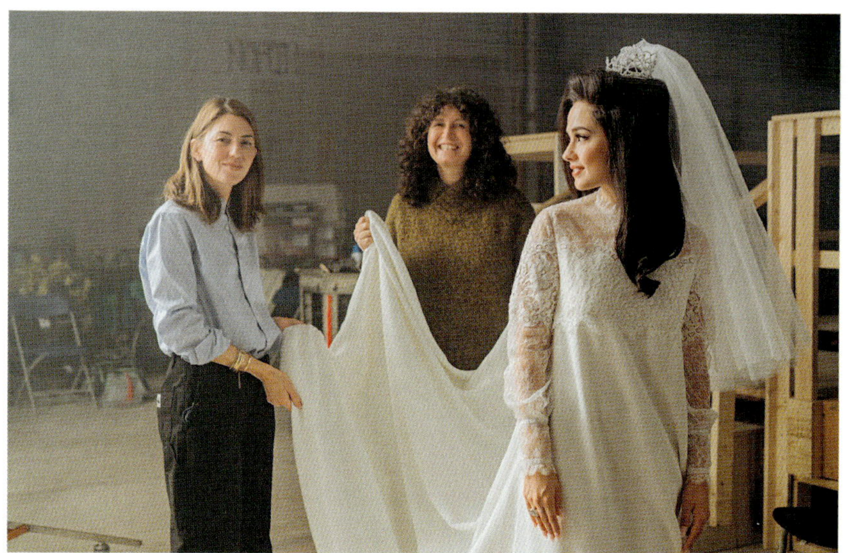

ABOVE: Coppola and costume designer Stacey Battat hold the train of the custom Chanel wedding gown designed for the film.

In terms of the look and style of the film, you might recall *Marie Antoinette*, all sugary sweetness with a bitter pill in its centre; a woman seduced by the frippery of the world presented to her only to realize it is a well-decorated trap. Coppola herself has said in interviews that *Priscilla* and *Marie Antoinette* share something like the same DNA. And what is Graceland if not the American Versailles, a grandiose monument to a king, where their women wander the halls bereft of purpose? The film opens with a memorable, girly-girl montage: a whoosh of wholesome 1960s doo-wop, a cloud of hairspray, pink shag rug and pink painted toes squishing into it. *Priscilla* knows its audience, and more importantly, it knows its subject. This is a girl whose head is turned by the near fairy-tale quality of Elvis' whirlwind life as a rock 'n' roll star, who is initially excited and then increasingly worn down by being fashioned into a sort of real-life doll for his enjoyment. There's a seductive pleasure to losing yourself in a glamorous and exciting romantic fantasy, but the slow erasure of Priscilla's sense of self or identity is what she gets in exchange.

To achieve the impact of *Priscilla* with only a $20 million budget, Coppola relied heavily on her set and production design, done by frequent collaborator with Guillermo del Toro, Tamara Deverell. In fact, her budget was so strained they lost a week of shooting in an already only 30-day shoot, and 10 pages from her script were cut in order to make it work, a disappointing outcome for a film which is already minimal in approach and elliptical in style. Coppola even said she considered selling off a date with Jacob Elordi to fund one more day of shooting. Still, it's an incredible coup to emerge from this challenge with such a gorgeous film; from the textiles of Graceland's curtains to the various musical cues, nothing feels undercooked.

'We talked about Graceland looking like a wedding cake. We wanted to have a real contrast between Germany and her arrival at Graceland,' Coppola told *The Hollywood Reporter*. 'In Germany, it's winter and grey. All the palettes of the clothes are muted. When she goes to Vegas and Graceland, it's all very colourful and heightened, and exciting. It was almost like Oz.'

In describing all of this luxuriant retro styling, it's hard not to get caught up in the chic beauty of it all; it's not exactly controversial to say that with films like *The Virgin Suicides* and *The Beguiled* under her belt, Sofia Coppola has always made female despondency look rather gorgeous. (And, at risk of sounding glib, who can blame her? If you're going to look sad wandering around your palatial house, why not wear something nice while you're doing it?)

For the question of what music to use, Coppola chose to see the Presley estate's refusal as a creative advantage. She was telling Priscilla's story, after all: emphatically *not* her husband's, no matter

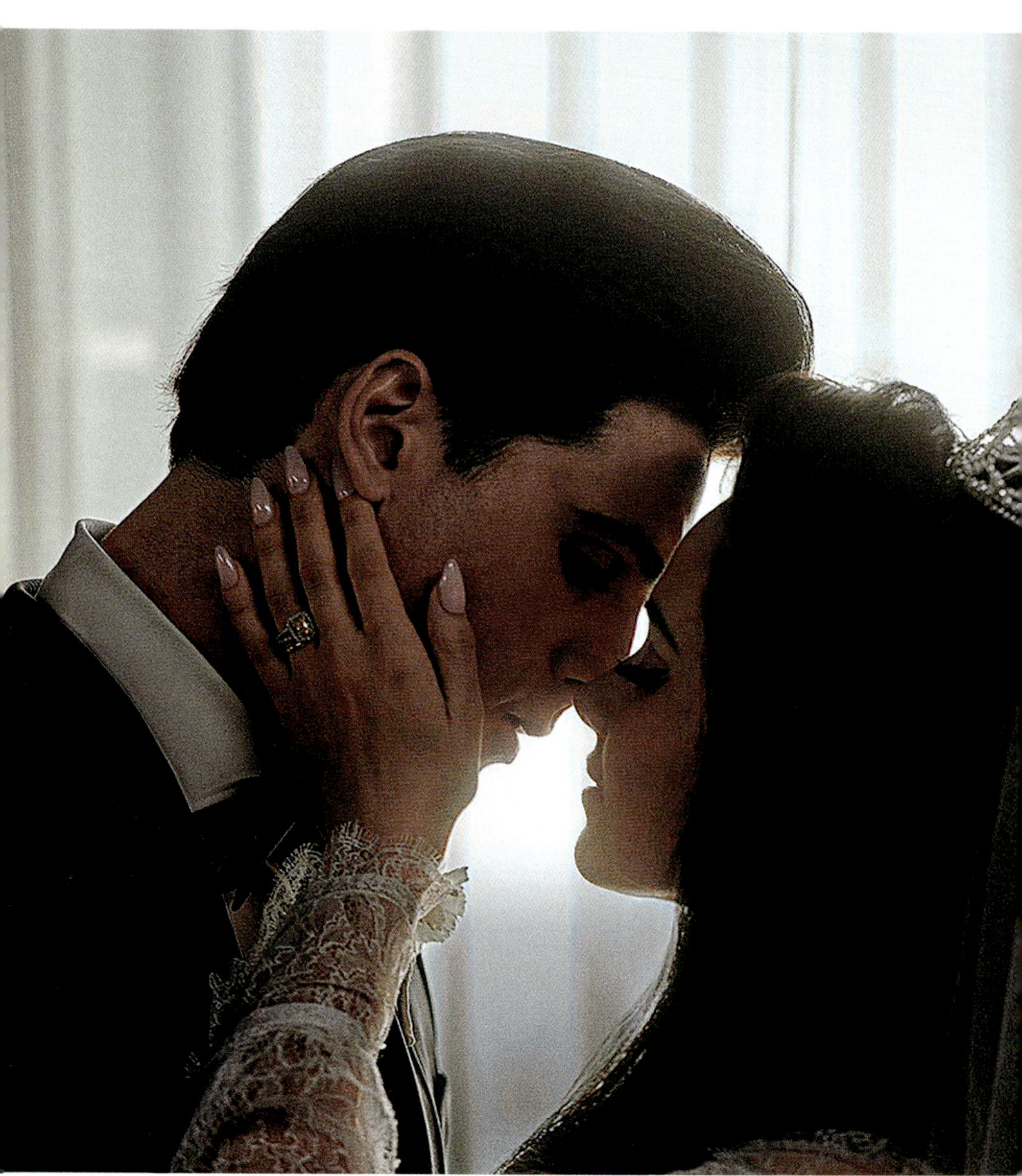

CHAPTER EIGHT

how intertwined they were. So in her typically playful anachronistic manner, she opens the film with what was originally a 1963 track by a saccharine-sweet girl group, The Ronettes' 'Baby I Love You', but chooses to use a bratty 1980 Ramones cover version instead. It feels oddly correct to the spirit of the film that there are no nostalgic distractions in the form of Elvis' own music; all of the snippets of Elvis songs you do hear are cover versions by Phoenix. Other films might feel curiously truncated or limited by this missing piece, but pushing Elvis' burnished legend to the sideline only further suits Coppola's thesis as a filmmaker.

In another key scene, Coppola leans into the unfurling, warm, sensual power of Tommy James and the Shondells' 'Crimson and Clover' to soundtrack a lissome slow-motion scene of teen Priscilla in her school hallway, daydreaming about Elvis. It can't help but to vaguely recall the slow-mo down a high-school hallway of Trip Fontaine in *The Virgin Suicides*; another scene maximized for depicting the urgency of female desire for lusciously handsome young men.

LEFT: Elvis and Priscilla's wedding day.

Sofia's makeup

It's perhaps unsurprising that a filmmaker as concerned with both the aesthetic and the feminine should have such a thorough interest and understanding of makeup artistry. Coppola – who herself has collaborated with luxury beauty brand Augustinus Bader on a series of subtle lip stains – cares about cosmetics in her movies. *Priscilla* is likely the most clear example, where hair and makeup crews were absolutely pivotal in transforming Cailee Spaeny across over a decade of different looks, ages and moods. From an au naturel teen to 1960s icon in her black cat-eye liner and white eyeshadow, the film also purposefully features the application of makeup as key to Priscilla's life and character. She has to become someone to please Elvis – thus a transformative makeover sequence showing her glam-up and trip to the hair salon. She forces herself to apply false eyelashes even as she goes into labour with her baby. And as Spaeny points out, as Priscilla grows more liberated and the 1970s approach, she relaxes into herself, wearing less makeup as a sign of her own comfort and distance from her husband's expectation.

Makeup is used again in *Marie Antoinette* as highly symbolic; take the brief fantasy sequence where the queen says her evil line 'Let them eat cake'. To exaggerate the hyperbole of this propaganda against her, Kirsten Dunst has jet-black lipstick applied, like she's a fairy-tale witch or a contemporary goth. We never see this lipstick at any other time in the movie. And in *The Bling Ring*, Emma Watson's Nicki and her pals are nothing without their all-important lip gloss. They carry it around like a mythic token, constantly pull it out of their designer bags to reapply it for selfies, performatively put it on in their car mirrors. It's an accessory, and an important one to boot.

This scene sets up the sense of Priscilla's long-simmering lust for Elvis, which goes unanswered and unfulfilled for a long time in her life at Graceland. Presley had some curious ideas about preserving her chastity, seeming to prefer to explore sex with other women (like co-star Ann-Margret) while keeping Priscilla at bay until their eventual marriage. And even still, the temperamental star, who called Priscilla 'my little one', saw her innocence as sacrosanct, essentially turning her into a play thing and an accessory but rarely attempting to satisfy her desire for him. This radiating sense of unsatisfied yearning is one of the many sources of discomfort for our melancholy protagonist; the intimacy she craves is denied repeatedly, and she turns to shopping and pill-popping to fill the void. It's not the first time Coppola has addressed the discontents of horny teenage girls in her work; sex is a key part of her exploration of feminine self-actualization.

Special care and attention was taken to capture some of the most iconic and well-circulated images of Elvis and Priscilla: their wedding day. Coppola films the sequences with a desire for both accuracy and gentle commentary, swapping format to 16mm film (this would have then been what was available for handheld filming at an event in 1967). Cailee Spaeny wore a custom-made Chanel wedding gown, and the hyper-stylish 1960s bride wore lashings of graphic cat-eye liner with her black hair lacquered high into a beehive on her head.

What we may not be aware of behind the iconography of the wedding photos is that the young bride in question had been sculpted and made over like a Barbie doll for Elvis' preferences, right down to her hair and makeup. Controlling and particular about aesthetics, Elvis wanted his young wife to look like an au courant rock 'n' roller's girl, and made no concessions to her own preferences about what she liked. In a scene where a giddy Priscilla is taken shopping by Elvis and a handful of his (male) entourage, she is encouraged to try on a whirling variety of expensive clothes but clearly has no say in what she takes home. Instead, Elvis acts as the final arbiter, with his cronies nodding along robotically.

The obsession with external appearances also spoke to Priscilla's own anxiety around looking good for her often absent and frequently adulterous heart-throb husband. In one striking scene, as she's going into labour with her first child, she stops to apply false eyelashes before leaving for the hospital (this was something she actually did, according to the real Priscilla). She arrives to give birth fully kitted out in go-go boots, and then emerges for her first public appearance to the media as a family-of-three in a resplendent fuchsia minidress. We see none of the sweat or pain of childbirth in the interim; simply the glossy, pain-stakingly manicured surface, and if you're a vintage-clothing lover, you'll be aware how little Lycra or stretchy fabric existed in fashionable clothes of this decade – not ideal for a woman fresh off the maternity ward.

RIGHT: One of the many gorgeous retro costume choices for the doll-like Priscilla.

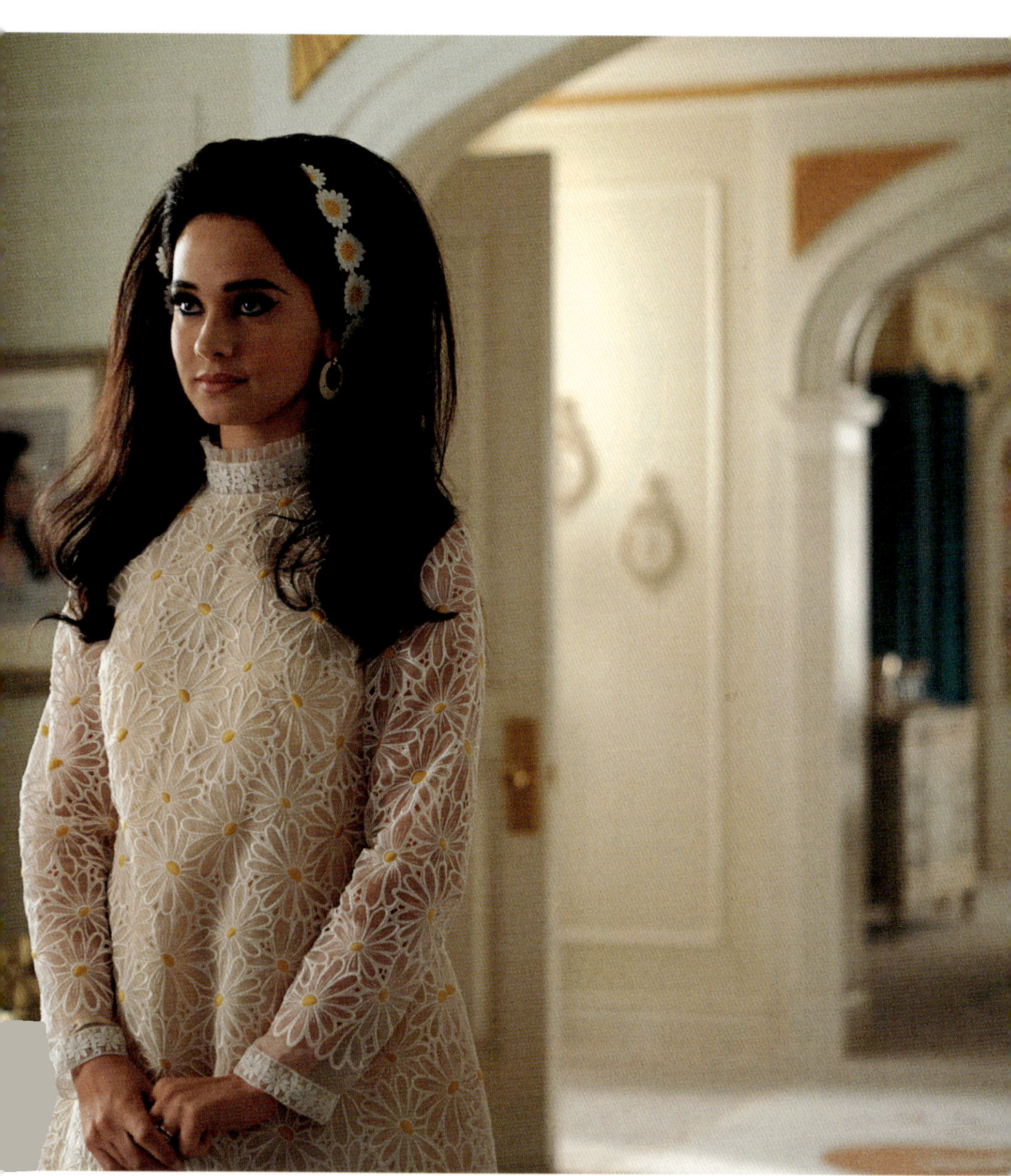

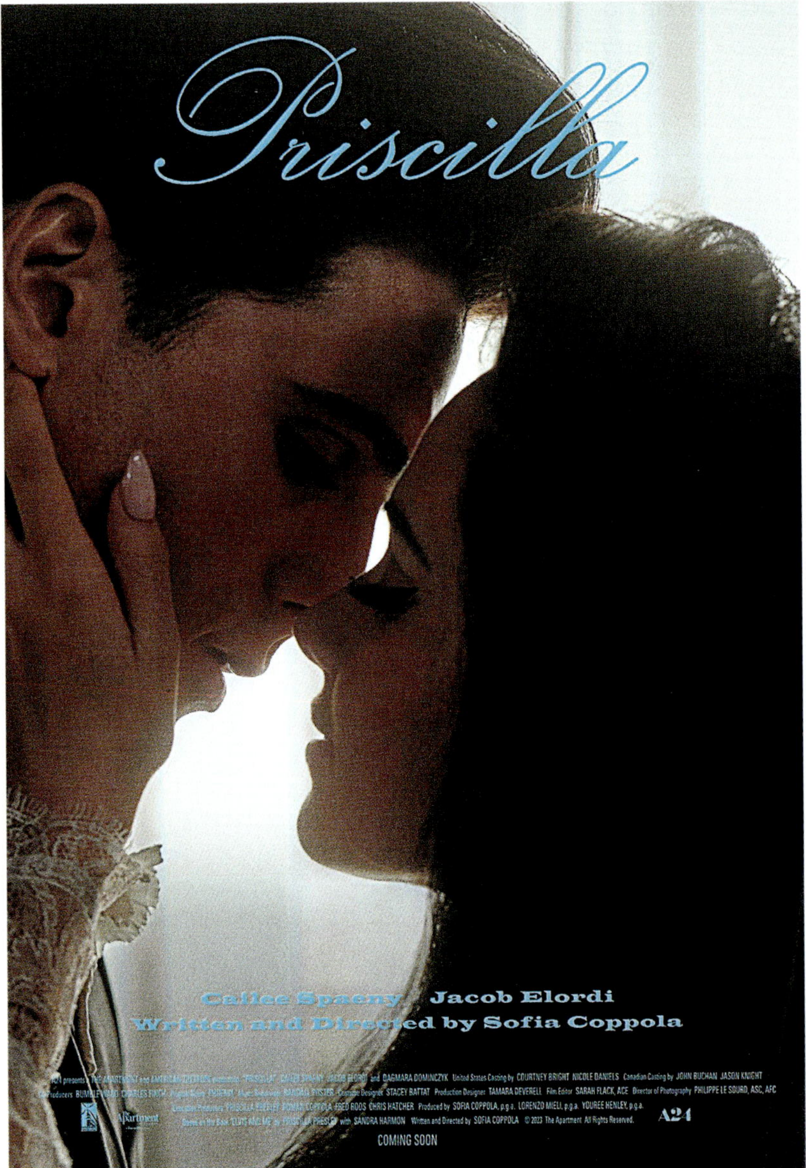

Priscilla
Cailee Spaeny   Jacob Elordi
Written and Directed by Sofia Coppola
COMING SOON
A24

Budget constraints meant that Coppola had to elide a scene she had originally planned which would show an eight-month-pregnant Priscilla riding a motorbike at Elvis' behest, another indicator of just how desperately the young woman wanted to share in her husband's interests and to keep his attention from wandering. Stacey Battat has also discussed that while Priscilla otherwise has a constant stream of brand-new outfits, she wears no new clothes or maternity outfits while pregnant because the real Priscilla had been obsessed with not gaining weight at that time. She was determined, sad as it now seems, to fit into her regular clothes during the pregnancy.

When *Priscilla* premiered at Venice Film Festival, the response was broadly positive, particularly for Cailee Spaeny's performance as the naive but bright Priscilla (Spaeny won Best Actress award at the festival). Some, though, made the same old complaints: all style over substance, a confection of a movie that had nothing on the inside. Added to this was the notion that Coppola was merely repeating herself, driving home her themes of isolated girlhood and the gilded cage without much fresh to say. Nothing could be further from the truth: *Priscilla* is her most delicate and anguished dissection of marriage yet, able to mine the deep faultlines of an uneven power dynamic and still sensitively portray how intoxicating the uniquely feminine dilemma of giving up your power can be. In *Priscilla*, style *is* the substance; it represents the feminine disassociation and desire for building a facade to disguise the cracks.

As ever, a certain degree of the personal makes it into the film too, although this time it's more abstract than in the more clearly autobiographical projects. In several interviews about *Priscilla*,

Coppola made reference to her mother Eleanor. She, after all, knew what it was like to be married to a famous, wilful and beloved male artist, and maybe even to be in his shadow. It's not an easy part to play. And while the expectation of that role has now changed significantly since the 1960s, the idea of subsuming one's identity into one's partner's is hardly a thing of the past. And as Coppola says, 'Living in a house with my dad, this big personality, a great artist and a lot of our life revolving around that. And seeing my mom's life, how she was trying to find her way within his, I could relate to that.' Many of her films touch upon female characters who seem to have no choice but to be looked at; they live in a kind of fishbowl with the prying eyes of others on them.

Intriguingly, in spite of the isolation and cruelty Priscilla felt as the result of her marriage, Coppola chooses a touching song to close out the powerful final scene of the film. As Priscilla bids goodbye to the familiar faces of Graceland – a place which felt like a trap but had also been her home from a young age – Dolly Parton's original rendition of 'I Will Always Love You' plays. Priscilla drives off and out of the gates for the final time, a courageous act in the days of divorcing such a powerful man. The song choice says that there's an enduring affection that remains, but there's also another sparkle of wisdom in it. Parton, then only a young budding singer-songwriter, wrote 'I Will Always Love You' in 1973 and was aggressively chased by Presley's team to sell her song to them so he could perform it. She courageously decided to turn down the paycheque and take the risk making it her own; everyone knows the rest of the story, and just how much Dolly's bravery paid off. It's a beautiful homage to female independence and ingenuity at a time when patriarchal values still ruled the roost.

'I wanted to convey that Priscilla got out and got to form her own identity,' Coppola told *GQ* magazine. 'She told us that she didn't even know what her taste was when she left – everything

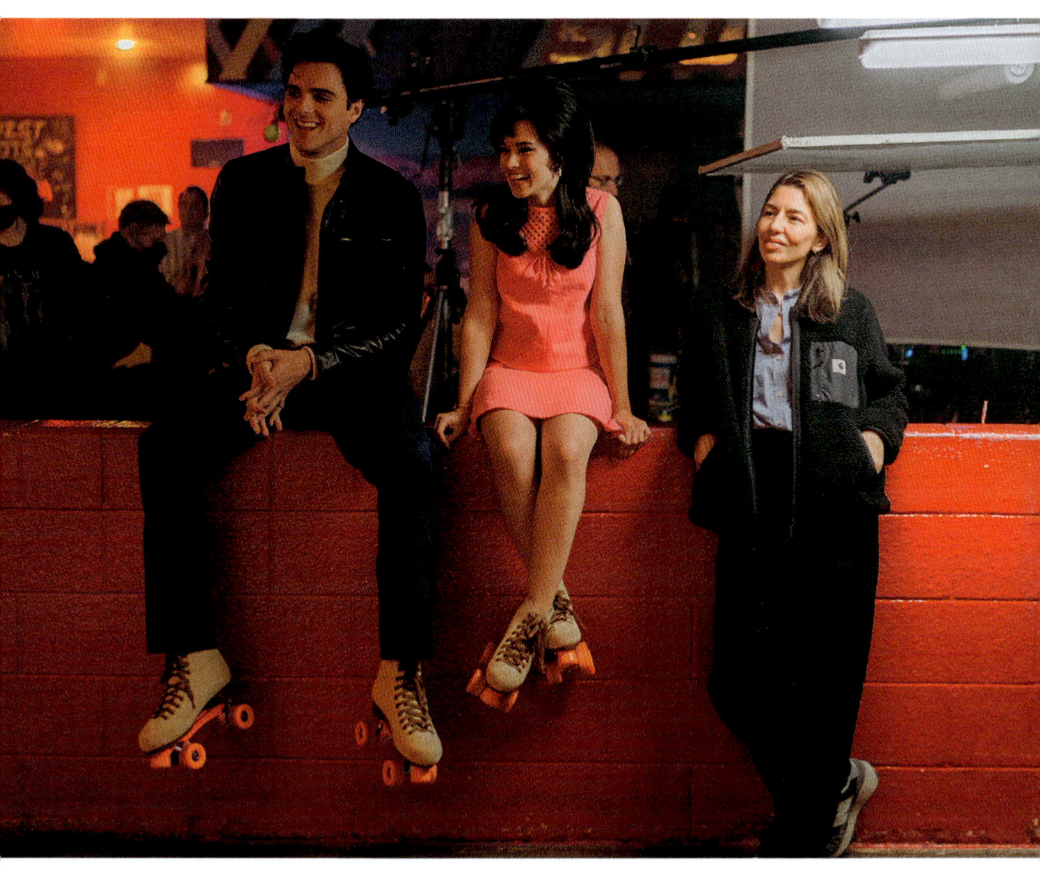

ABOVE: Elordi, Spaeny and Coppola enjoy a break while filming a roller-rink sequence.

had been Elvis' taste,' Coppola said. 'So by leaving, she got to have a whole life of her own.' *A life of her own*: if ever there were a few words to summarize the thesis of Coppola's cinema of girlhood, it might be these.

Resources

Chapter one

'The Virgin Suicides Roundtable', Entertainment Weekly, YouTube, 18 June 2020

Interview with Jeffrey Eugenides, 4K release, 2018

'Sofia Coppola on making The Virgin Suicides: "When I saw the rough cut I thought: Oh no, what have I done?"' The Guardian, 25 January 2018

Lodge, Guy, 'Sofia Coppola: "I never felt I had to fit into the majority view"', The Guardian, 2 July 2017

Weston, Hillary, 'Intimate Apparel: A Conversation with Nancy Steiner', The Criterion Collection, 31 August 2022

Ferrier, Aimee, 'Sofia Coppola names the turning point of her career: "I just tried different things"', 9 August 2024

Chapter two

Stern, Marlow, 'Sofia Coppola discusses Lost in Translation on its 10th anniversary', The Daily Beast, 12 September 2013

Nayman, Adam, 'We'll never know everything about Lost in Translation', The Ringer, 26 September 2023

Kemp, Ella, 'Killer Queen: the deep, delicious impact of Sofia Coppola's Marie Antoinette', Letterboxd, 23 September 2024

Ferriss, Suzanne, BFI Film Classics: Lost in Translation, Bloomsbury, 9 March 2023

Bose, Swapnil Dhruv, 'A complete list of Sofia Coppola's favourite films', Far Out, 26 January 2022

Harding, Michael-Oliver, 'How Phoenix and Sofia Coppola influence each other', Dazed, 23 June 2017

Bland, Simon, '"I never expected people to connect with it so much" – Sofia Coppola on Lost in Translation at 15', Little White Lies, 26 August 2018

Pitts, Johny, 'Lost in Tokyo – in search of Sofia Coppola's lingering influence through the luminous streets of Japan's capital city', Conde Naste Traveller, 1 October 2023

Dawson, Nick, 'The Music of Sofia Coppola', Focus Features, 8 November 2012

Chapter three

'The Making of Marie Antoinette', DVD Extra

Bell, Keaton, '"It Was Like Hosting The Ultimate Party": An Oral History of Sofia Coppola's Marie Antoinette', British Vogue, 30 October 2021

Kemp, Ella, 'Killer Queen: the deep, delicious impact of Sofia Coppola's Marie Antoinette', Letterboxd, 23 September 2024

Cook, Pam, 'Portrait of a lady: Sofia Coppola and Marie Antoinette', BFI, 22 October 2021

Bergeson, Samantha, 'Sofia Coppola admits Marie Antoinette was a "Flop" that "Nobody Saw", but she's happy "It's Lived On"', IndieWire, 25 August 2025

French, Philip, 'Marie Antoinette – review', The Guardian, 22 October 2006

Chapter four

'The Making of Somewhere', Blu-ray extra, 2011

Buchanan, Kyle, 'Stephen Dorff on Somewhere, Personal Turmoil, and His Inability to Keep His Clothes On', Vulture, 15 December 2015

Berning, Beverly, 'Interview with Sofia Coppola and Stephen Dorff, the Director and Star of Somewhere', CultureVulture, 21 December 2010

Barnard, Linda, 'Interview: Sofia Coppola', The Star, 8 January 2011

'Sofia Coppola and Stephen Dorff', Interview Magazine, 19 November 2010

Macaulay, Scott, 'An Interview with Somewhere's Sarah Flack', Focus Features, 17 December 2010

Jennings, Sheri, 'Sofia Coppola's Somewhere wins Venice Golden Lion', Screen Daily, 11 September 2010

Chapter five

'Making the Bling Ring', The Bling Ring Blu-ray special features, 2013

Sales, Nancy Jo, 'The suspects wore Louboutins', Vanity Fair, March 2013

'The Scene of the Crime with Paris Hilton', The Bling Ring Blu-ray special features, 2013

Masters, Tim, 'How Sofia Coppola tackled the Bling Ring', BBC News, 5 July 2013

Kasman, Daniel and Cook, Adam, 'Dialogues: Sofia Coppola's The Bling Ring', Notebook, 17 May 2013

Gamble, Ione, 'Sofia Coppola on the Girlhood Trend, Gracie Abrams and Never Growing Up', Polyester, 2024

Chapter six

'A Southern Style', The Beguiled Blu-ray special features

McGilligan, Patrick, Clint: The Life and Legend, HarperCollins, 14 May 2010

Le Sourd, Philippe, 'Eye Piece: DP Philippe Le Sourd Shoots the Human Textures in Sofia Coppola's The Beguiled', MovieMaker, 31 January 2023

'A Shift in Perspective' The Beguiled Blu-ray special features

'The Colour of The Beguiled', The Beguiled Blu-ray special features

Cusumano, Katherine, 'How French Band Phoenix Transformed the Music in Sofia Coppola's The Beguiled', 3 July 2017

Bastién, Angelica Jade, 'How The Beguiled Subtly Tackles Race Even When You Don't See It', Vulture, 10 July 2017

Coppola, Sofia, 'Sofia Coppola Responds to The Beguiled Backlash', IndieWire, 15 July 2017

Chapter seven

Kohn, Eric, 'Sofia Coppola on the Identity Crisis That Led Her to Make On the Rocks with Bill Murray', IndieWire, 12 October 2020

Hattersley, Giles, 'We Didn't Know We Were Making A Period Movie: Behind The Scenes Of On The Rocks With Sofia Coppola', British Vogue, 11 October 2020

'Manhattan Mellow Drama from On the Rocks Cinematographer Philippe Le Sourd', Musicbed

Tafoya, Scout, 'On The Rocks review', Roger Ebert, 23 October 2020

'Esther Perel in Conversation with Sofia Coppola and Rashida Jones', Apple TV+ On the Rocks Bonus Feature

'Sofia Coppola on Directing On The Rocks and Casting Rashida Jones and Bill Murray', BAFTA Guru, YouTube, 22 March 2021

'On The Rocks Q&A with Sofia Coppola & Bill Murray, moderated by Jim Jarmusch',

American Cinematheque, YouTube, 14 February 2021

Chapter eight

Bergeson, Samantha, 'Sofia Coppola Reveals Presley Estate Turned Down Using Elvis Music for Priscilla', IndieWire, 23 August 2023

Newland, Christina, 'In Priscilla, Sofia Coppola tells a story that is frighteningly familiar', Dazed Digital, 5 January 2024

Keegan, Rebecca, 'Priscilla Presley Entrusts Sofia Coppola to Tell Her Story: "I Felt She Could Get Me"', The Hollywood Reporter, 23 August 2023

Strong, Hannah, 'Sofia Coppola on struggling to get Priscilla made: "Straight men with money don't always relate to me"', GQ, 30 December 2023

Garside, Megan, 'Priscilla's budget was so tight Sofia Coppola considered selling a date with Jacob Elordi', Games Radar, 3 October 2023

Silver, Jocelyn, 'How Priscilla's Production Designer Brought Graceland Back To Life', British Vogue, 11 November 2023

DeLucci, Theresa, 'Priscilla: The True Story of Elvis' Hangups About Sex and Virginity', Den of Geek, 3 November 2023

Picture credits

Alamy Stock Photo: Alamy Stock Photo: 4/5, 15, 67, 140, 141, AJ Pics; 115, ABACAPRESS; 22 ©Paramount Classics/Courtesy Everett Collection; 6, 12, 30/1, 84/5, 116/7, 132/3, 181, 192, 195, 198/9, 204, 210/1 Album; 37, 178, 197 BFA; 11 Celebrity Archives; 42/3, 46/7, 51, 52/3, 68, 70/1, 72/3, 74, 89, 90, 94/5, 106/7, 112, 121, 122/3, 126/7, 128/9, 131, 134/5, 137 Cinematic Collection; 111, 148/9, 108/9 Collection Christophel; 63 dpa; 164/5 Entertainment Pictures; 167, 172/3, 186/7, 191, 200/1, 212 Everett Collection; 202/3, 206/7 FlixPix; 100/1, 105, 48 ©Focus Features/Courtesy Everett Collection; 41, 60/1, 38 kpa Publicity Stills; 168, 171, 176/7, 189 bottom, 215 Landmark Media; 9, 19, 78/9 Maximum Film; 87 Moviestore Collection; 28/9 Photo12/7e Art/American Zootrope; 175, 189 top Photo12/A24/American Zoetrope/JoJo Whilden; 145, 159 Pictorial Press; 44/5, 64, 97 PictureLux; 16, 24/5, 93, 98 RGR Collection; 142, 150, 156/7, 160/1 Ron Harvey; 57 SilverScreen; 77, 81 ©Sony Pictures/Courtesy Everett Collection; 33, 119 TCD/Prod.DB; 147, 162 TCD/Prod.DB; 20/1, 54, 152/3 155 ZUMA Press.

Acknowledgements

With thanks to Andrew Roff and Paul Martinovic.